IMAGES
of America

LAKE CAREY

On the cover: Participants in the Lake Carey Labor Day regatta of 1939 pose on the Stevens/Herrick dock, the sails of their Comets luffing behind them. They are, from left to right, (first row) crews Bobby Stevens, Lindsey Coon, Jim Ridgway, Ken Heffran, Byron Sleppy, Ruth Quin, Peg Ridgway, Jo Boston, Rowland "Bubba" Tewksbury, and Cordelia "Corky" Bergman; (second row) skippers Ab Folsom, Hardy Coon, Bob Selingo, Al Fassett, Ruth Stevens, Bill Quin, Dick Ridgway, Clarence Boston, Hank Dunn, and Nat Stevens Jr. (Skipper Brad Sleppy and his crew Fred "Zook" Billings, pictured on the far right in the original photograph, could not be included when the image was sized to fit the cover.) Regatta sponsor, Adm. Harold R. Stark, then chief of naval operations, was not present at the event having been called back earlier to Washington on this weekend when Britain, France, Australia, and New Zealand declared war on Germany formally beginning World War II. (Fassett collection.)

IMAGES
of America

LAKE CAREY

Walter Broughton

ARCADIA
PUBLISHING

ISBN 978-0-7385-5518-8

Published by Arcadia Publishing
Charleston, South Carolina

Printed in the United States of America

Library of Congress Catalog Card Number: 2007929953

For all general information contact Arcadia Publishing at:
Telephone 843-853-2070
Fax 843-853-0044
E-mail sales@arcadiapublishing.com
For customer service and orders:
Toll-Free 1-888-313-2665

Visit us on the Internet at www.arcadiapublishing.com

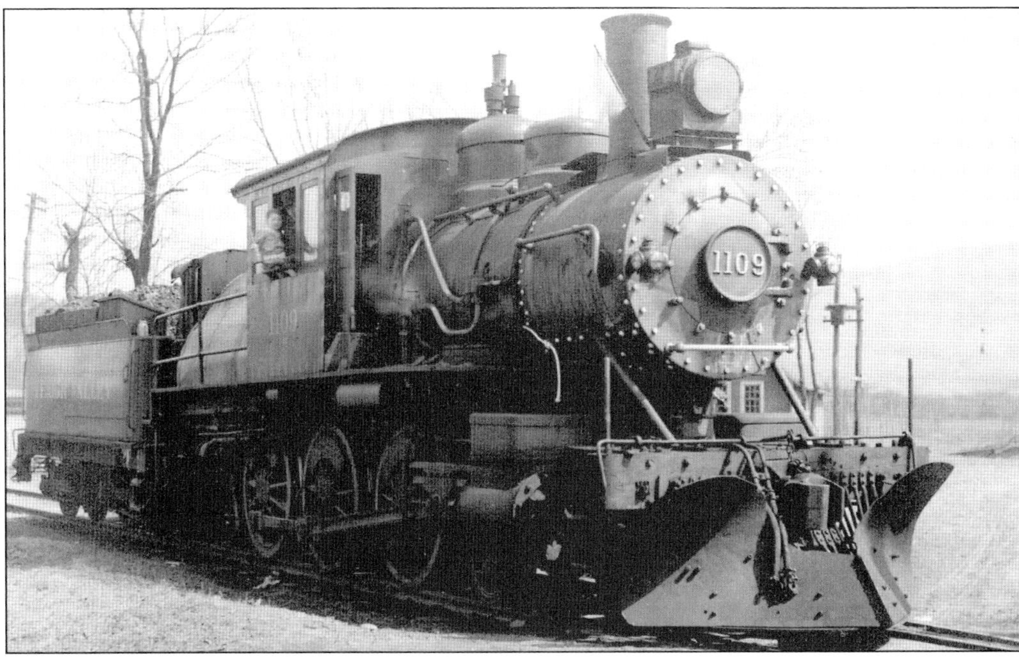

The 1109 moved freight and passengers on the Montrose Railroad from 1903 until 1923 when it was scrapped. Cottagers still recall the screech of the train's wheels as it rounded the curving track on the west shore. (The boy at the engineer's window in this real-photo postcard is prepared to oil the engine's moving parts.) To cottagers, it was affectionately known as the "hardlyable" or, for unknown reasons, the "pumpkin." (Author's collection.)

Contents

ACKNOWLEDGMENTS

I am indebted to the work of the Wyoming County Historical Society whose clippings, files of lake ephemera, and earlier sketches of Lake Carey history got me going. Robert and Robbie Fellows have been an unfailing source of images and reliable accounts of lake life. Peggy Stevens shared materials collected earlier by the lake's short-lived historical society; Elizabeth Tidball generously loaned the Davis/Quin family photographs her late mother had archived as a member. John Fassett provided several important volumes and the book's cover image. Kenny Weaver gave me access to his extensive postcard collection and boyhood recollections and gladly set out to secure images and facts I needed. Charles Petrillo supplied some rare images and the clues with which to unravel the history of the Picnic Grounds. Nancy Klimas of the office of the Wyoming County Recorder of Deeds cheerfully assisted my searches there.

I am deeply indebted to an additional 11 past or present residents who shared their recollections and family photographs, tolerating my awkward attempts to record facts and family trees. They are Doris Banis, Doris Cochran, the late Sally Farr, James Fitzsimmons, Elizabeth "Bumpy" Herman, Buck Kelly, Bill McLaughlin, Marcy Pitkin, Martha Redding, Betty Robic, and Kittie Roemer.

Because this is an illustrated history I am especially grateful to those who shared their personal collections of real-photo postcards and/or family photographs. In addition to those acknowledged above, they are Debbie Bell, Marlene Butler, Dick Daniels, Pam Dewitt, Michele Fitzsimmons, Chuck Givler, Kay Lumi, Patrick Robinson, Jeff Russell, Bertha and Eleanor Sturman, Laura Tinner, and Sally Willoughby.

Marywood University and my colleagues there provided help scanning images, as well as editorial, reference, and clerical support. Joe Fennewald granted me continuing encouragement and his skilled reference services. His able nephew, Tim O'Gorman, helped solve the mystery of the "Jewish boys camp(s)."

Finally, I am deeply grateful to all who thanked me beforehand for creating a lasting record of life at Lake Carey. I hope your faith in me is warranted and that you will not be disappointed.

Introduction

Lake Carey, one of Pennsylvania's largest natural lakes, lies amid the rolling Endless Mountains almost 1,000 feet above the Susquehanna River. Here a summer community grew after the Civil War. In the victorious northern states, it was an era of rapid industrialization, urbanization, and immigration. It was also a time when enormous wealth was generated for new elites and rising standards of living for the region's working and middles classes. These changes created a demand for summer retreats in the mountains, at the ocean, or at the lake.

The most famous and best documented of these retreats—the estates of Newport, Rhode Island; Durand's Great Camps in the Adirondacks; the "cottages" of the Berkshires and Bar Harbor—are those of elites. The summer communities of the old middle classes are less well known and recorded. Their founding families were local not national, their architecture more modest, and they were often tucked away in less dramatic sites. Over time, some were relegated to the rural poor or succumbed to urban sprawl. A few, near prosperous small towns yet far from urban centers, Lake Carey among them, preserved their architecture, scenic beauty, and cohesive communities.

The character of their summer life was strongly influenced by the moral convictions and economic interests of their residents. While elites indulged in ostentatious displays of wealth and social connections as they jockeyed for positions of national power, the old middle classes practiced self-reliance and self-discipline, honed their business skills, and built a community where neighbors shared with and supported one another.

Regardless of class, the summer retreat was sought to escape the clamor, ugliness, and even violence of the 19th-century city. For elites this could be accomplished sailing ever larger and more expensive yachts, or hosting ever more lavish events in scenic sites. For the independent businessmen and professionals of the region's small towns and cities, summer at the lake or ocean provided an opportunity to practice the rural virtues of their forebears—feeding one's family with the fish one caught oneself or filling the cottage with extended family or friends, three, four, or more to a bedroom.

Ironically, underlying the growth of all these summer communities were the railroads—intimately linked themselves to urbanization and industrialization. The speed and ease of transportation and communication they created is difficult to appreciate today. Railroads yoked together communities previously separated because they lacked a common river. They reduced travel time for freight, passengers, and mail from weeks to days and from days to hours. And they lowered the cost of shipping goods, promoting a dramatic rise in the standard of living for all. Now people could travel quickly and easily to more distant and more scenic sites, while still communicating with the folks at home. Money once needed for the necessities of food, clothing, and shelter could be spent on travel or a summer cottage. And men could continue to work in town and still devote their weekends to families in the mountains, at the shore, or at the lake.

Development at Lake Carey was made possible by the Montrose Railroad. This uncertain venture was chartered in Springville in 1869, when many small-town investors viewed railroads as a sure way to create wealth for themselves and their communities. The corporation's shareholders hoped to link the Lehigh Valley Railroad in Tunkhannock to the Albany and Susquehanna in Binghamton, but their plans soon foundered on a lack of funds. Instead, the three-foot-wide, narrow-gauge track (itself an economy) was laid only from Tunkhannock to Montrose. Even then, it was the Lehigh Valley that supplied the rails, ties, spikes, and splices. Its president, Asa Packer, had married a Springville girl. Full service began in 1874 with two 15-ton Baldwin locomotives (one named the *Asa Packer*), two passenger cars, one baggage car, three boxcars, two flatcars, and eight gondolas. There was a turntable in Tunkhannock, as well.

The Tunkhannock papers were enthusiastic. Lake Carey was to be a resort of exceptional beauty, far surpassing Harveys Lake or Crooked Lake (Lake Winola). Families and parties of young people began to camp. Others rented rooms from local farmers. Plans for a hotel were reported, and within three years, German immigrants Herman Oscar and Christina Pollner opened one on the west shore.

Residential development at the lake began shortly thereafter when Draper Billings and his wife bought 15 acres from east shore farmer George Washington Stark. Apparently Billings wanted to build a community. Instead of selling off lots, he formed an association among his Tunkhannock friends and business associates. It was chartered in April 1880 to maintain a private park and to promote skating, boating, trotting, and fishing. The initial directors—seemingly all solid members of the middle class—were Albert Townsend (a local tailor), Ziba Billings (owner of Tunkhannock's Packer House hotel), E. G. Sampson, S. Judson Stark (son of banker Samuel Stark and a partner in the Tunkhannock Toy Company), Frank E. Bunnell (three-term U.S. representative and Tunkhannock banker), Peter Miller, Felix Ansart (civil engineer and attorney), and A. B. Woodward (Tunkhannock physician and owner of a witch hazel factory). Shares entitling the owner to the use of a 40-foot lakefront lot cost $25. They sold briskly. Editor Alvin Day, himself a shareholder, soon referred to the resulting cluster of cottages as "Billings City."

Draper Billings's next development on the west shore, with Felix Ansart as his partner, was more conventional. Ansart and Billings lots were put up for individual sale, beginning in 1884. Apparently land had appreciated considerably—in the first year these lots sold for $91 to $205. Again the buyers were largely members of the old middle class, but now they were drawn also from Wilkes-Barre, Pittston, and other nearby towns along the Lehigh Valley Railroad line.

Within 20 years of the Montrose Railroad's arrival, there were more than 50 cottages and two hotels on Lake Carey's shores, at least one steamboat on its waters, and a picnic grove operated by English immigrants John and Mary Wrigley. An attractive community had been formed with appropriate institutions, including the Lake Carey Fish and Game Association, incorporated in 1894.

For many families, the new community was embodied most fully in Union Chapel, chartered in 1888. Its founders included many of the important figures in the lake's early history, including Draper Billings, E. L. Diefenderfer, and John W. Wrigley, as well as a number of its early cottagers (S. Judson Stark and William Marcy, to name but two). It became an enduring institution where many of the lake's longtime resident families, including the Coolbaughs, Weils, and Cassidys, worshipped every summer. To this day, the chapel bell rings in July and August at 9:30 a.m. and then again at 10:00 a.m. when Sunday services begin.

The developmental patterns at Lake Carey were typical of summer resorts of this era. These communities were often promoted as rustic havens from the discomforts of urban life, and railroads typically spurred their growth, as at Lake Carey. But there is little evidence that Lake Carey attracted big city folks in its early years or that the poorly financed Montrose Railroad actively promoted or underwrote its development (as railroads elsewhere often did). The mix of camping, hotels, and cottages is also common. But there is no surviving evidence that future cottagers here were first drawn to the lake by its hotels and then, after one or more summers as their guests, chose to settle at the lake as residents, a pattern typical in the Adirondacks, Bar Harbor, and some other resorts. Finally, it is interesting to note that, although many of the lake's developers were small-town entrepreneurs with deep roots in Tunkhannock, the lake also attracted recent immigrants who found attractive business opportunities here and often settled in with the community of cottagers.

In the chapters that follow I will describe the origins of Lake Carey, its heyday as a regional resort before World War I, its architecture, and the texture of its summer life. It is the story of a community of some charm and much good fortune, a place to which people returned again and again. Its architecture and social life are those Hollywood has long celebrated as quintessentially American. It has and continues to provide "a wonderful life." Yet, the community has also known tragedies. Businesses failed, children and adults died of accidental drowning, and two world wars and a depression exerted their toll on lives and livelihoods. (And countless summer romances doubtlessly led to broken hearts not long thereafter.)

As I researched the county's deed books, my efforts were frequently frustrated when cottages passed down from mother to daughter, not father to son. Thus a cottage built by a Stark might be sold one or more generations later by a Billings. Or a cottage sold by a Harding might have been built by a Marcy. Some cottages, and family businesses too, I noticed were purchased by women. These facts challenge the conventional view of the subjection of Victorian women to their patriarchal husbands and fathers. At least in the old middle classes, women often controlled the resources they inherited. It was women too who typically maintained family ties through time and across the family tree. Thus it was to daughters, who often displayed the greatest attachment to the cottage where the family had summered happily, that their widowed mothers might will it. Whether a cottage was transmitted through women or not, the number of families who have summered at Lake Carey for three, four, or even five generations attests to the lake's enduring beauty, the material comforts to be found there, and the strength of its community.

The images in this illustrated history were scanned from vintage photographs or real-photo postcards—with the exception of four lithographic postcards, themselves prints of photographs. Although photographers often framed their images with care, and posed their subjects artfully, what you see is what existed when the shutter was triggered (sometimes a little more; check out the diver on page 59). At the same time, I can only include images someone thought to record with a camera and someone else to preserve in an old shoebox or the back of a dresser drawer. While the record they provide of Lake Carey is especially rich, some gaps exist. Few photographs were taken here before Eastman popularized photography, and fewer yet of these survived into this century. On the other hand, the lake's public summer appearance during the real-photo postcard craze (roughly 1907 to 1919 at Lake Carey) is well documented. Indeed, there are far more photographs of Elsmere (later Sunbright) cottage, the Picnic Grounds, and its steamboat the *Rosalind* than I could include. Still I was never able to find photographs of Union Chapel, picnickers at Wrigley's Grove, the cottages of Hillbilly Village, the water-driven mills at the outlet, winter ice cutting, cottage interiors (with one exception), or the important founding figures.

I have also chosen to cover only the first 75 years of the lake's history as a summer place—a period stretching from 1870 to 1945. As a result, some important institutions, most notably the fire company, and the history of the last 60 years are not described. Despite many conversations with older residents, some important facets of community life in the first 75 years surely have escaped the net of interviews I cast. I have also limited for lack of space my coverage of the lake's cottages to those of the first generation built before World War I. The bungalows of the 1920s and 1930s have not been included.

I should also warn the reader of sins of commission as well as omission. While I have attempted to root the book's basic chronology in contemporary newspaper accounts and courthouse records of charters and deeds, some errors undoubtedly lumbered in. I also regret that I was unable to explore the identities and careers of the lake's professional and amateur photographers. In short, there's much left to be done in the next history of Lake Carey.

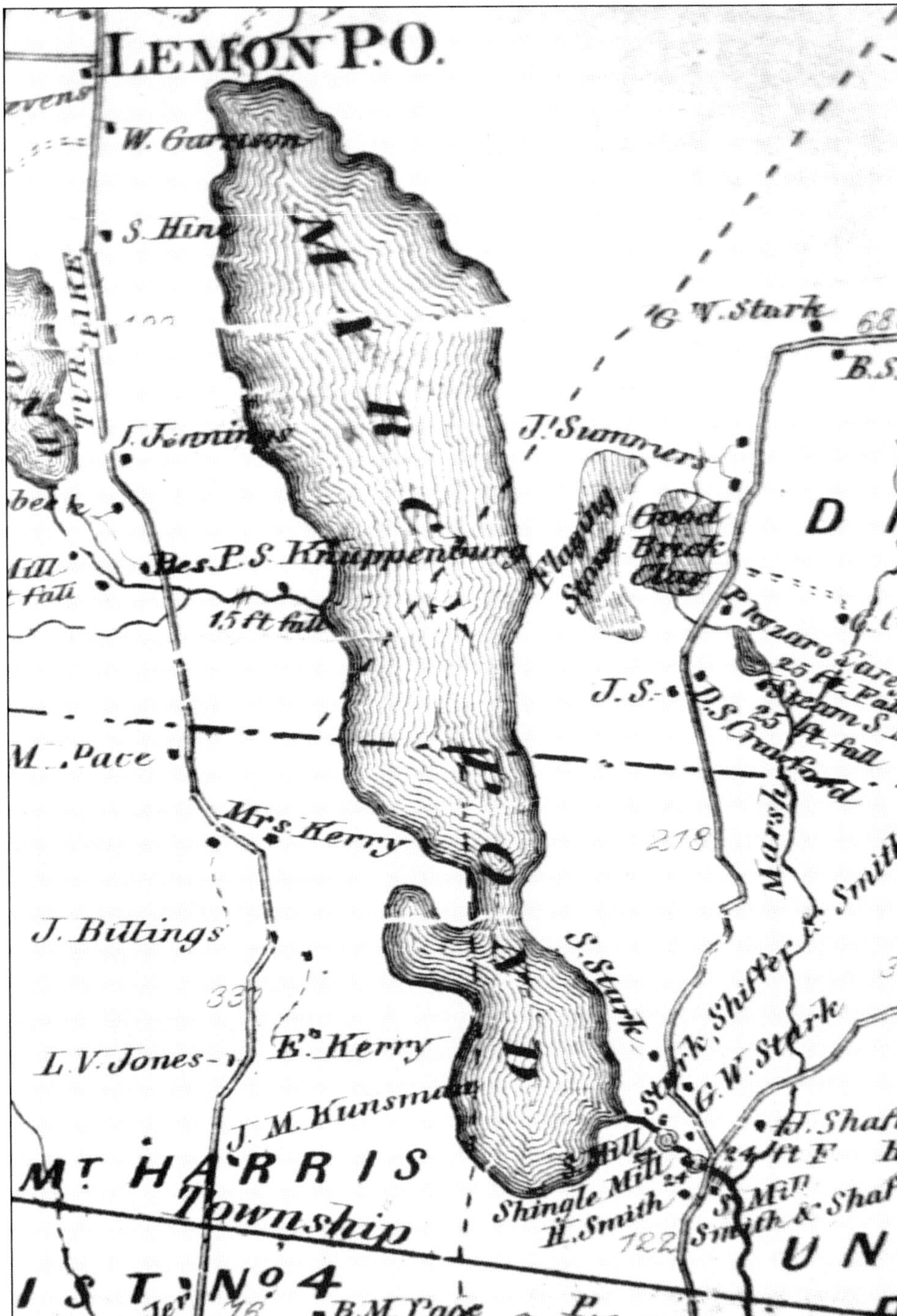

This 1869 map includes the lower lake or Flow Pond created when the outlet was dammed to yield more waterpower. The Starks' shingle mill and sawmills are marked, but there are neither farmhouses nor cottages yet. Economic resources of the time—clay beds, quarry sites, and waterpower—are carefully noted. The causeway and its bridge have not yet been built. (Wyoming County Court House.)

One

Promoting Marcy's Pond

Brothers Alvin and John Day came to Tunkhannock as young men to publish a local newspaper. They here discovered Marcy's Pond, as it was then known. It was love at first sight. Readers of the *Wyoming Democrat* were soon informed of its many charms—and the need for a more appropriate name. Here is one example, taken from Alvin Day's account of a trip to the Carey farm on the west shore:

> The lake is entirely surrounded by primeval forests, except where forest fires have swept through the southern shore and left only a fringe of second growth, berry bushes and wild flowers; but, being out upon the broad waters, on all sides, where the eye could turn, nothing met it but the mirror-like surface of the lake, the azure blue of the skies and the dense setting of the woods. So rich and fleecy are the outlines of the forest, on the northern shore, that scarce an opening can be seen, the whole earth, from the mountain top to the waters edge, presenting one unvaried hue of unbroken verdure; and . . . [as if] vegetation were not satisfied with a triumph so complete, the trees overhang the lake itself, shooting out towards the light, and there are many places where a boat might pull beneath the arches of the dark Rembrandt-looking hemlocks, quivering aspens and melancholy pines.

Here was nature, pure and wholesome, unsullied by the forces of civilization and progress. With its hillsides of hemlock and pine and its shorelines shaded by water elm and river birch, Lake Carey offered an undisturbed and solemn beauty comforting to the soul. What reader could resist it, and what reader would disagree with Day that it richly deserved the more fitting name Lake Carey.

Alvin Day was writing only one year after the railroad began running between Montrose and Tunkhannock. At this time, there was only a hamlet and two mills at the lake's outlet and the Dan Carey and Asa Stevens farmsteads on the west shore, as well as a simple railroad depot. The lake was as yet undisturbed by many visitors.

As soon as railroad service was in place, the Careys and the Stevens began to clear picnic sites, sell food and drink, and rent rooms, fishing rafts, and small boats. Parties of young people discovered the pleasures of camping at the lake. One group of eight from nearby Factoryville carried in pies and cakes and puddings, baked beans and pork, bread, pickles, butter, eggs and meal, canned cherries, coffee, sugar, salt potatoes, onions, lemons, and apples. In addition, they loaded their wagon with lanterns, hatchets, matches, quilts, robes, blankets, salves, rags, crockery, tin cups, spiders, kettles, a rifle, an axe, fish hooks, hammocks, rods, and bats. All this for three July days in 1878. They stabled their horses in Dan Carey's barn and rented a boat and a scow with which to ferry their supplies to the east shore. With their tents raised (one for the men and another for the young women), they picnicked, fished, sang, danced on a platform at Stevens's farmhouse and visited the two-year-old toy factory at the outlet.

The volume of visitors, however, was soon greater than the hospitality of two farm families could manage. Herman Oscar and Christina Pollner opened the first hotel in 1877 on a rise south of the Carey farmhouse, near the first railroad depot. Their establishment, with a capacity of 60 guests, served the lake for 12 years, until destroyed by a tornado in 1890. Apparently disheartened, the Pollners left for Oregon.

The lake's second hotel endured for almost a century. It too was the vision of a German American. In 1882, E. L. Diefenderfer, a physician from Ashley, purchased land on the west shore, including Asa Stevens's farmhouse and its popular spring. The remodeled farmhouse opened on August 24, 1887, as the Spring Grove House to much fanfare. There was an afternoon ice-cream festival to raise funds to improve the new train station opening behind the inn. Cottages were decorated with lights; a boat parade and carnival were included. A special train left Tunkhannock at 8:00 p.m. for the dinner and dancing to begin at 9:00 p.m.

Diefenderfer began by selling 50-foot lakefront lots several years before he opened the hotel, presumably to capitalize the venture. But his development was actually the second at the lake. Draper Billings's Lake Carey Park Association was first, followed shortly by his sales on the west shore.

In the early 1890s, Eugene Martin planned a fitting hotel to serve the growing resort. Martin, a newspaperman with the New York *Telegraph* had been a cottage owner on the east shore since 1883. Fern Cliffe opened in the summer of 1894 on an east shore ridge with a splendid view of the lake. With 100 rooms or more, however, it was too large. Stories soon appeared in the local papers of rowdy behavior in the hotel's bar. Within 10 years the venture was bankrupt. Two years later Fern Cliffe burned to the ground. With Fern Cliffe's demise, the lake was left with the Spring Grove House, several boardinghouses, and various rental cottages. They proved sufficient as the era of the railroad resort drew to a close and World War I approached.

After the war, the prosperity of the 1920s brought new residential development. George Washington Stark's son, John M. Stark, developed the east shore of the Flow Pond. One-story bungalows with lake rights sprang up rapidly in "Hillbilly Village" there. John Kilcoyne platted over 100 lots on the lake's causeway and the Flow Pond's west shore. Lots on the causeway, many with fine views of the large lake, sold well, and small cottages soon followed. Edward Hinchcliffe, another member of the Stark family, attempted to develop a second tier on the east shore, but the Depression interfered. Plans by Clarence Toole to develop second- and third-tier cottages on the Spring Grove Hotel property also faltered in the hard times of the 1930s.

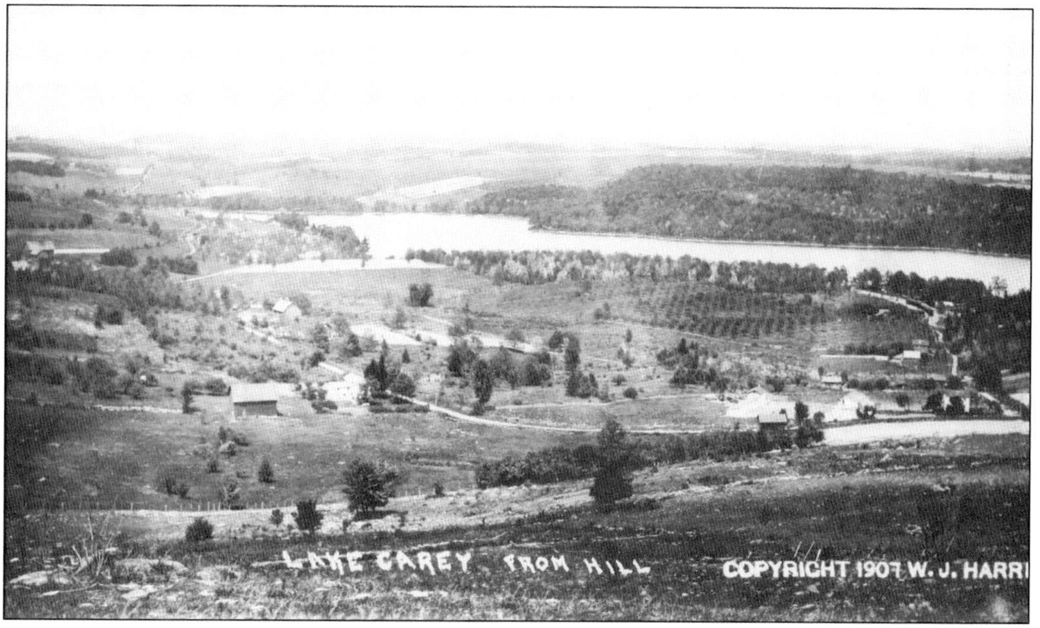

The view on this real-photo postcard in 1875 inspired Alvin Day, editor of the *Wyoming Democrat* and early lake booster, to write, "The . . . view from Mount Airy is magnificent. To the right is Waverly . . . while immediately before you is Lake Carey; its surface smooth as glass and its waters as limpid as pure air; while on either hand are finely cultivated farms, attractive residences and orchards laden with fruit." (Russell collection.)

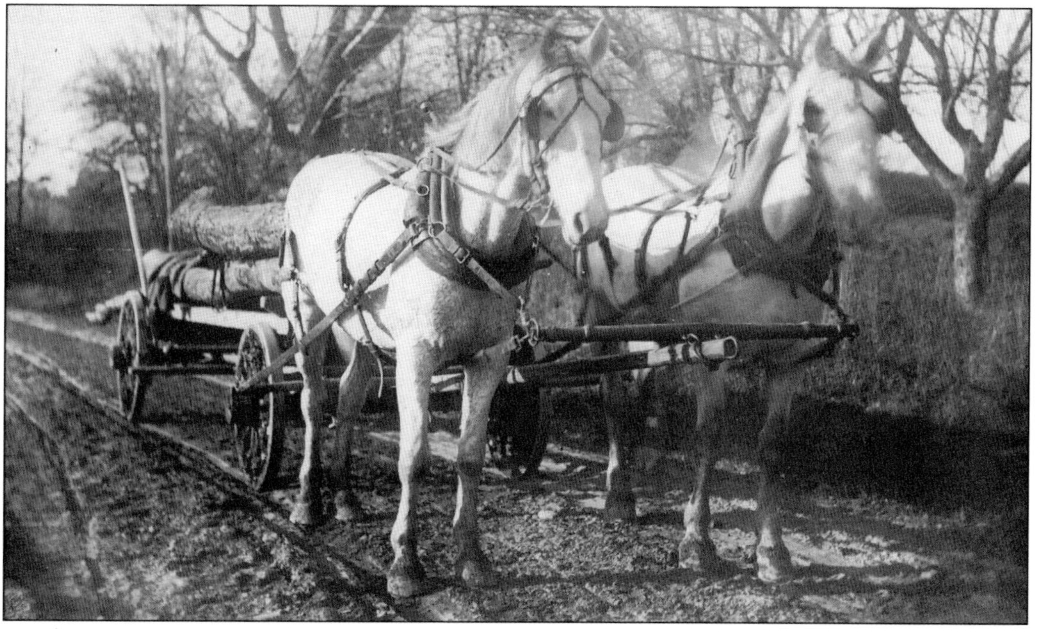
Lumber was an important industry at the lake for over a century. After they were felled, the trees were skidded or dragged to a road and then carted, as pictured in this real-photo postcard, to the lake's millpond. A water-driven sawmill belonging to George Washington Stark and his descendants operated at the outlet until the 1940s. A toy factory, later a gristmill and cider mill, also was located there. (Author's collection.)

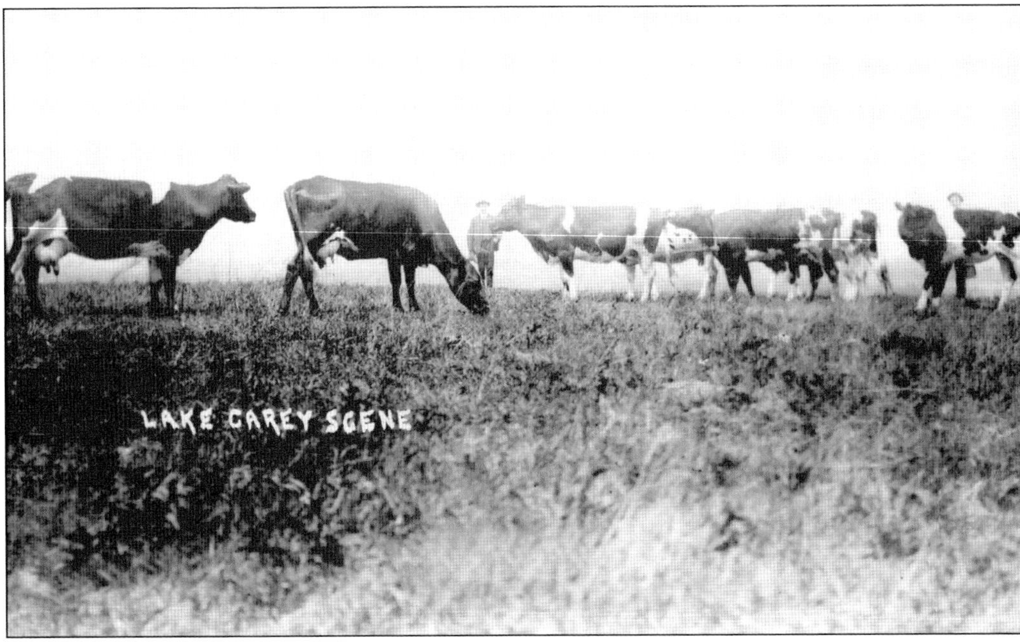

Dairy farming was important as well. In this real-photo postcard, Guernsey cattle graze on a misty morning around 1907. East shore farmers John W. Wrigley and Asa Stevens both were registered breeders then of the more popular Jersey cattle. (Russell collection.)

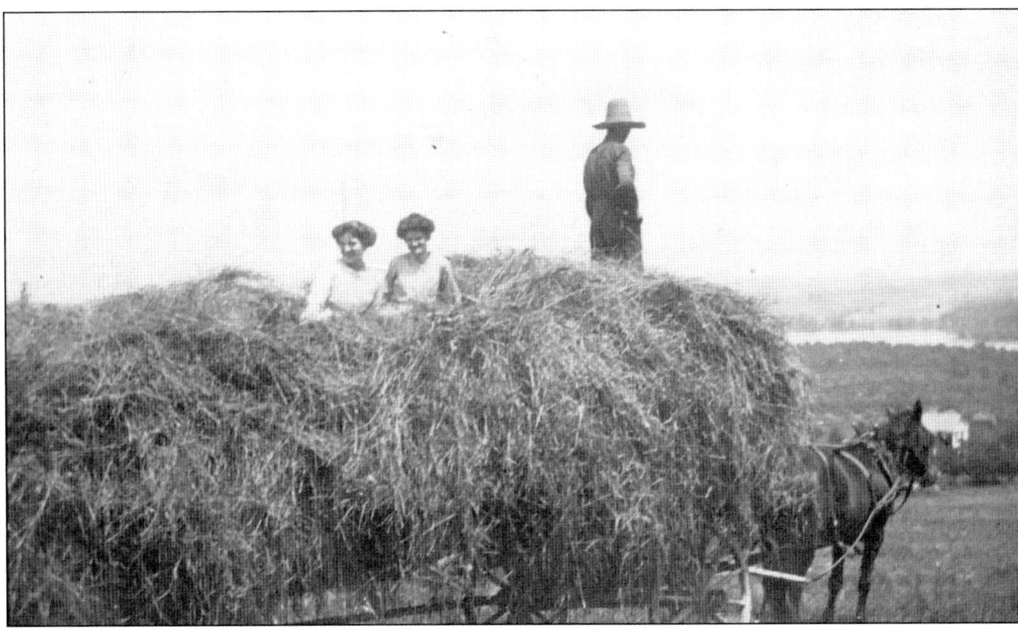

Two women enjoy a hayride on Mount Airy above the lake in this real-photo postcard. Hay was an essential part of the area's agricultural economy; for the lake's summer residents, hayrides were a rustic treat. (Robinson collection.)

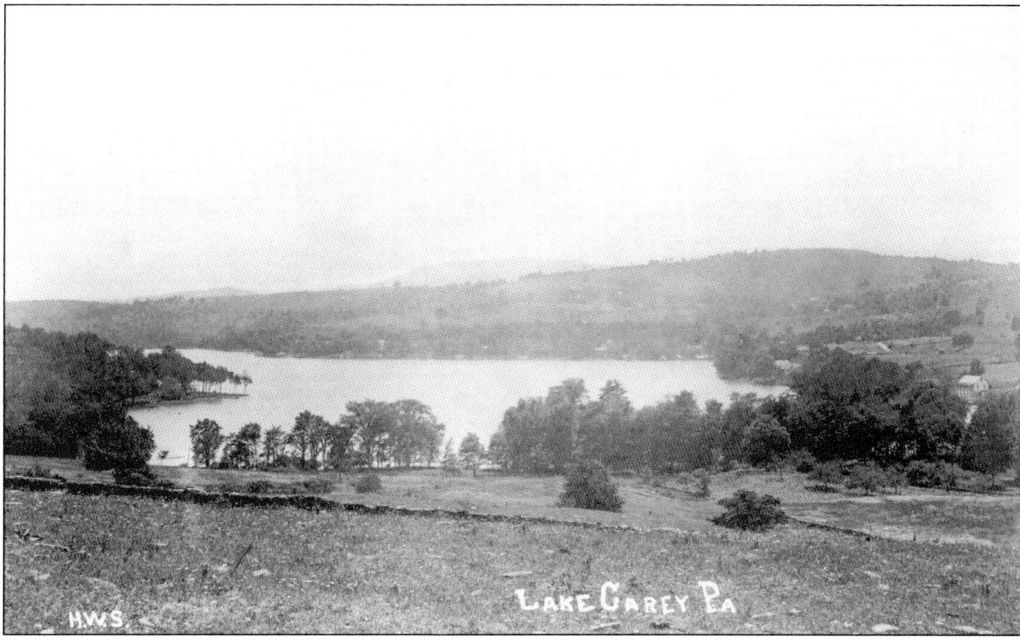

Here is a real-photo postcard view to the south-southwest from a hillside on the Stevens farm at the lake's northeast end. Kilkenny cottage is visible to the far right. (Russell collection.)

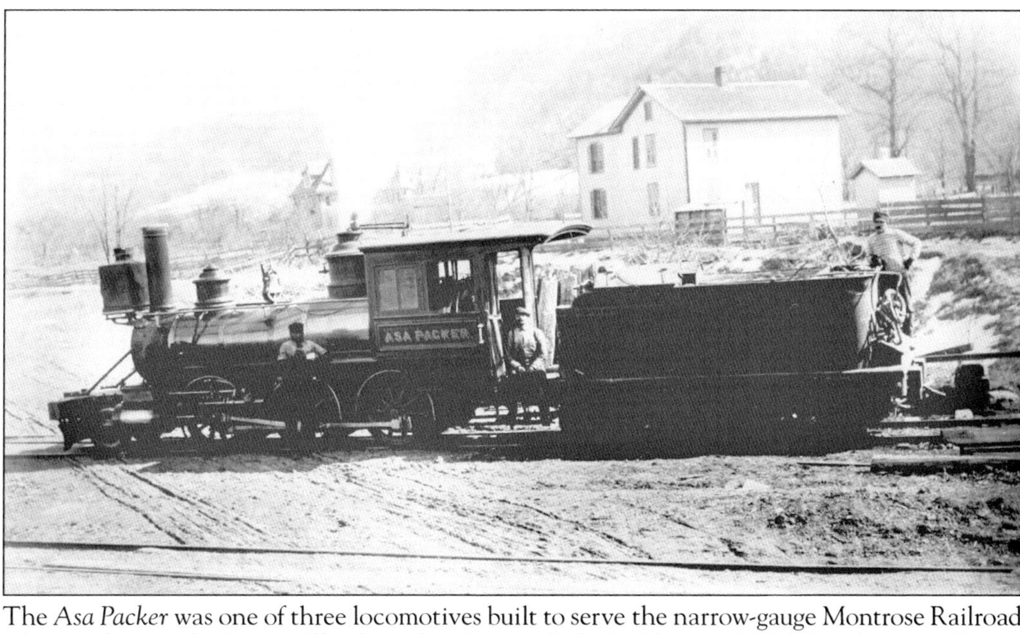

The *Asa Packer* was one of three locomotives built to serve the narrow-gauge Montrose Railroad. Chartered in nearby Springville, the railroad was to link Tunkhannock with Binghamton. Capital for this ambitious project proved difficult to raise, but the Lehigh Valley Railroad's Asa Packer offered his help in return for a controlling interest. (Petrillo collection.)

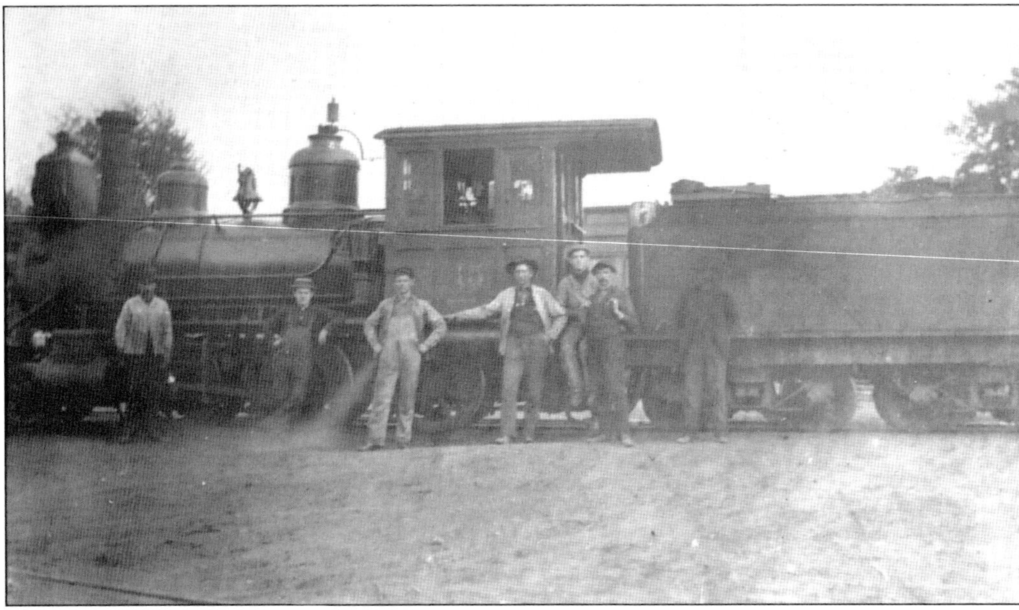

Full service between Tunkhannock and Montrose began in 1874. Engine 15, built by the Baldwin Works in 1882, was another of the line's early locomotives. With three engines, the railroad scheduled three round trips daily. The fare from Tunkhannock to the lake and back in 1880 was 25¢. (Wyoming County Historical Society.)

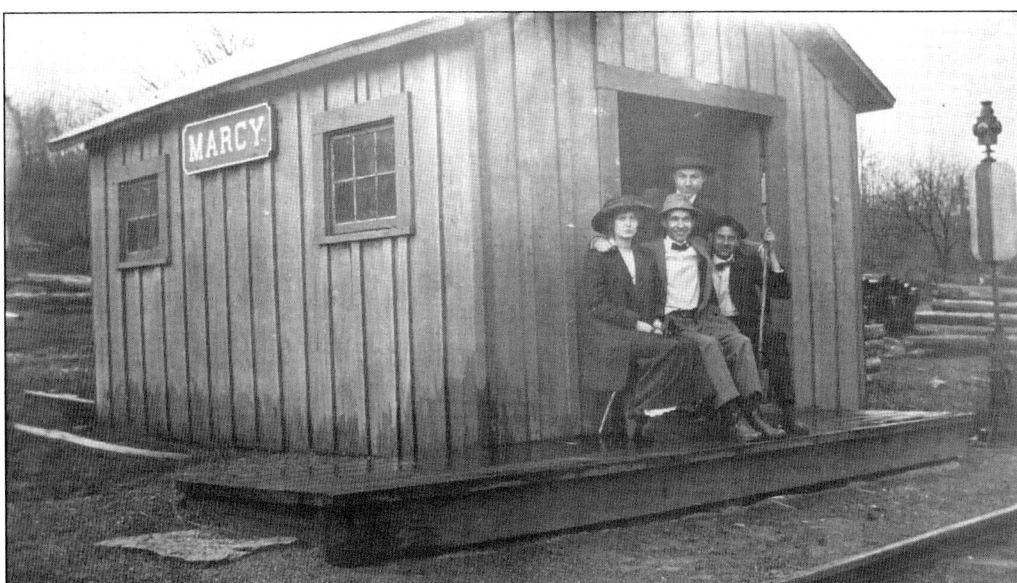

The railroad followed the "back way" to the lake—a gentler climb—crossing several country roads. Marcy Station was located a half-mile south of the lake at what is now Marcy Road. Here passengers, baggage, or freight could be picked up or delivered. Indeed, the train would stop wherever someone flagged it down. (Petrillo collection.)

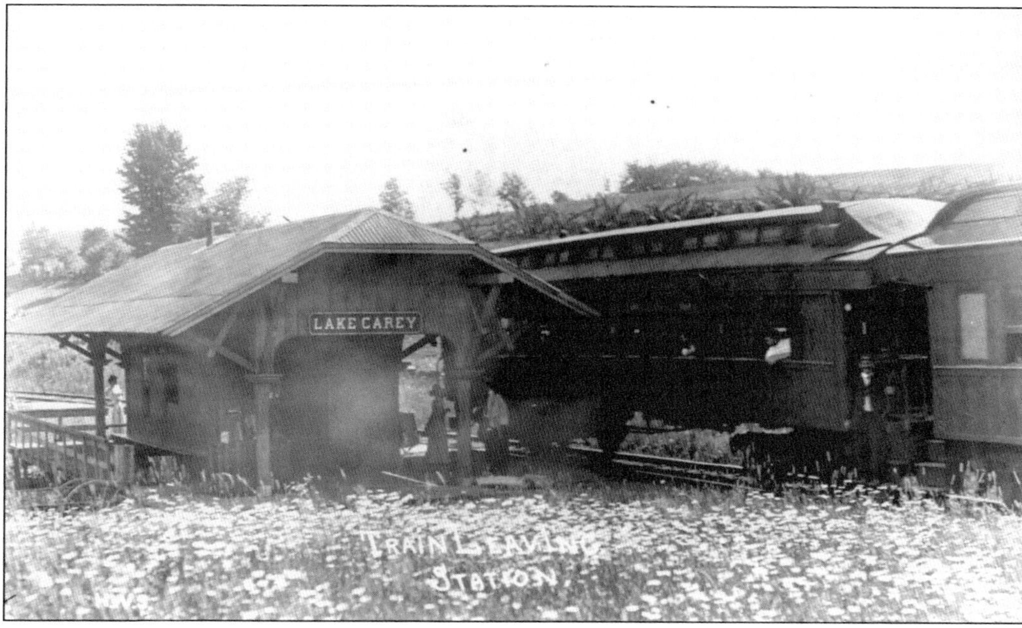

The line followed the lake's west shore to this depot constructed halfway up the large lake in the mid-1880s. A traveler could leave New York on the Lehigh Valley's *Black Diamond Express* at 8:50 on a summer's morning and arrive at this handsome station set in a field of wild daisies at 2:52 the same afternoon. (Petrillo collection.)

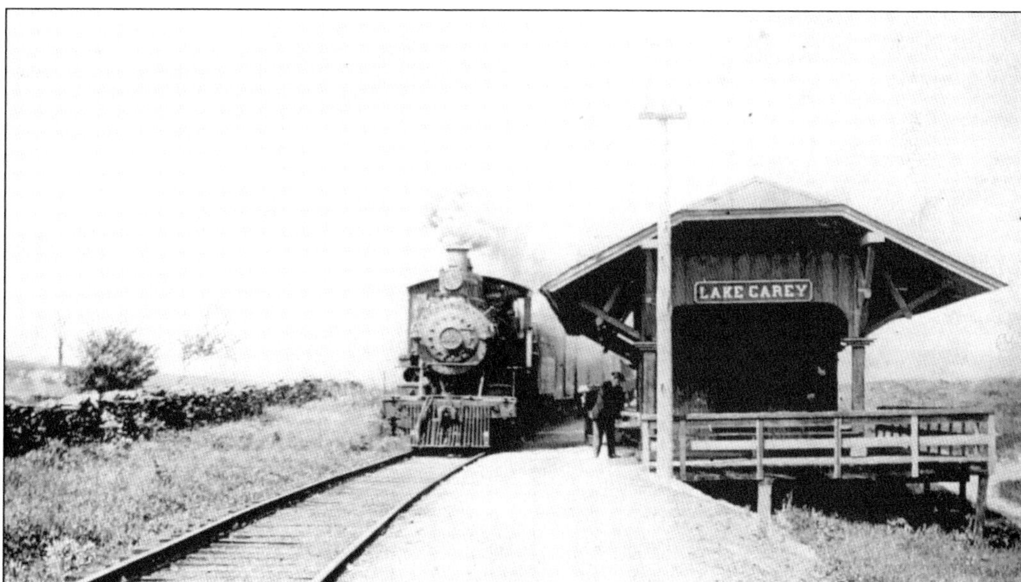

The Lehigh Valley, now the railroad's formal owner, spent $86,000 in 1903 to replace the original rails with standard gauge. The old locomotives were sold and replaced with two 4-6-0 Baldwin-built engines, the 1099 and 1109. In this photograph, the 1109 stands at the station en route to Tunkhannock. (Weaver collection.)

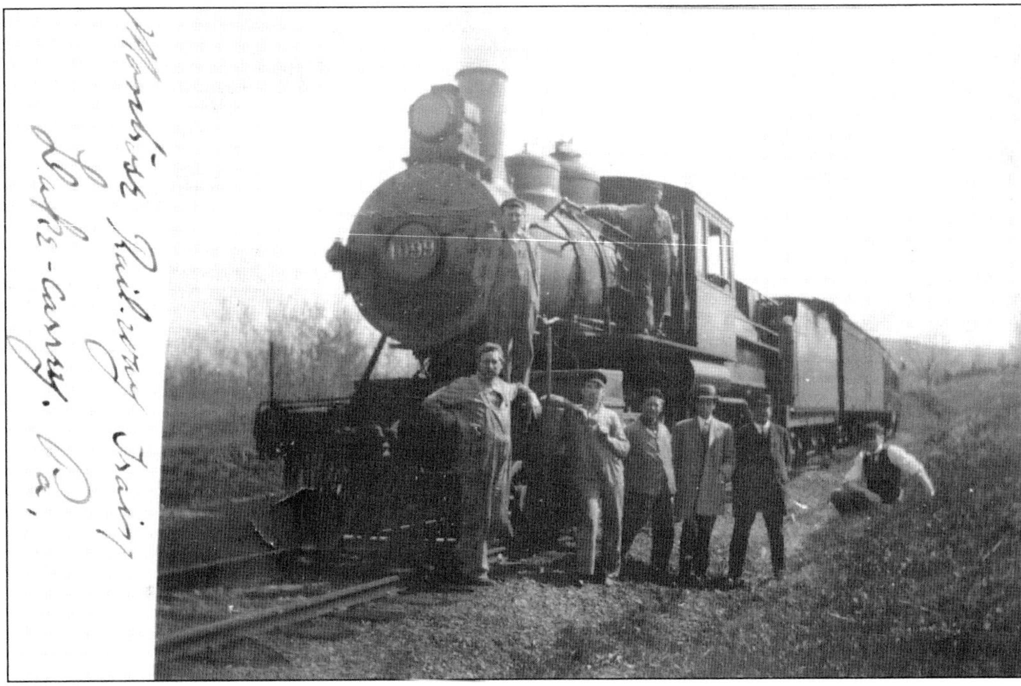

This is the 1109's sister, the 1099, with its crew. The card's 1910 message from Arthur Wall (who may have taken the photograph on this real-photo postcard) offers to take the South Montrose recipient's picture, if he will flag down the train the next time Wall is aboard. (Russell collection.)

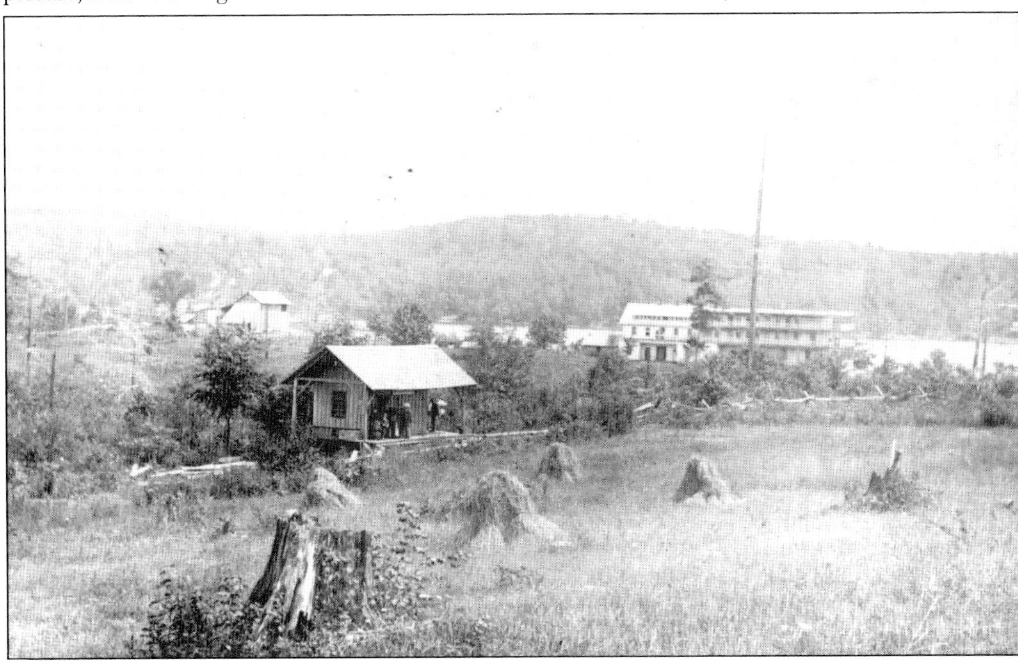

Herman Oscar and Christina Pollner opened their hotel in 1877 on a five-acre site once part of the Carey farm. They added a three-story addition in 1883, only to lose this successful business to a tornado and fire in 1890. Note the lake's first, simple railroad station in the foreground where a family awaits the train. (Petrillo collection.)

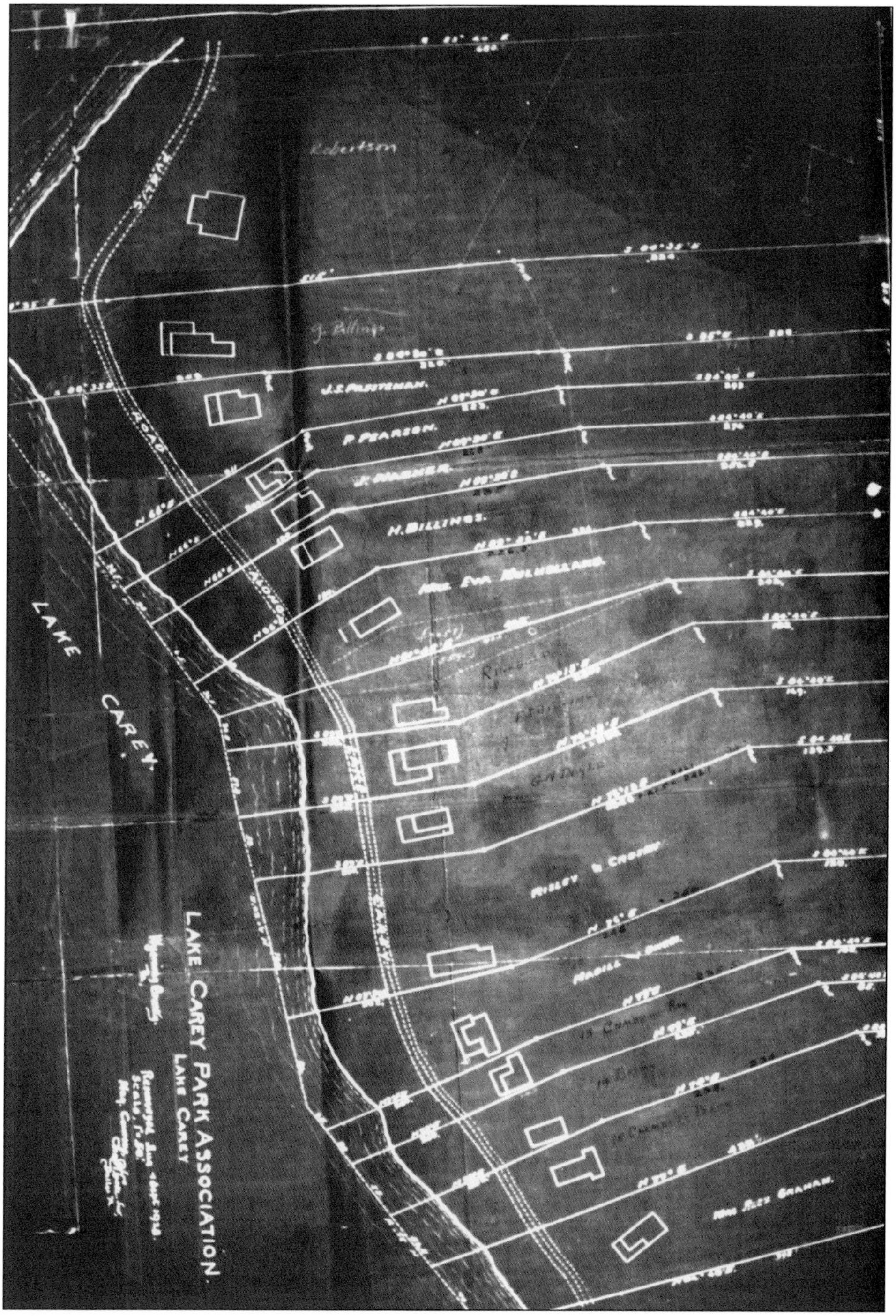

The Lake Carey Park Association on the lake's east shore was its first residential development. Draper Billings purchased 15 acres there for $375 in July 1879. He then sold association shares to friends and acquaintances, entitling them to a cleared lakefront lot—clearing cost $12 and the lot itself $13. The diamond-shaped park has disappeared by the time of this 1928 resurvey; the Mulholand/Rinebold property line was redrawn through its center. (Wyoming County Recorder of Deeds.)

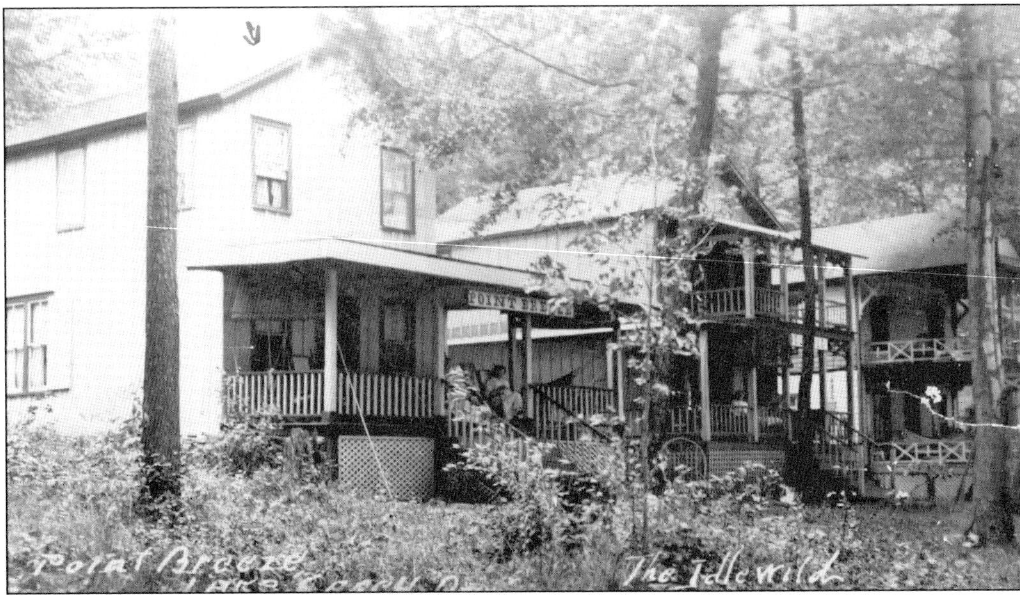

Looking south in this real-photo postcard, the early park association cottages Point Breeze, Idlewild, and Summer Rest face the lake in heavily wooded lots. They later succumbed to a 1927 fire, which began in the Rubrights' neighboring cottage (located up the hill on the left) after a poker party broke up. (Author's collection.)

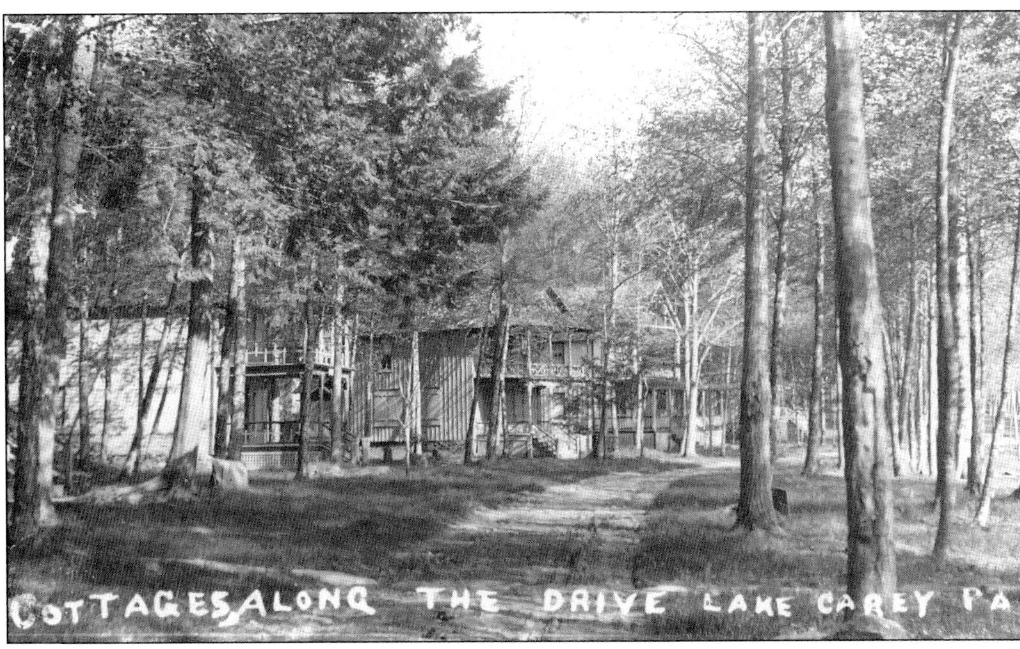

Further south, Thistle, Bayview, and Auto Rest are still shuttered in this early spring real-photo postcard from 1907 or so. Bayview was then Eleanor Rinebold's cottage—she sent the postcard. These three cottages survived the fire, but Auto Rest was demolished in the 1980s. (Author's collection.)

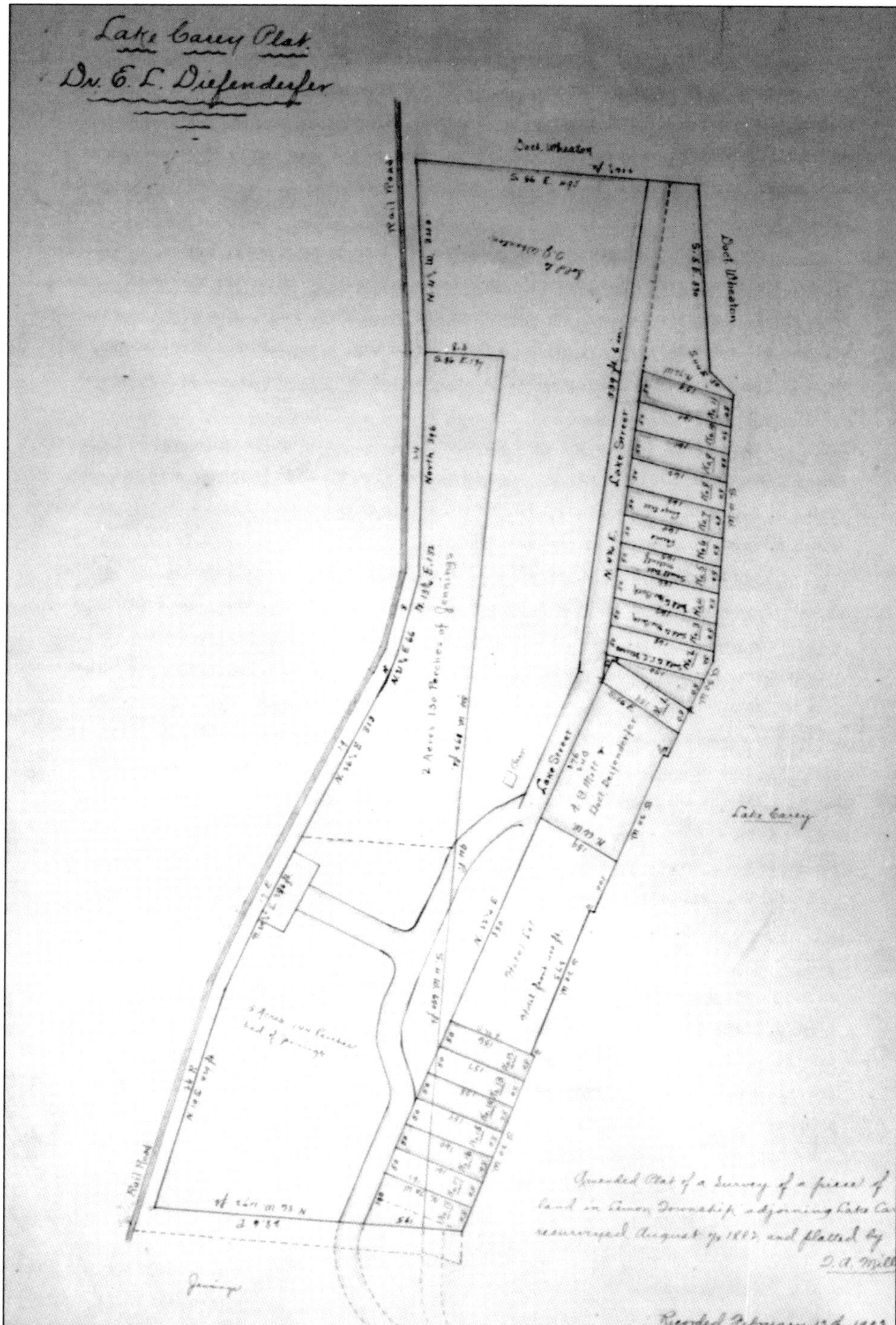

Development on the west shore followed soon thereafter. E. L. Diefenderfer purchased 23 acres of the Stevens and Jennings farms in 1882 and laid out 18 lots. He reserved a large one for himself and friend A. B. Mott and another, containing the Stevens farmhouse and a spring, for a hotel. (Wyoming County deed book.)

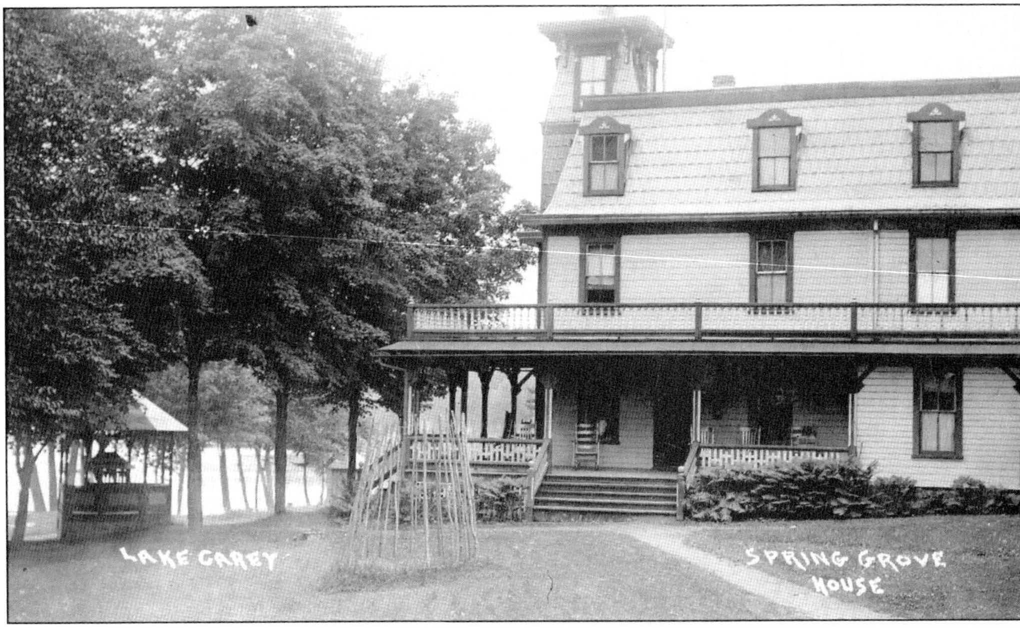

E. L. Diefenderfer "modernized" the Stevens farmhouse five years later in the fashionable Second Empire style to create an enduring and popular lake institution, Spring Grove House. This real-photo postcard view of the north facade reveals the wraparound porches, tower, and third story (under a Mansard roof) he added. (Author's collection.)

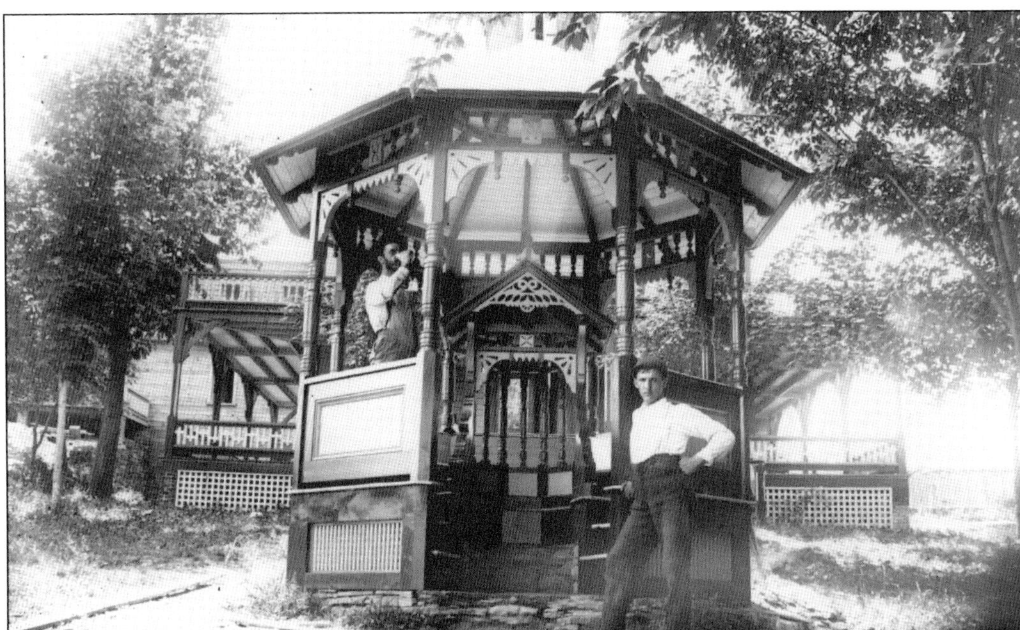

Here the hotel's ornate springhouse gets a fresh coat of paint in 1898. This image is from an original glass plate presumably by F. C. Shook. (Daniels collection.)

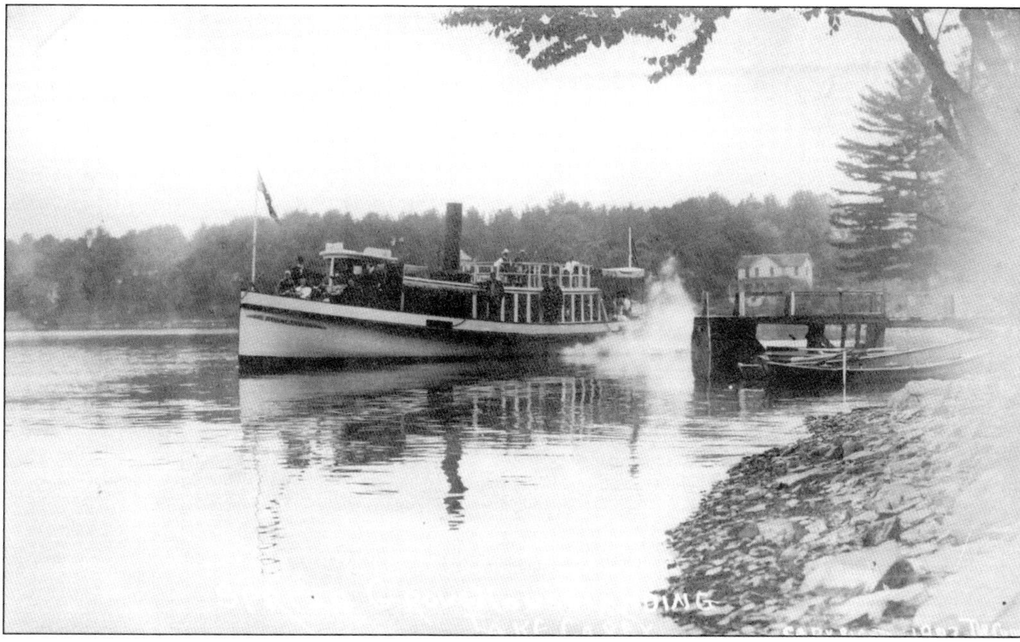

The *Rosalind* sits at the Spring Grove House landing in 1907 in this real-photo postcard; Ed Stevens's boardinghouse (later that of P. J. Ryan) is in the background. (Weaver collection.)

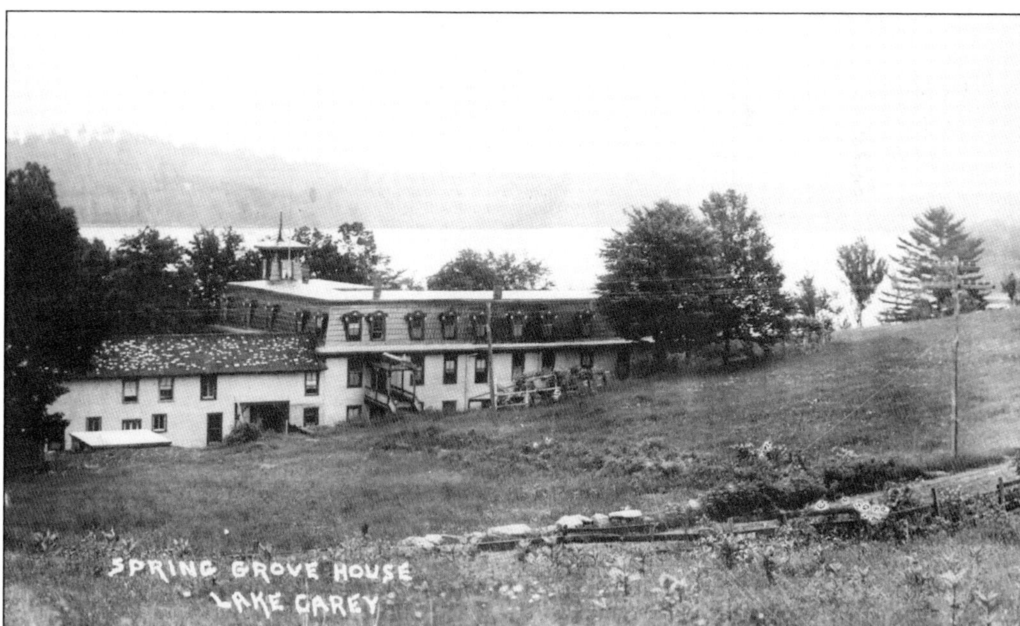

The back of Spring Grove House faced the train station. Guests arriving by train could walk down the lane in mid-picture to the second-story entrance at the rear in this real-photo postcard. (Russell collection.)

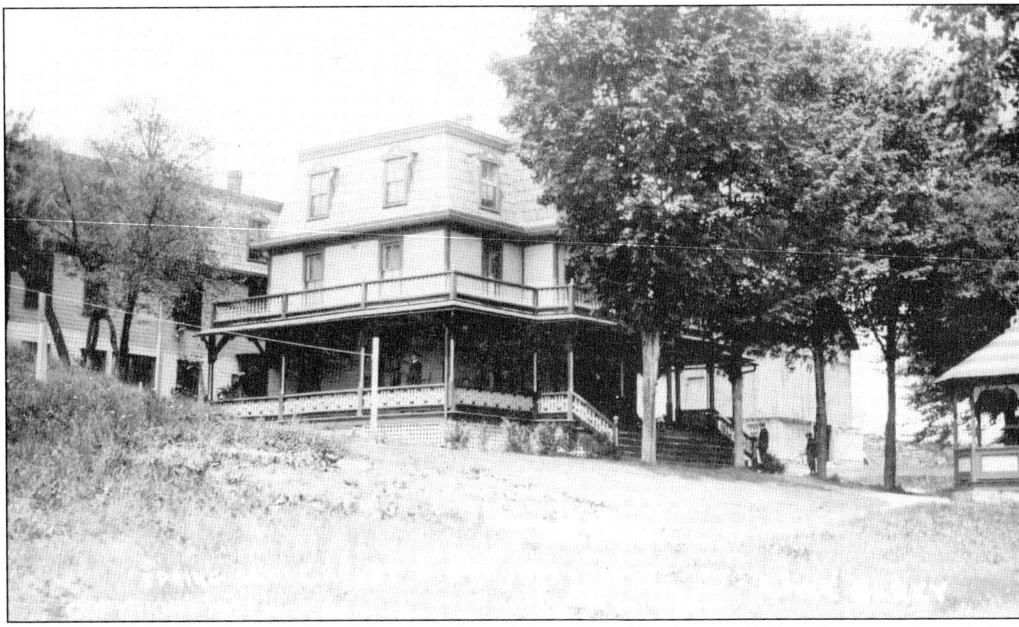

This real-photo postcard view of the south and east facades also includes the now-demolished bank barn on the right rear—a reminder of the hotel's past as a working farm. During E. L. Diefenderfer's ownership, the hotel was managed by Grant Tinsley, John H. Jones, and, in the final years, by John Stark Coolbaugh of Buena Vista cottage. (Sturman collection.)

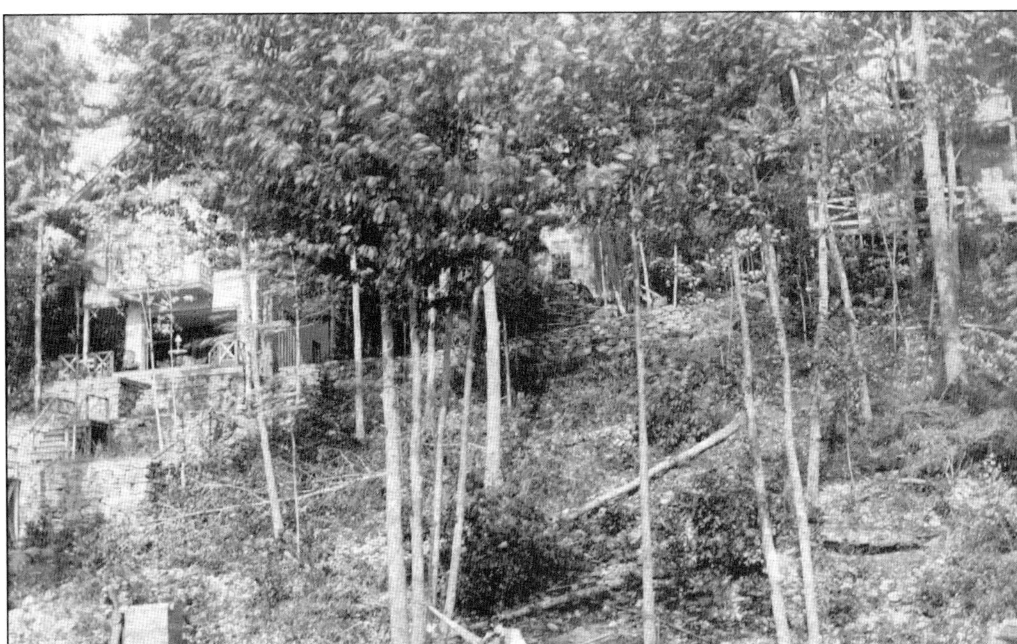

Fern Cliffe, the Bijou, and Maple Lodge stand above the lake before the Fern Cliffe Hotel was built on this east shore site. Note the open gable, elegant balcony, and wide entrance of Eugene Martin's board-and-batten Ferncliffe cottage in this early photograph by C. F. Cook of Wilkes-Barre. (Daniels collection.)

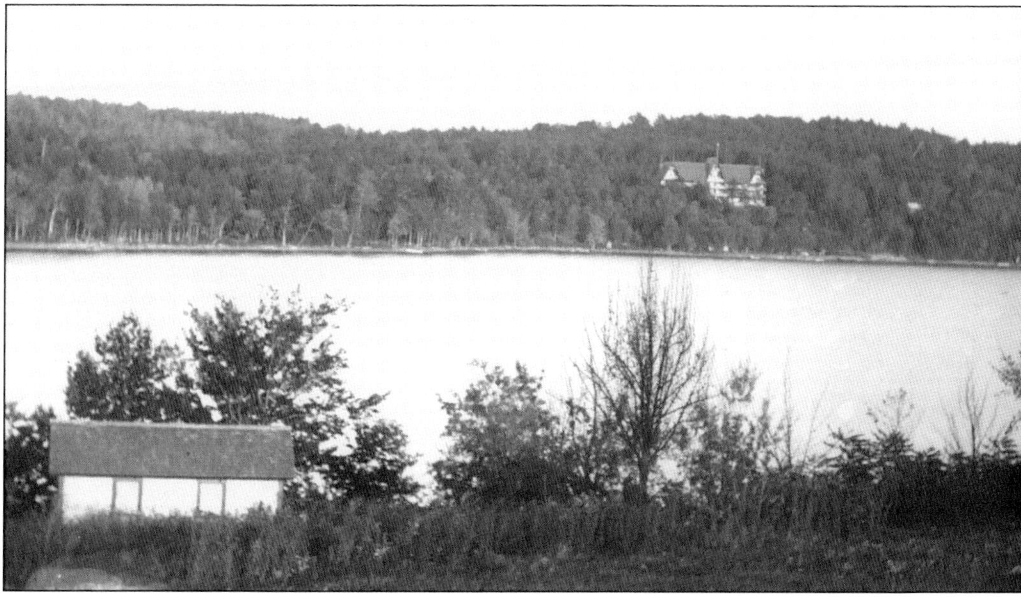

The three-story Fern Cliffe Hotel was built to hold 250 guests for $8,000 in 1894. Never a success, its furnishings were sold 10 years later in a sheriff's sale. The hotel, acquired that year by John Redington's Lake Carey Land and Improvement Company, was destroyed in an early morning fire on March 5, 1906. This original glass plate is dated October 6, 1898. (Daniels collection.)

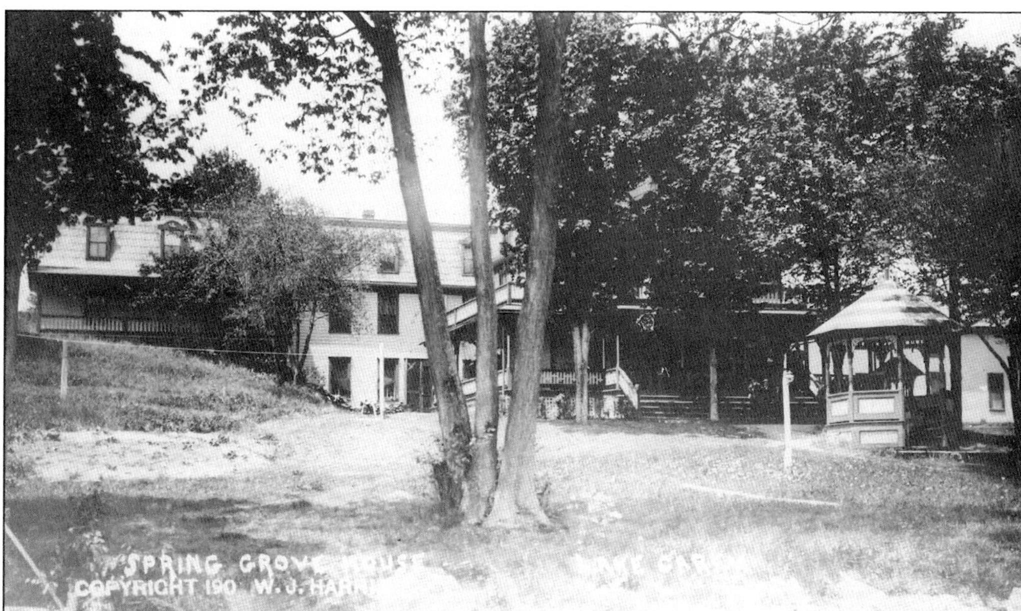

After Fern Cliffe Hotel came to an end, Spring Grove House was the lake's only hotel. Frank McGee purchased it for $4,000 from E. L. Diefenderfer's widow, Sara, the year of the Fern Cliffe fire (and only one year before W. J. Harris took the photograph on this real-photo postcard). On McGee's retirement in 1913, he sold the hotel to Joseph W. and Elizabeth Oliver, who promptly closed the bar. (Author's collection.)

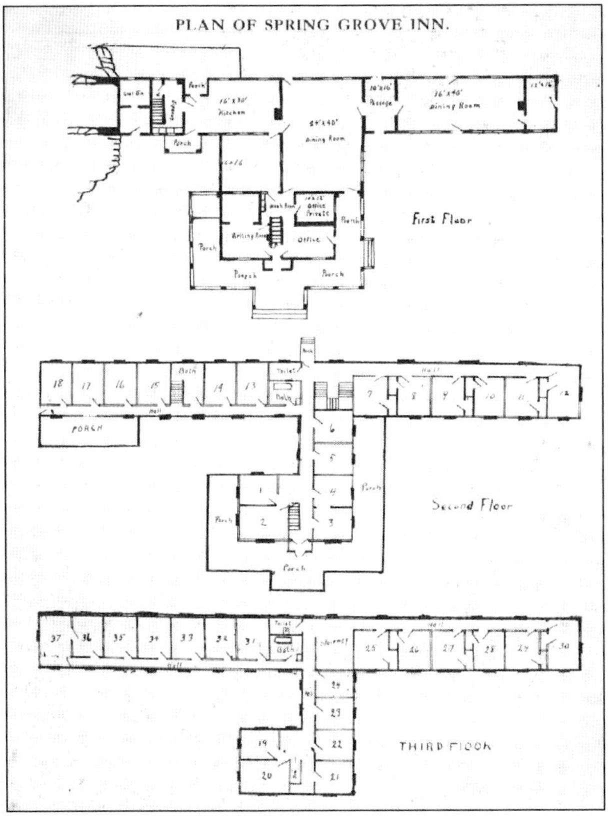

The Olivers expanded the hotel, adding the north wing (on the right), which contained a new dining room and an additional 12 rooms. They renamed it the Spring Grove Inn. New bathrooms were installed, one to a floor, with hot and cold running water. Rooms were $2 to $2.50 a night or $12 for the week (initially, references were required). (Fellows collection.)

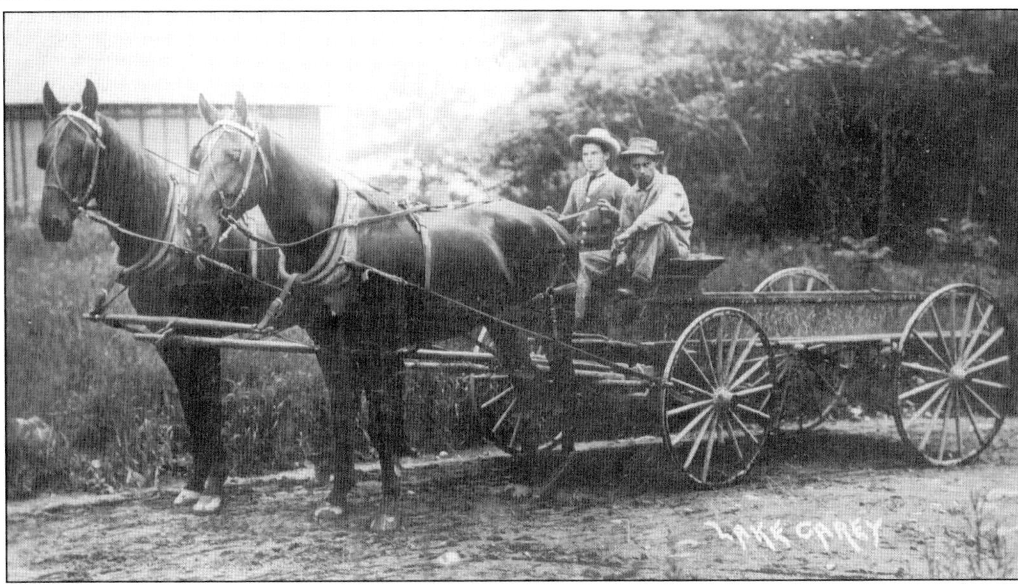

These two men on the road behind the hotel in this real-photo postcard may have been employees. A Wyoming County directory of 1900 lists a chambermaid, Lizzie Pritchard; a domestic, Mary Pritchard; and a porter, James B. Gorman, as employed there. During the summers, Elizabeth Oliver drew on students from the Indian Industrial School at Carlisle to staff the hotel and work its farm across the road. (Russell collection.)

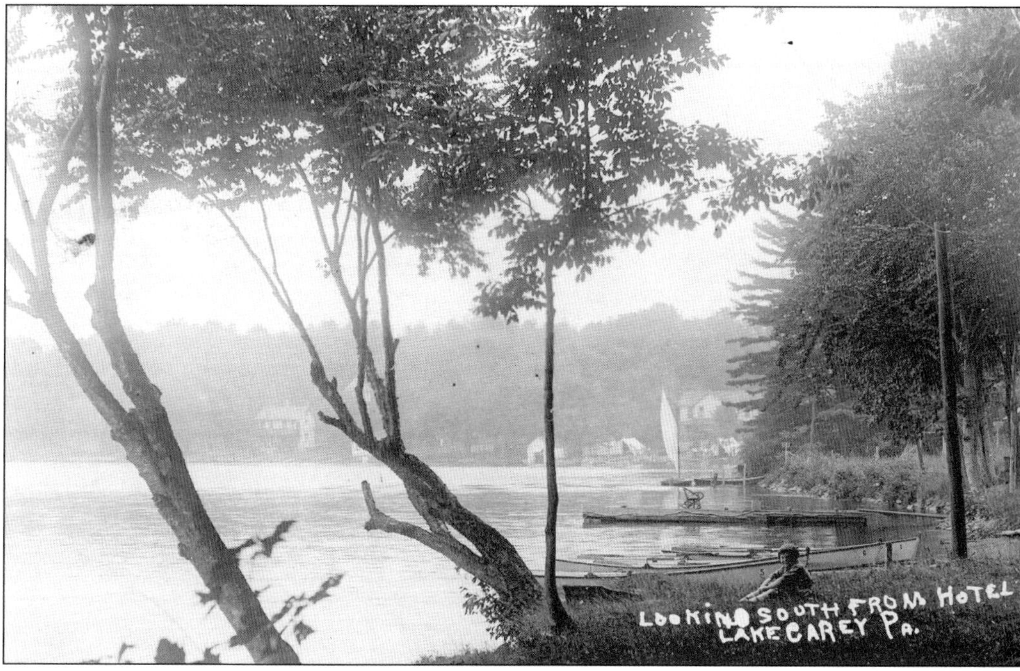

This real-photo postcard captures the west shore visible from the hotel's lakefront on a hazy day. Note the small boy looking at the camera in front of the hotel's rowboats numbered 5, 8, and 1. The Stevens/Ryan boardinghouse is just visible beyond the large pine tree. (Author's collection.)

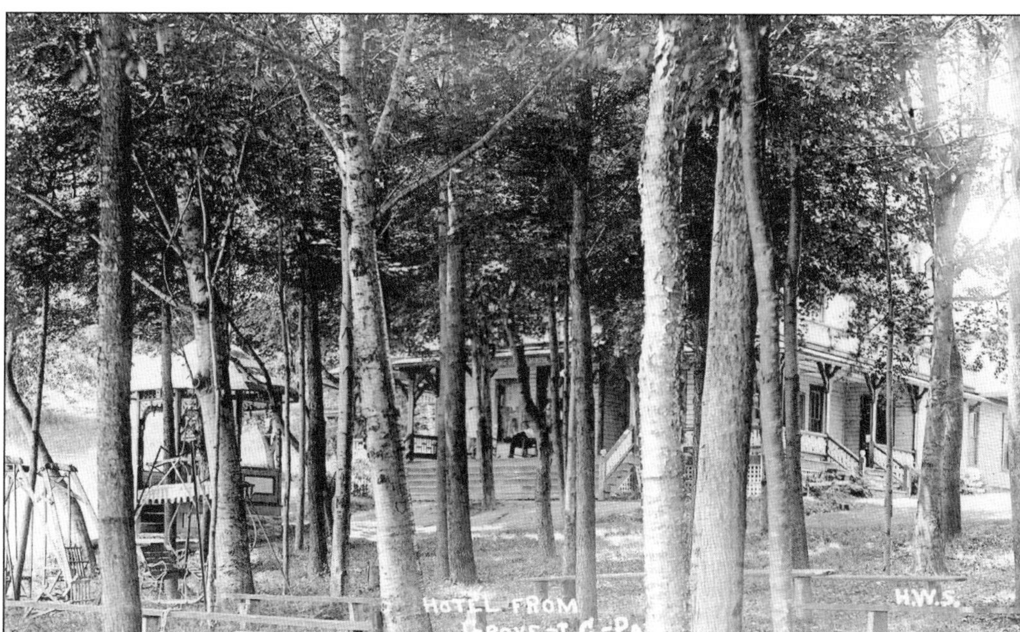

On Sunday evenings cottagers would gather in boats decorated with Chinese lanterns to sing hymns with the Olivers' guests who were seated on the benches in the foreground in this real-photo postcard. Leland Stearns led these "services" for years. (Author's collection.)

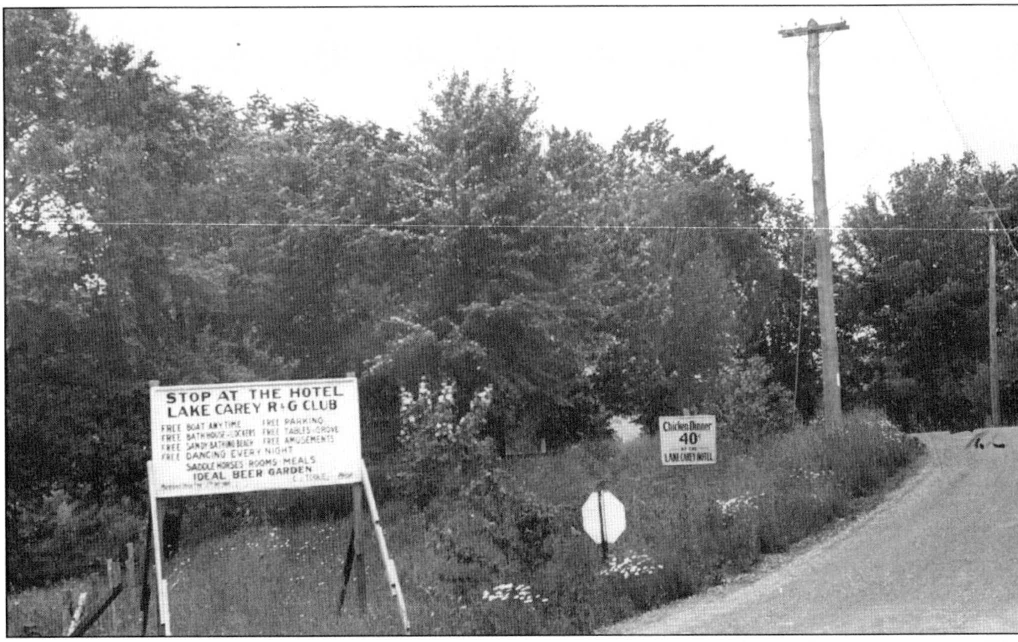

In 1930, Clarence J. Toole bought the Spring Grove Inn with a $300 down payment. The Depression, however, disrupted his plans to develop 20 cottages there. By 1937, the hotel was a rod and gun club. This sign at the lake's entrance announces seven free benefits; but there is a $2 annual membership fee (in very small print). After 97 years of service, the hotel was destroyed by fire in 1983. (Weaver collection.)

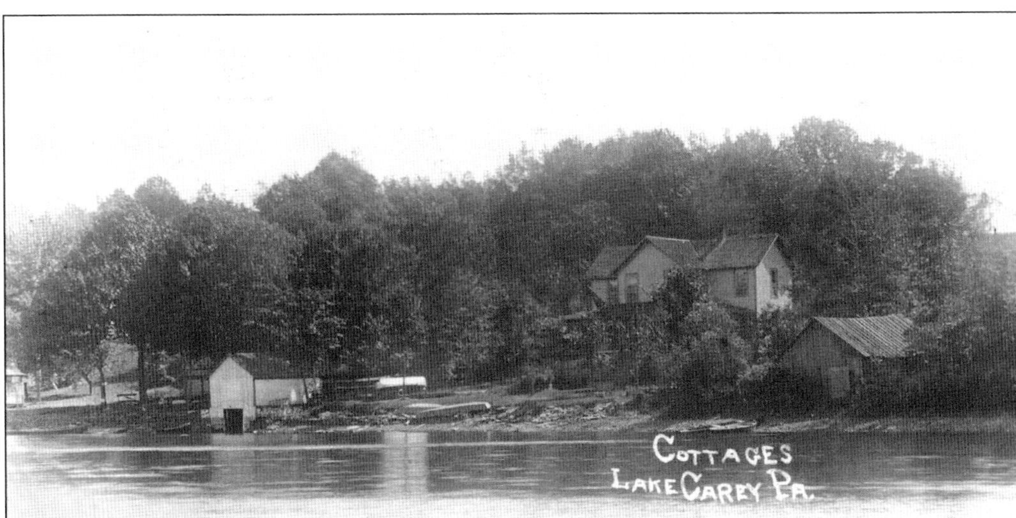

Edwin Stevens and later Patrick James and Mary Ryan operated a popular boardinghouse just visible against the trees in this real-photo postcard. Stevens also operated the *Lily of the Lake* (described as a raft with a steam engine-driven paddle wheel) and a store. He built rowboats as well. (Russell collection.)

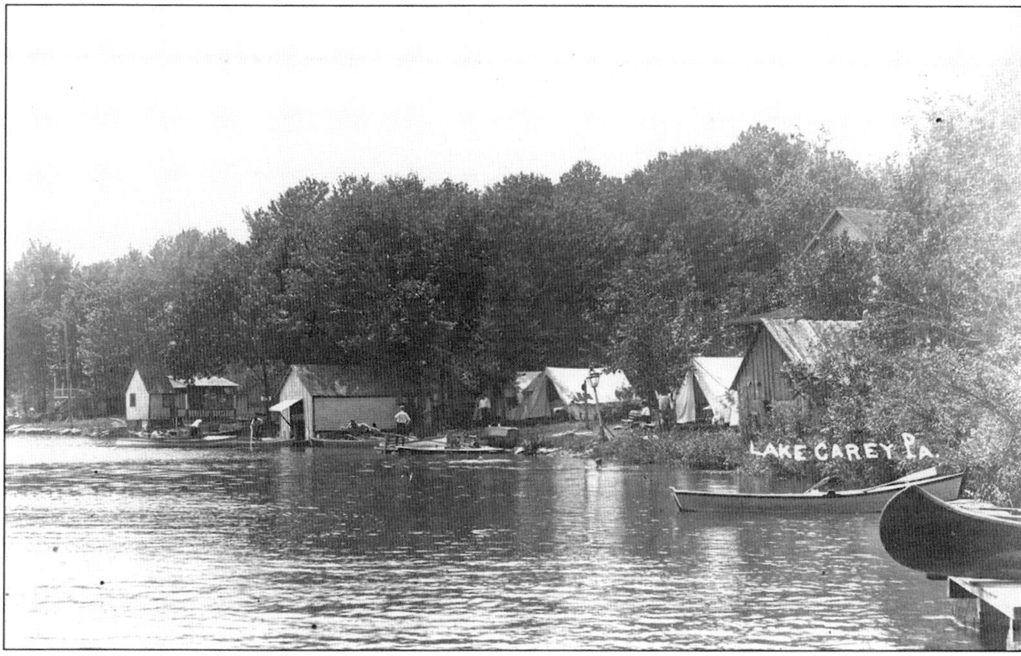

The Stevens/Ryan guests could rent a room or a tent by the shore. Rowboats could also be hired. (The dock and canoe in the foreground of this real-photo postcard are part of Camp Pokanoket.) Note the acetylene lamp on the lakeshore. (Author's collection.)

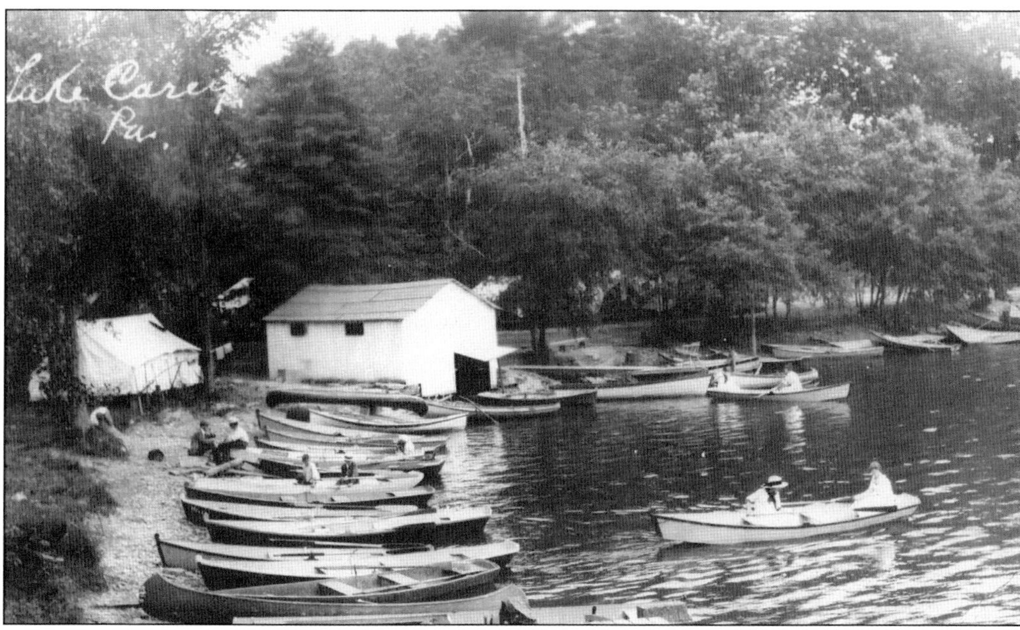

Renting a canoe or boat was a popular pastime. This boat livery operated on a pebble beach beside the Stevens/Ryan boardinghouse. The boathouse and tents of Camp Pokanoket are visible beyond in this real-photo postcard. (Russell collection.)

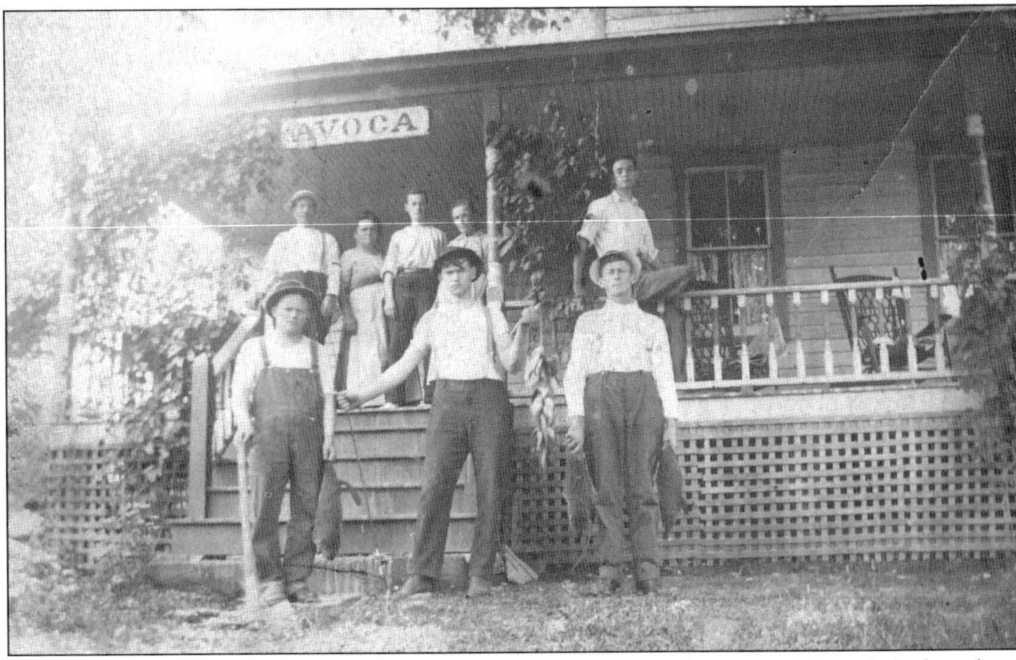

P. J. and Mary Ryan (far left on the porch) and son James (on the ground directly before them) pose with the catch of the day in this real-photo postcard. Groundhog, as well as fish, were served at the lake. One longtime resident recalls that her mother prepared woodchuck, which she first boiled in vinegar and water and then fried. The Ryans' cottage, Avoca, was demolished in the early 1970s. (Fitzsimmons collection.)

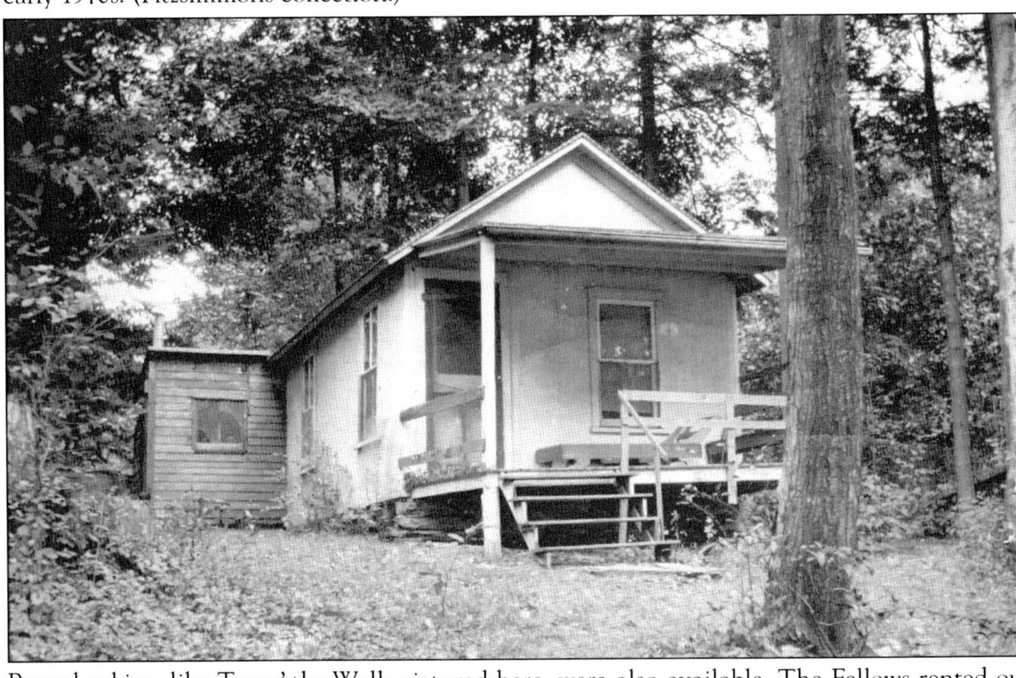

Rental cabins, like Top-o'-the-Walk pictured here, were also available. The Fellows rented out this east shore two-room structure—a dirt-floored kitchen and large all-purpose room with a coal stove—to pay their property taxes. (Fellows collection.)

Lean-tos and tents were commonly used for shelter before the first hotels opened. They remained popular with young men well into the 20th century. Here such a camper in period bathing suit and straw hat confronts the camera in his lean-to. (Weaver collection.)

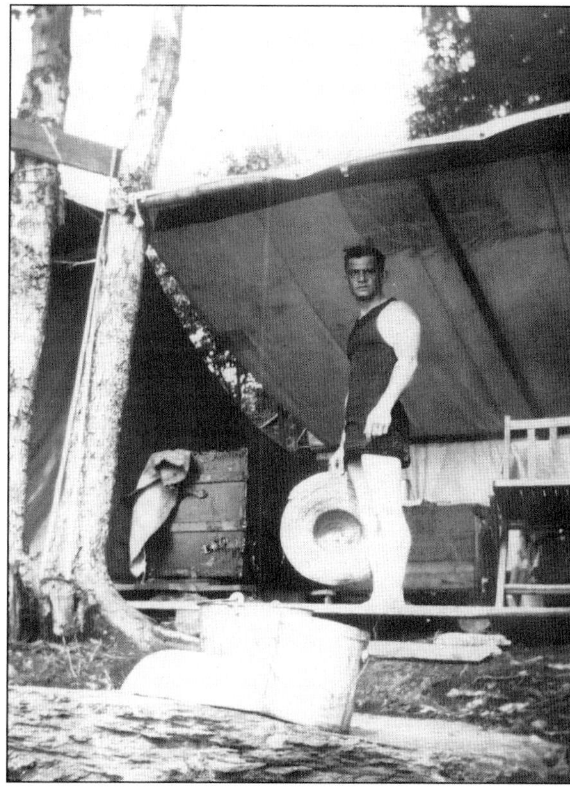

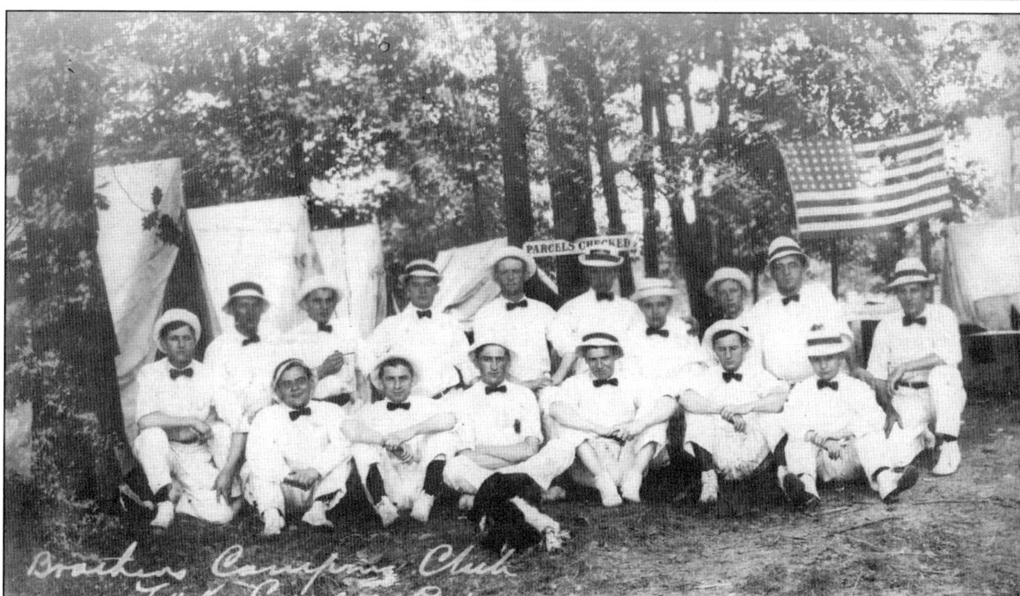

Members of this camping club from Luzerne County pose in bow ties in a campground thought to have been located near the Picnic Grounds on the west shore. In this real-photo postcard, the sign "Parcels Checked" may have indicated that alcohol was not allowed when this photograph was taken as the temperance movement neared its peak; the card was mailed just five years before Prohibition became law. (Weaver collection.)

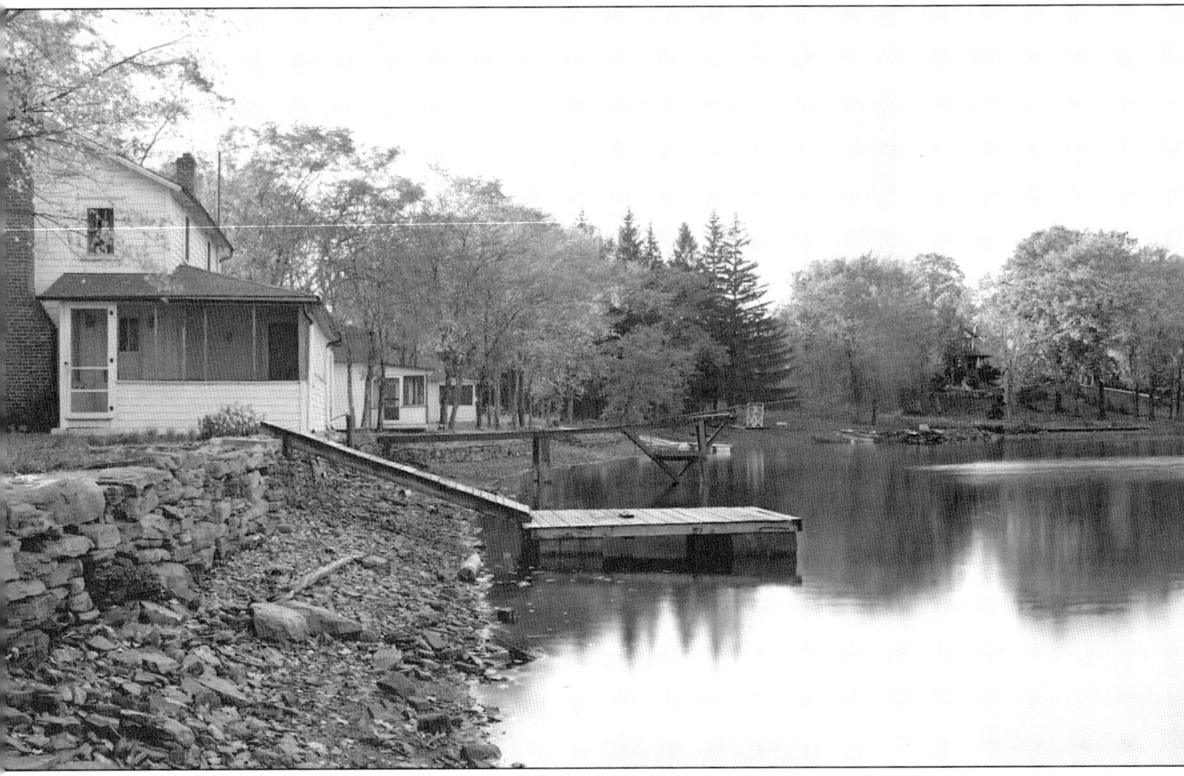

The most ambitious development in the lake's history, Lakewood Park was conceived by John Kilcoyne, who dominated lake real estate for 40 years. Lots on the causeway sold well, and by the

mid-1930s, a row of one-story bungalows lined the road there. This 1937 photograph by *Scrantonian* staff photographer John Anneman reveals the fine view they enjoyed. (Weaver collection.)

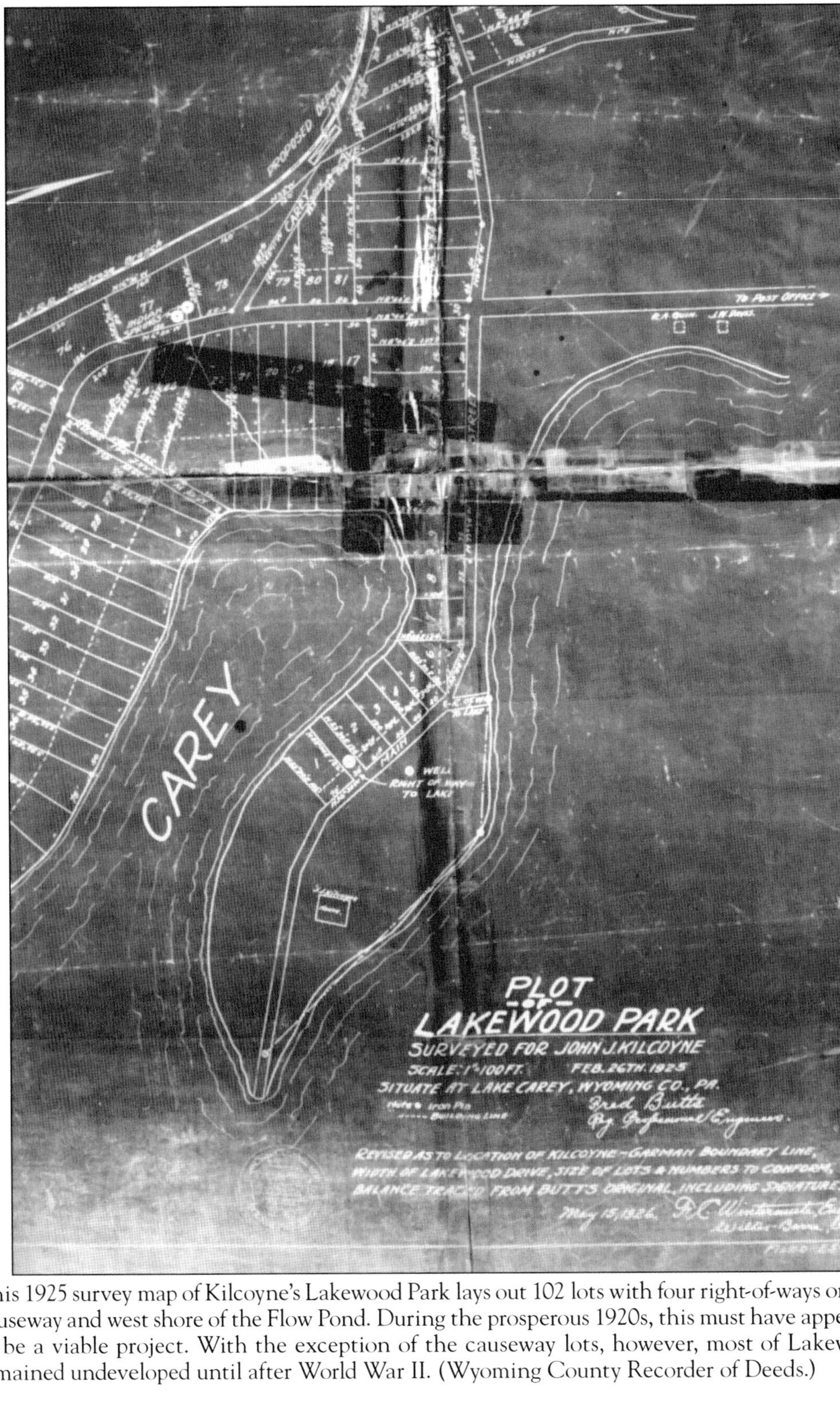

This 1925 survey map of Kilcoyne's Lakewood Park lays out 102 lots with four right-of-ways on the causeway and west shore of the Flow Pond. During the prosperous 1920s, this must have appeared to be a viable project. With the exception of the causeway lots, however, most of Lakewood remained undeveloped until after World War II. (Wyoming County Recorder of Deeds.)

Two

America's Most Popular Summer Resort

From the 1890s until World War I, Lake Carey featured attractions that brought large numbers of visitors from the surrounding counties and beyond. The popularity of its picnic grounds and children's camps, however, were rooted in patterns of social life that were undergoing steady change. Nowhere were these changes more visible and dramatic than in the emerging life stage of adolescence.

At the beginning of the 19th century, Americans received little or no formal education, moving directly from childhood into adulthood at early ages. A century later, however, small but growing numbers were beginning to enroll in high school, where they were no longer children but not yet adults. As the 20th century progressed, the nation's burgeoning industrial economy would require more and more education to provide the skills it depended upon. Longer years of education would foster student peer cultures, diminishing the influence of parents and family. Rising standards of living would provide pocket money for teenagers and the family automobile would offer increasing freedom from parental supervision. These changes and the adolescent life stage they would create, however, were still on the horizon when Lake Carey became a popular summer resort.

As the 19th century drew to a close, most students left school at 14 years of age after only completing the eighth grade. In the rural economy, young men and women were pressed into service on family farms at early ages and, as they matured, became full-time workers valued for their strength, stamina, and youthful good spirits. In the nearby cities, urban youngsters too began their working lives early—there were no child labor laws. As teenagers neared marriageable age, perhaps 16 or 17, they began a public courtship in mixed groups of young men and women under the watchful eyes of parents or church members. Family outings, church socials, and Grange picnics all served this important function. When a young man became serious about a girl, he would approach her for permission to call on her and later her father to gain her hand. Courtship as a serious couple then began in the parlor or on the porch with her protective father well within earshot.

In this social matrix, Wrigley's Grove and the lake's Picnic Grounds prospered. The grove was established in 1882 by John and Mary Wrigley next to the east shore farmhouse they constructed that year. Here they hosted the Granger's picnic every August until John's death in 1907. The Grange was then a powerful political force and a source of community cohesion in rural America. Thousands of farm families flocked to the lake for this event. The Montrose Railroad pressed every available piece of equipment into service to meet the demand for transport—benches were set up on flatcars and inside boxcars. The steamboats ran from the depot to the grove all day. Civil War reunions, Sunday schools picnics, and family reunions were all held here as well.

In 1904, John A. Redington of Wilkes-Barre and Harveys Lake opened the Picnic Grounds on the west shore, offering serious competition. Redington was an experienced manager of tourist attractions. He owned a Wilkes-Barre hotel and also briefly managed Harveys Lake's popular Oneonta Hotel. It is likely that he had strong working relationships with the Lehigh Valley Railroad as well; he later assumed the management of their picnic grounds at Harveys Lake. The Lake Carey Land and Improvement Company and the Lake Carey Boat Company Redington formed here, however, had no obvious connections to the railroad. Still the Lehigh Valley must have had a strong interest in the development of the grounds. The year before they had invested substantial sums to convert the Montrose line to standard gauge.

The park appears to have been an immediate success. An optimistic Redington and his fellow investors purchased Fern Cliffe Hotel on the opposite side of the lake in 1904. In 1905, they acquired the steamboat *Rosalind*. In 1907, they introduced a Ferris wheel and other attractions. By then the railroad was booking almost daily summer excursions to the grounds. Trains arrived, presumably in the late morning, with passengers and a band aboard. People picnicked, rented boats, enjoyed the rides, took the *Rosalind* around the lake, had their photographs taken, and danced in the pavilion until the train's departure in the evening.

In 1909, three years after the Lehigh Valley leased its Harveys Lake park to Redington, he sold his corporations at Lake Carey. Redington's base was clearly Wilkes-Barre, and the railroad's offer likely was attractive. He also must have suffered a financial loss when the underinsured Fern Cliffe Hotel burned three years before. It is possible that attendance at Lake Carey's park also was faltering.

The new owner, John Kilcoyne, bought the corporations with the announced intention of running them as Redington had done. In the winter of 1911–1912, however, Kilcoyne and/or Walter Cassedy moved the dance pavilion over the ice to a new site in front of Cassedy's west shore store. It is probably around this time that an abandoned *Rosalind* sank in the lake beside the grounds. In 1918, Kilcoyne sold most of the site where the grounds stood to J. Wallace Davis for family cottages. In 1923, Kilcoyne sold the railroad spur beside the unnamed brook (and a cottage he built on adjacent land) to Minnie Thickens Quin, whose descendents still summer there. The era had ended.

Young people continued to flock to the lake's two dance halls, but family, church, and community outings diminished greatly. While younger teenagers still attended in single-sex or mixed peer groups, the era of dating had begun. Now young people formed self-absorbed couples, free from direct parental and community supervision. Double dating, going steady, and exchanging high school rings become stages in a courtship ritual that would not change until the 1960s. At Lake Carey young men now checked out the young women at Weill's dance pavilion, then worked up enough nerve to ask for a date, which might set them back several weeks' pocket money. If the relationship grew serious, amorous couples began petting in the back seat of the family car or, somewhat precariously, on a blanket in the bottom of a canoe on the darkened lake.

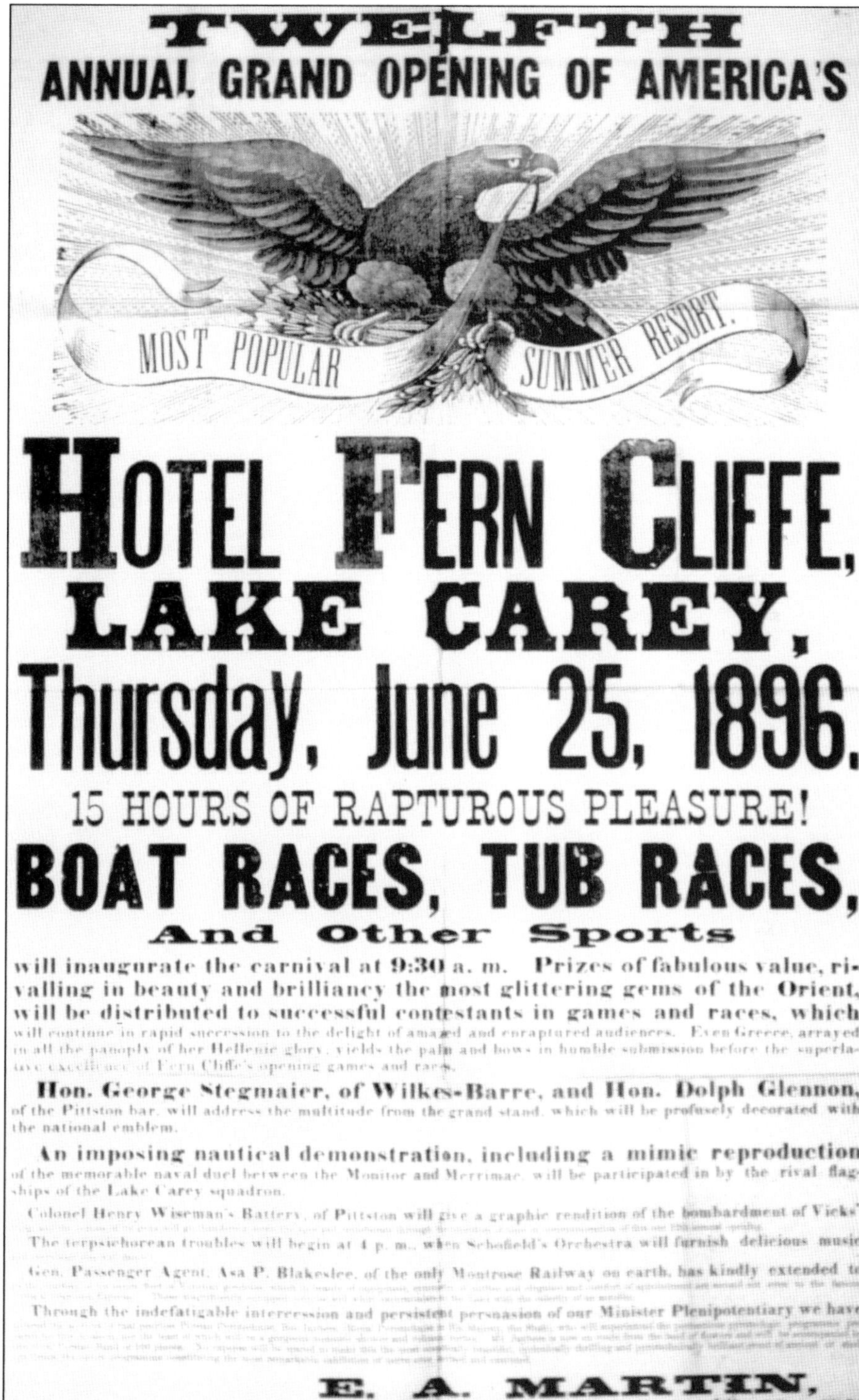

What other lake could offer 15 hours of rapturous pleasure? Hotel owner Eugene Martin seems to have brought his purple prose to the lake from the New York *Telegraph* where he once worked. (Wyoming County Historical Society.)

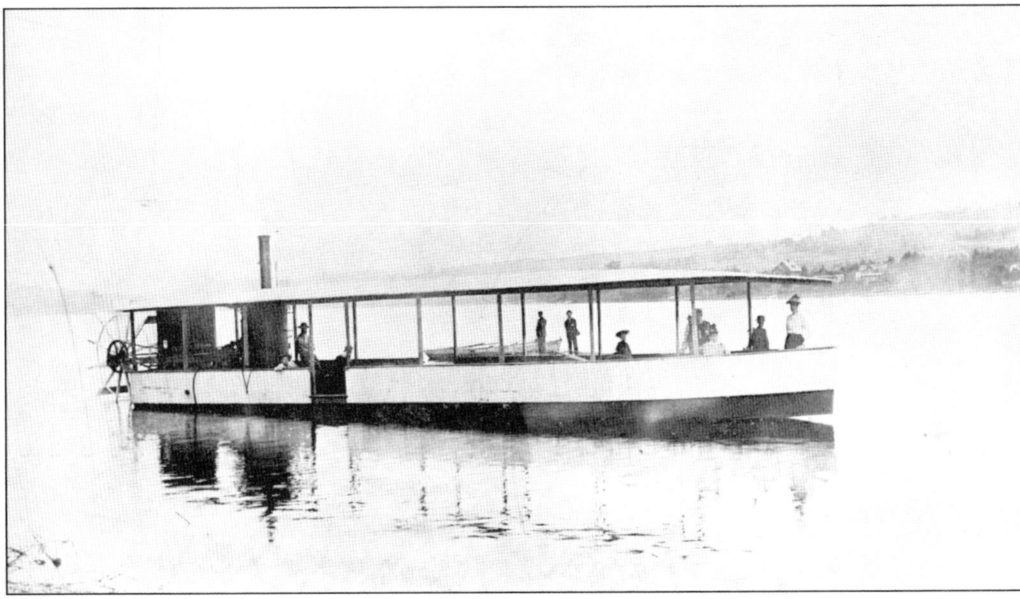

The lake's most popular event for over 30 years was the Granger's picnic held on the second Thursday in August. Asa Stevens's *Empress of the Lake*, pictured here, ran steadily all day. It cost 5¢ to cross and 10¢ for a trip around the lake. For a penny or two, enterprising boys (and at least one girl) from the cottages would row the picnickers across. The walk from the station to the picnic site on the dirt road around the lake was free. (Petrillo collection.)

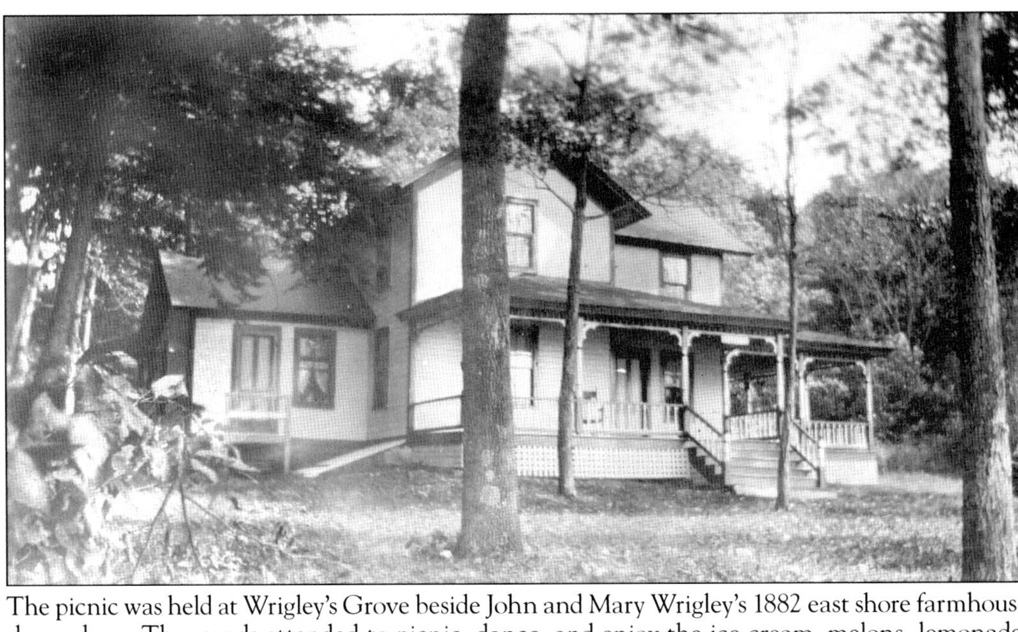

The picnic was held at Wrigley's Grove beside John and Mary Wrigley's 1882 east shore farmhouse shown here. Thousands attended to picnic, dance, and enjoy the ice cream, melons, lemonade, and cigars Wrigley sold. Some men, however, crossed the lake for the stronger stuff served at the Pollner House bar. (Banis collection.)

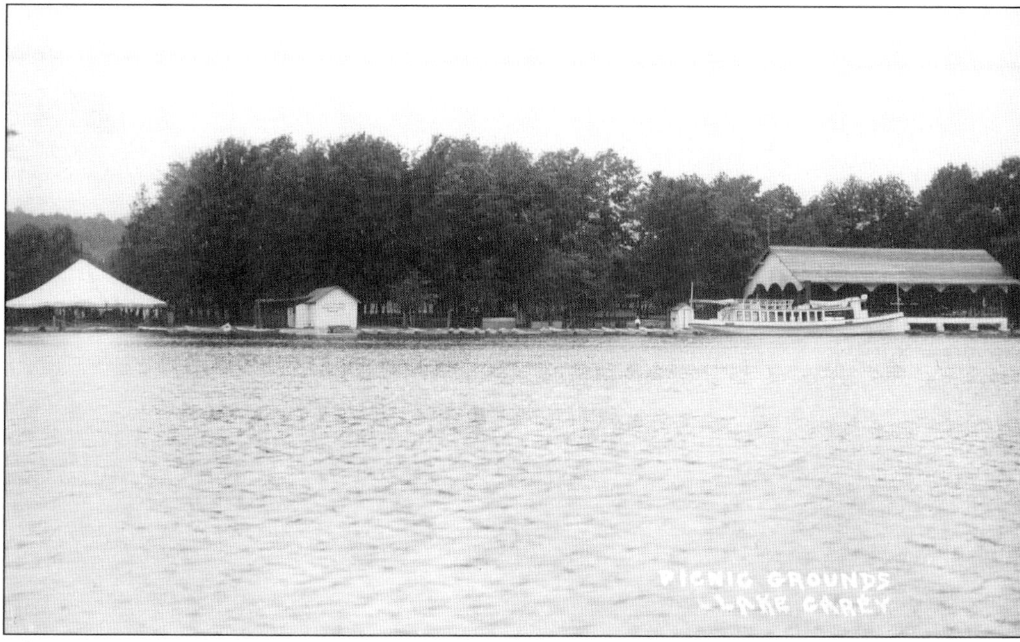

John A. Redington, a successful businessman at Harveys Lake, opened the Picnic Grounds in 1904. A spur of the now Lehigh Valley Railroad ran to the lake's edge beside a brook to the left of the large tent visible in this real-photo postcard. A white photography studio is in the center, and the *Rosalind* sits at her dock beside the dance pavilion on the right. (Russell collection.)

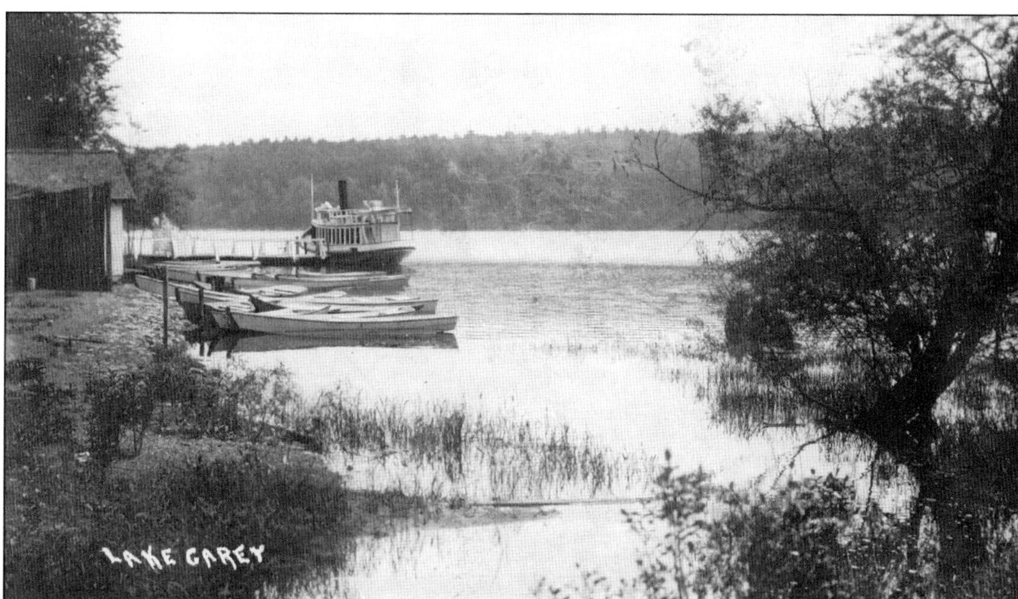

The photograph on this real-photo postcard was taken standing at the end of the railroad spur, looking north toward the boat livery, photography studio, and the *Rosalind*. The unnamed brook that flows from Stevens Lake to Lake Carey is in the foreground. (Russell collection.)

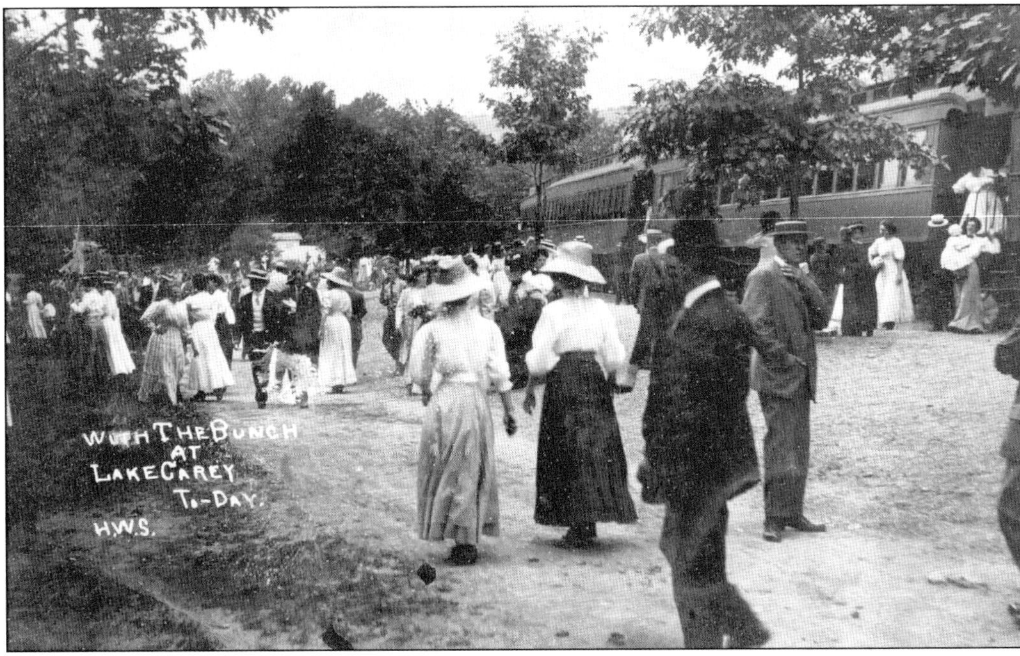

A large, formally dressed crowd detrains under a conductor's watchful eye in this real-photo postcard. The Lehigh Valley ran excursion trains throughout the summer; 78 were already booked by June 1907. It is likely that the railroad, having just invested in new track and locomotives, was a significant partner in Redington's venture. (Russell collection.)

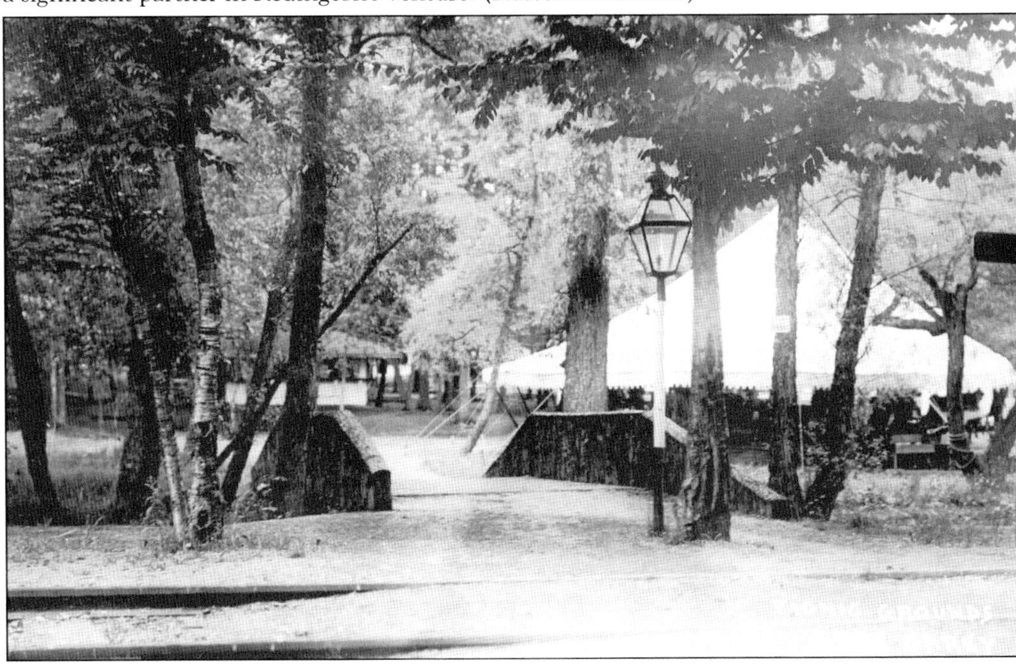

Passengers crossed the tracks in the foreground of this real-photo postcard and then took the rustic, log-sided bridge over the brook to enter the grounds themselves. The road was later relocated to the right, but the foundations of the old bridge can still be seen upstream. There is an acetylene lamp beside the bridge. (Russell collection.)

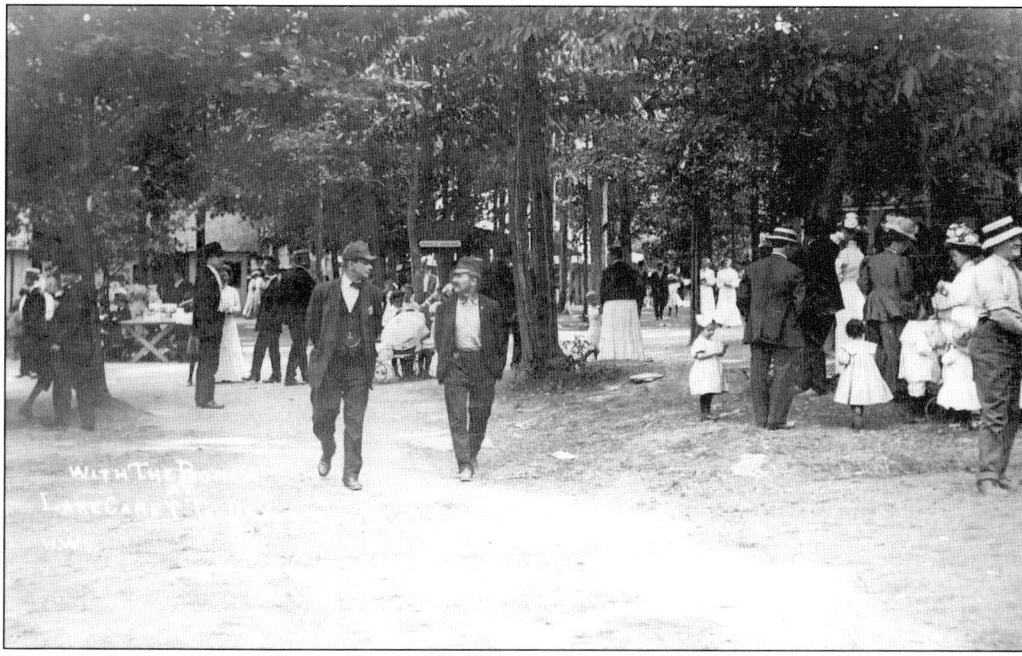

Two railroad officials stroll toward the lake, amid chatting men and women whose children are as yet uncertain what to do, all in their Sunday best in this real-photo postcard. (Russell Collection.)

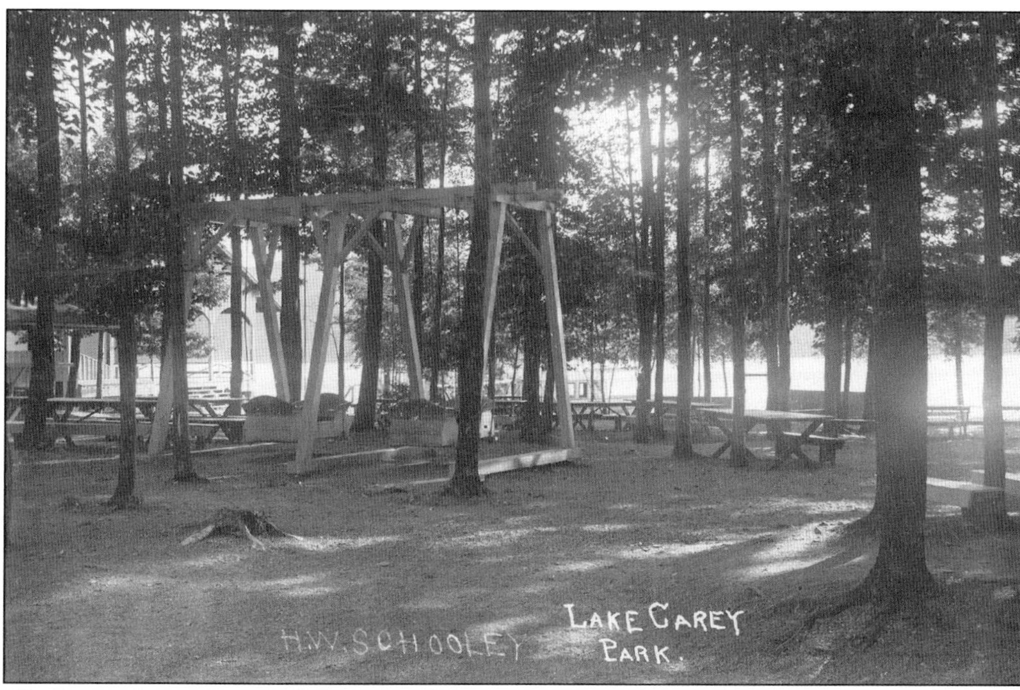

The Picnic Grounds are well shaded in the strong morning light captured by Harold W. Schooley in this real-photo postcard. Picnicking was a major activity, as the many tables attest. A sturdy, double glider provided simple pleasures. The *Rosalind* is visible through the trees at her dock. (Author's collection.)

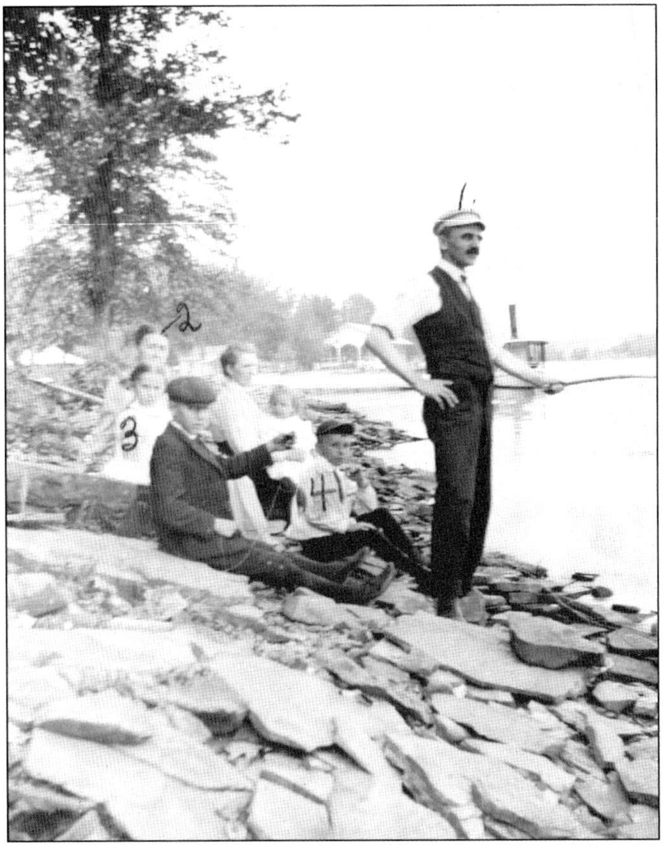

Some parties preferred the rocky shore for seating. This 1904 Sunday school group includes Marion DeFrehn (marked 3), who later married Thomas Jefferson Wheaton's grandson Frank W. Kelly. Note the pavilion in the background. The tall-stacked steamboat beside it could be the *City Charter*, which was brought to Lake Carey from Harveys Lake in 1895. (Kelly collection.)

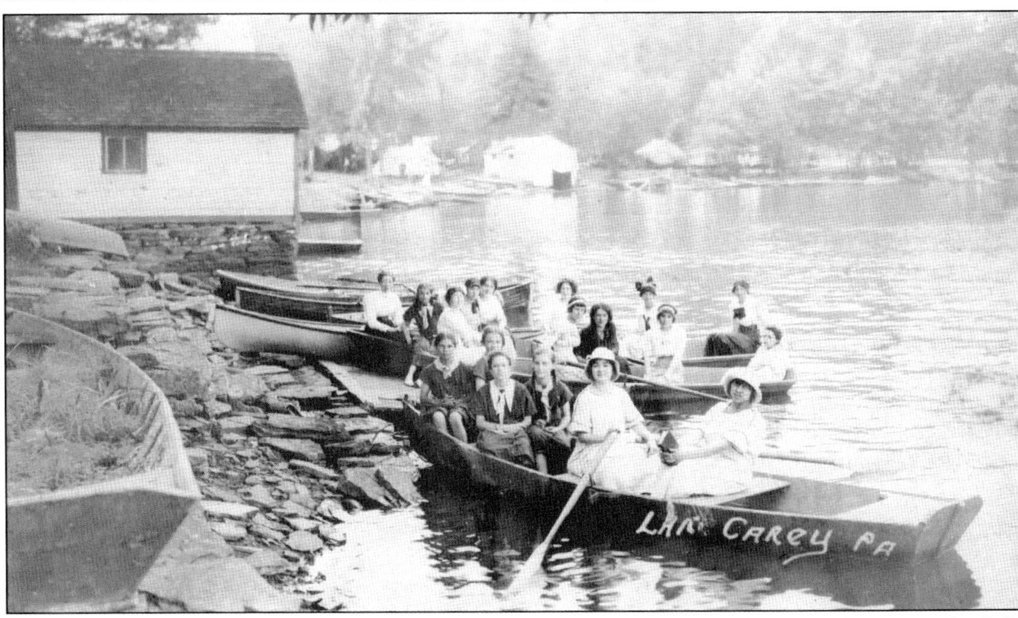

An organized party of girls and young women prepares to land on the west shore, up the lake from the Picnic Grounds. Four girls appear to be wearing a uniform—but it is not that of the Girl Scouts, Girl Guides, or Camp Fire Girls. (Redding collection.)

A party of five young men and women (and two chaperones?) poses for the photographer in his studio at the Picnic Grounds in this real-photo postcard. They have been photographed outside the studio against a canvas backdrop dated 1910. One also could have a tintype taken here. (Author's collection.)

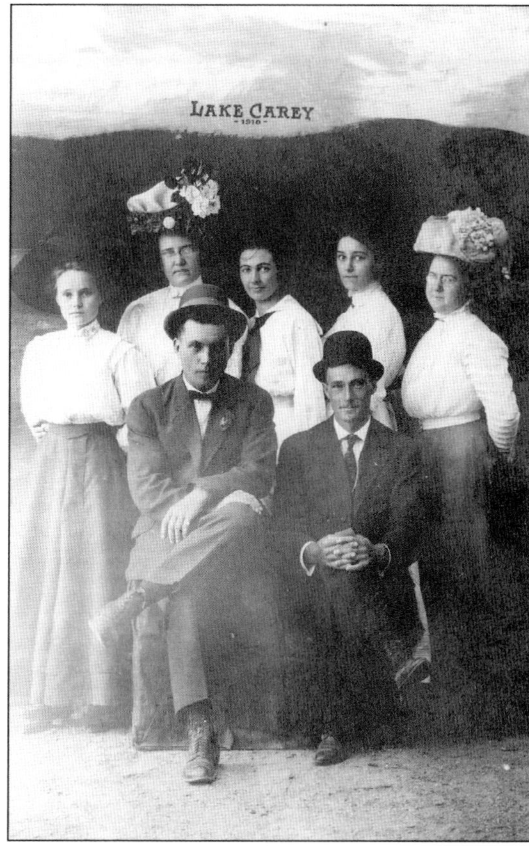

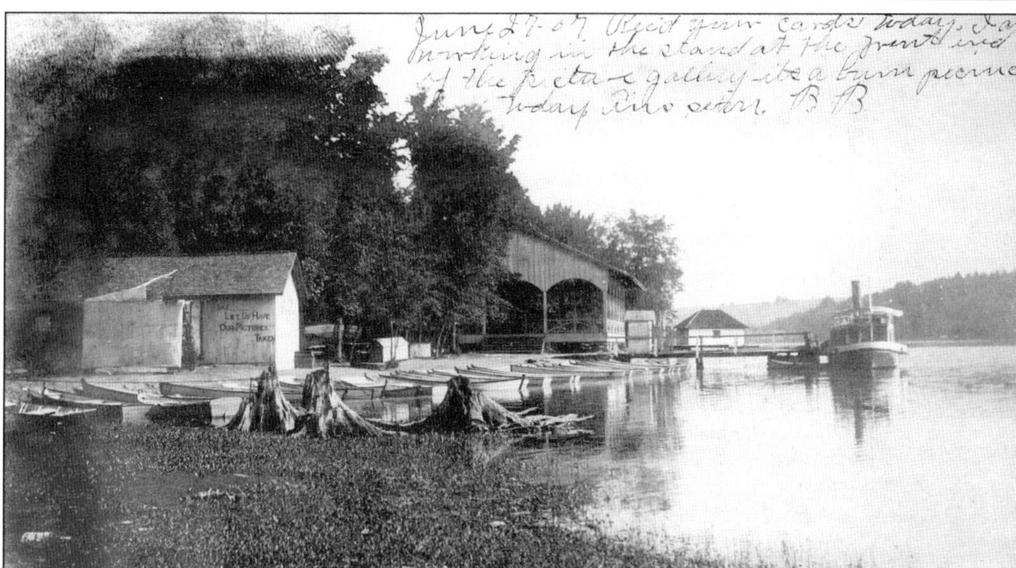

The romantic image in this real-photo postcard includes the photography studio ("Say Let Us Have Our Picture Taken"), the boat livery, the dance pavilion, and the *Rosalind*. The canvas backdrop in the image above can be clearly seen where it has been rigged beside the studio. (Author's collection.)

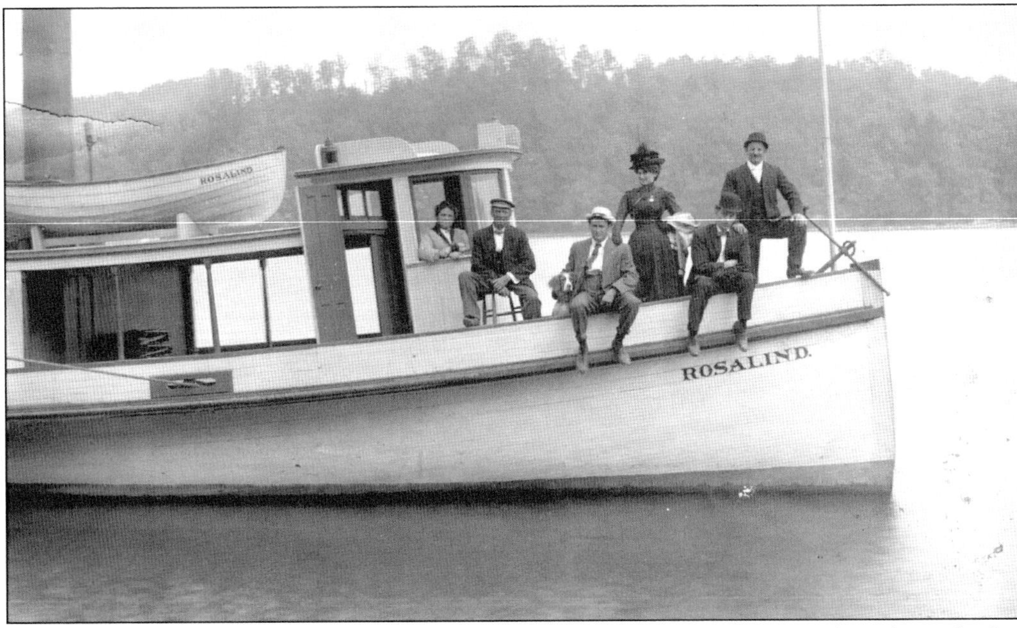

The *Rosalind*, shown here, was shipped by John Redington from Harveys Lake, where she had been built in 1893, on three gondola cars in 1905. Her single-action steam engine with a 40-inch four-bladed propeller could achieve 11 miles per hour. The men pictured here could be Ruben L. Shaver (her skipper), Redington, Miles Shepherd, and James S. Monks—all four were investors in the venture. (Tidball/Davis collection.)

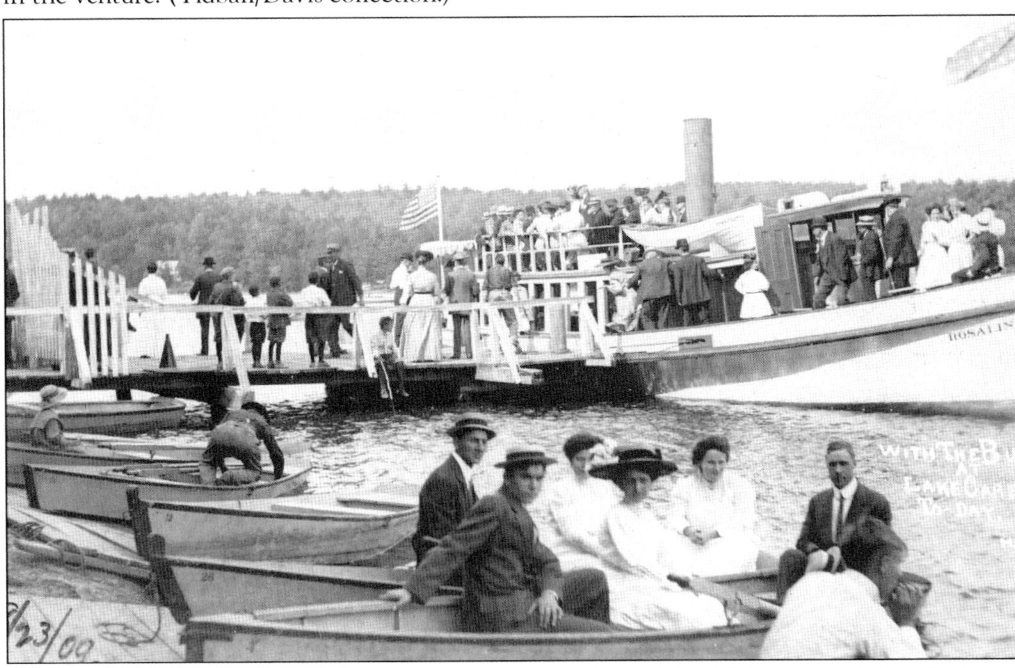

Men in suits and women in floor-length, white dresses board the 60-foot *Rosalind* at the Picnic Grounds in this real-photo postcard dated 1909. At 75 or so passengers, she is near capacity (note the single lifeboat behind the pilot house). A teenage boy smokes in the foreground while a party of three young men and women pose in rental boats just beyond him. (Russell collection.)

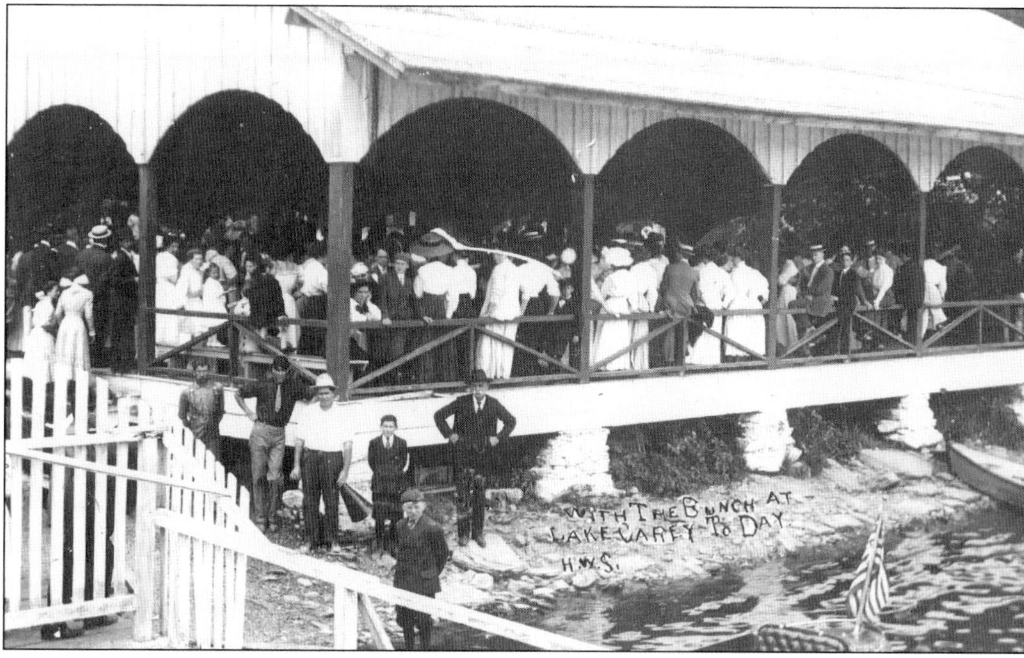

The dance pavilion is packed in this Harold W. Schooley photograph taken from the deck of the *Rosalind* in this real-photo postcard. Note the stern of a centered engine motor launch at the bottom right. (Russell collection.)

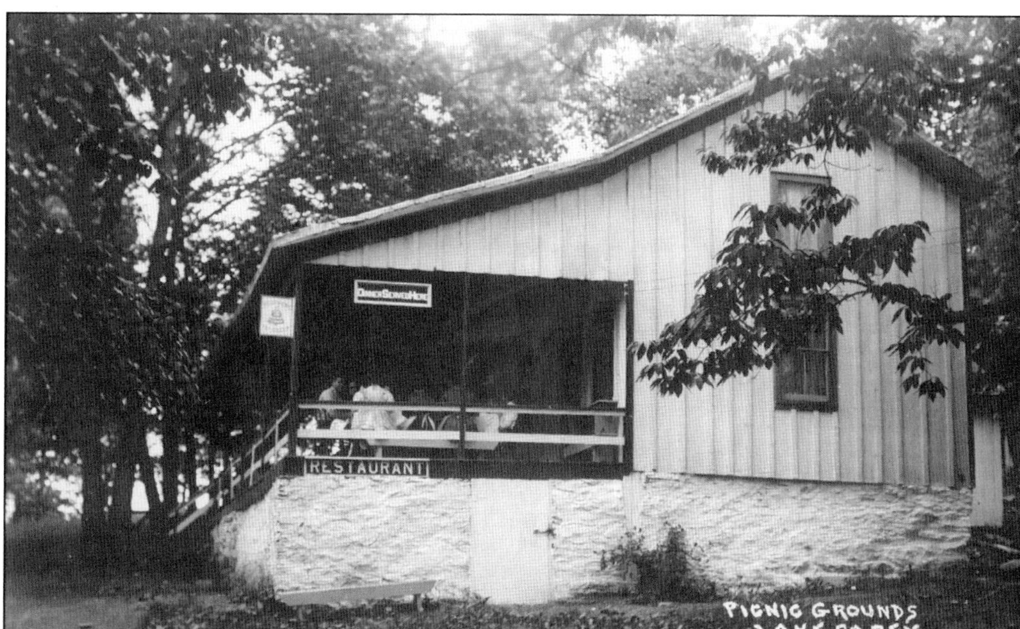

The grounds also included this pleasant board-and-batten restaurant with an open dining room on its porch pictured here in this real-photo postcard. It also offered a telephone pay station. (Russell collection.)

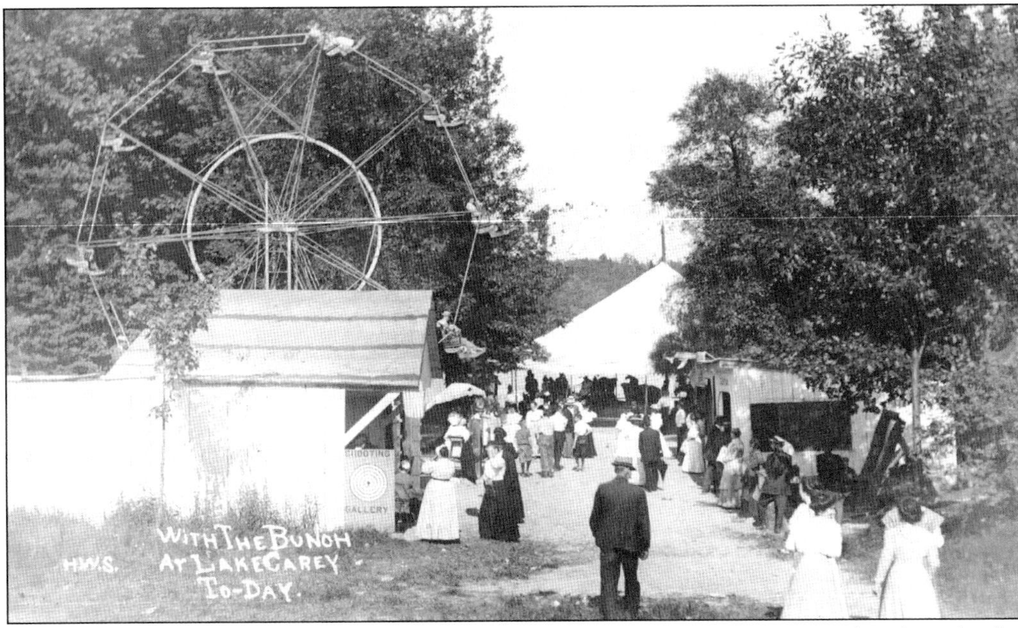

In 1907, John Redington's company introduced a Ferris wheel, miniature railroad, and other attractions. A merry-go-round and shooting gallery, as well as the Ferris wheel, are visible in the Harold W. Schooley photograph in this real-photo postcard. Most of the wheel's gondolas are occupied—imagine the thrill the ride must have been in 1907 (14 years after the wheel's introduction in Chicago). (Weaver collection.)

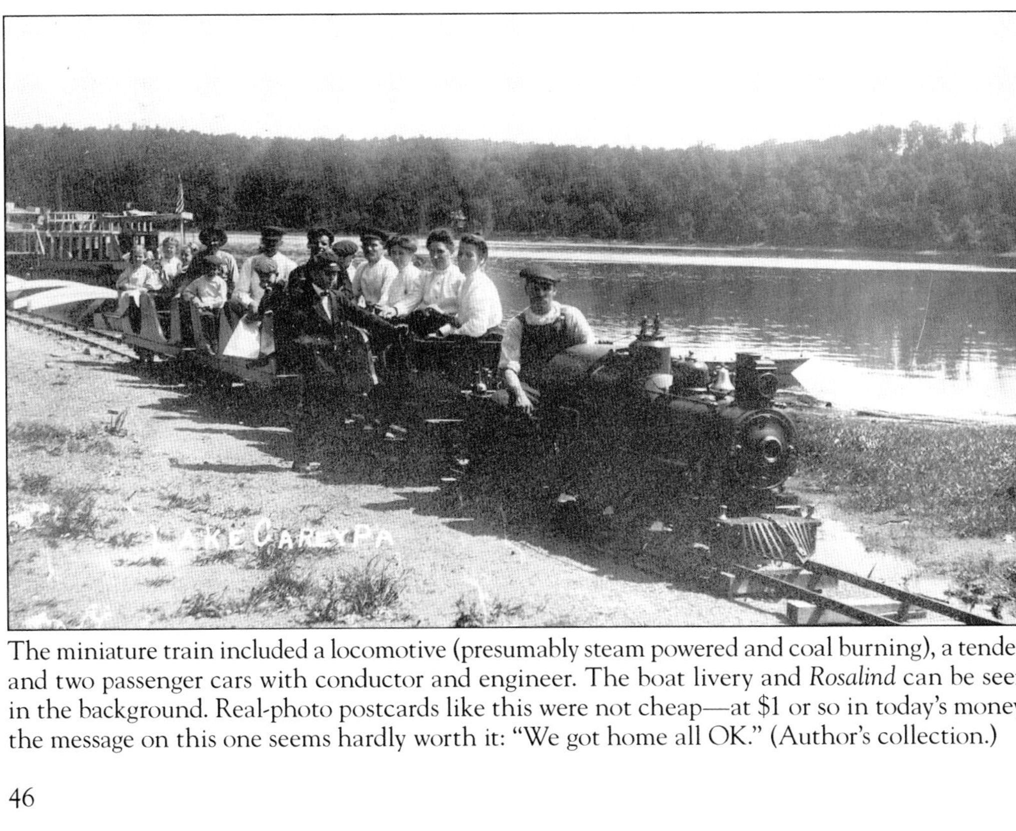

The miniature train included a locomotive (presumably steam powered and coal burning), a tender, and two passenger cars with conductor and engineer. The boat livery and *Rosalind* can be seen in the background. Real-photo postcards like this were not cheap—at $1 or so in today's money, the message on this one seems hardly worth it: "We got home all OK." (Author's collection.)

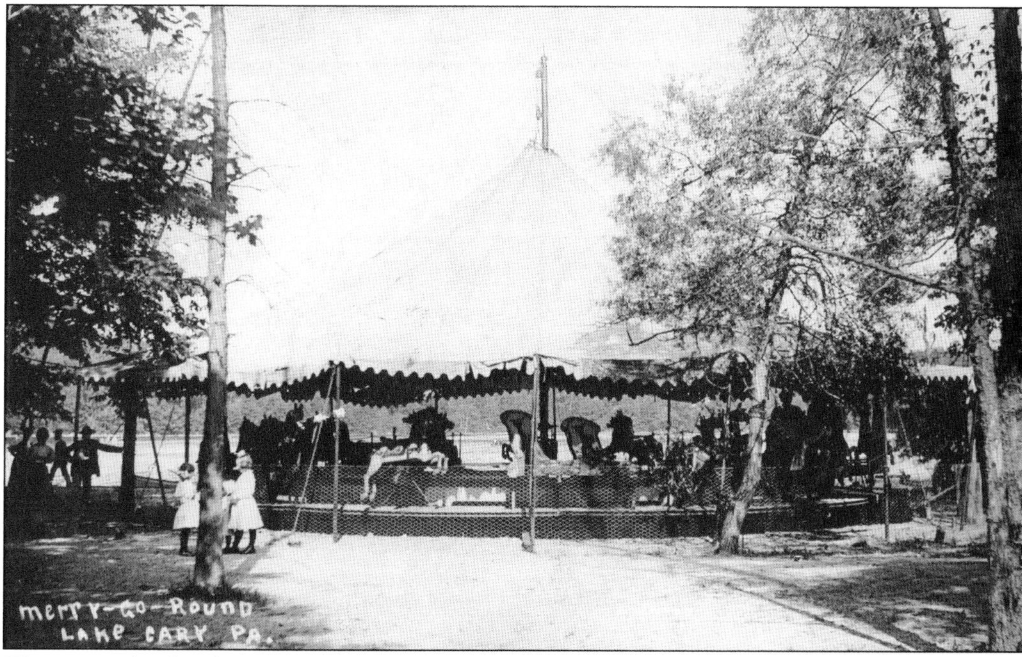

The grounds also featured this traveling steam-powered carousel manufactured by Charles Dare of New York City. Dare's work featured horses on moving wishbone platforms, and his two-seat chariots were often decorated with fish or sea serpents, as they are in this real-photo postcard. There is a steam boiler and flywheel barely visible under the canopy on the far right. (Weaver collection.)

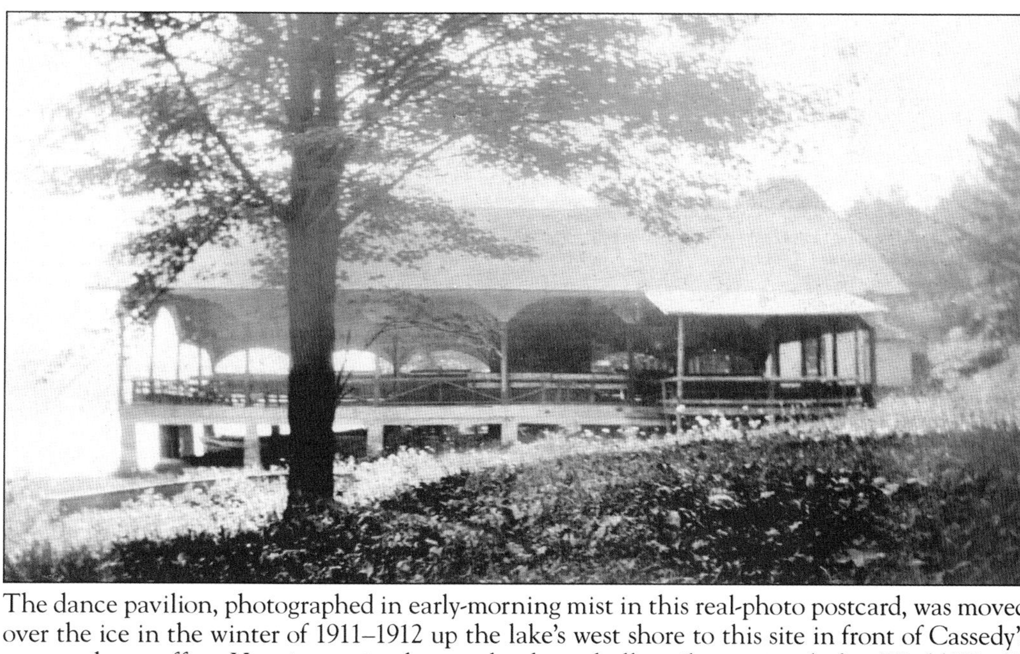

The dance pavilion, photographed in early-morning mist in this real-photo postcard, was moved over the ice in the winter of 1911–1912 up the lake's west shore to this site in front of Cassedy's store and post office. Here it remained a popular dance hall until sometime before World War II. (Russell collection.)

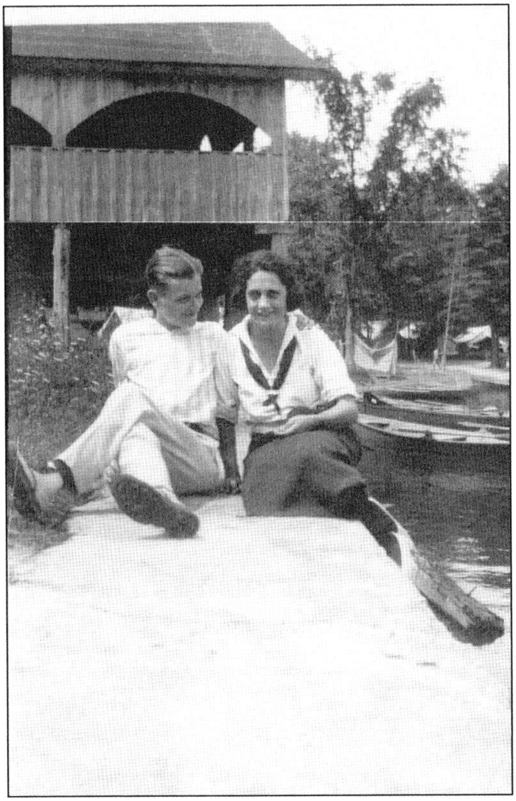

Ruth Marcy Trembath poses with her beau of the time, Curtis Logan, on the wall of the Stevens/Ryan boardinghouse. The pavilion, in the background, fell into disuse and disrepair 15 years or so after Ross J. and Mary Weill's purchase in 1923. (Pitkin collection.)

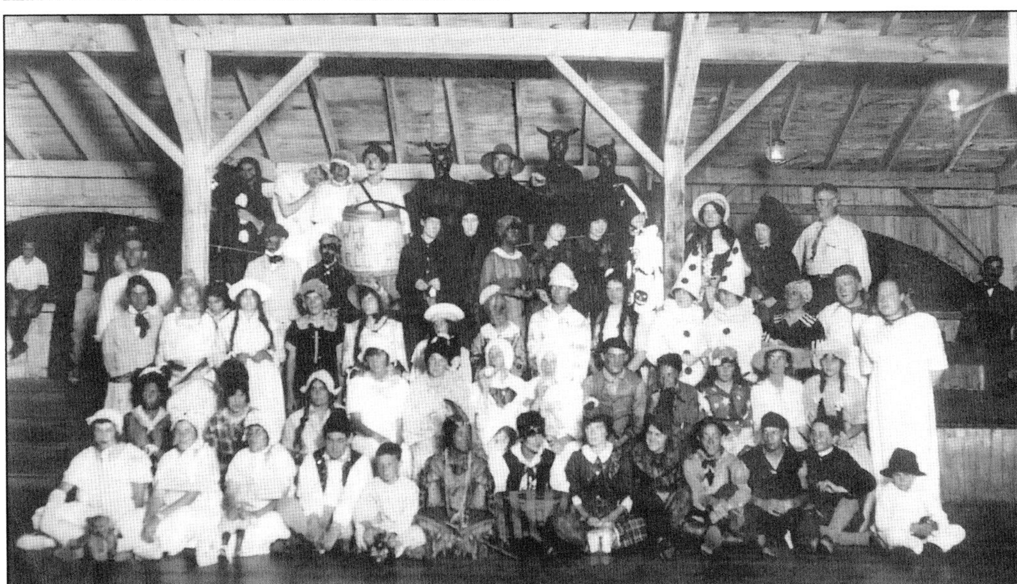

At its new location, the pavilion was used for public dances as well as private parties such as this costume ball attended by the young crowd from the lake's cottages. Note the infants, devils, Native Americans, Pilgrim maiden, Dutch girl, clowns, Little Bo Peep, and other popular icons. Joseph W. Oliver, third row far right, appears out of place and ill at ease in shirt and tie. Eleanor Reinbold stands to the left of him in a bonnet next to the pillar. (Pitkin collection.)

Some photographers retailed "moonlit" shots of the lake like the one in this real-photo postcard. Is that the moon over the lake's western shore? Is it even Lake Carey? (Author's collection.)

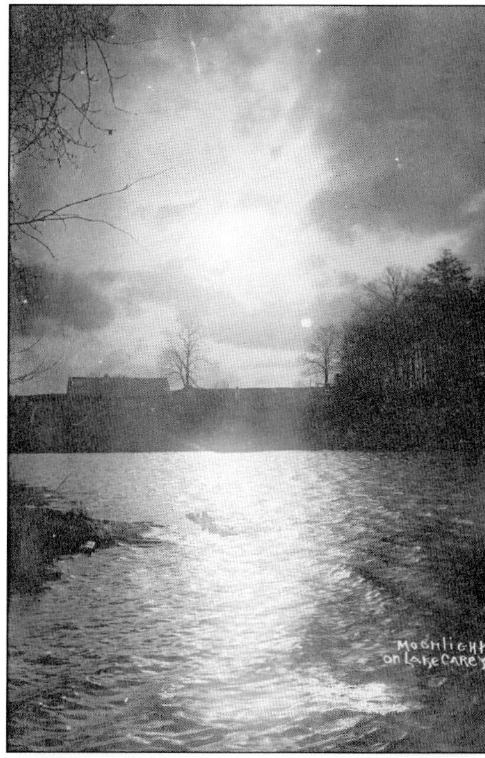

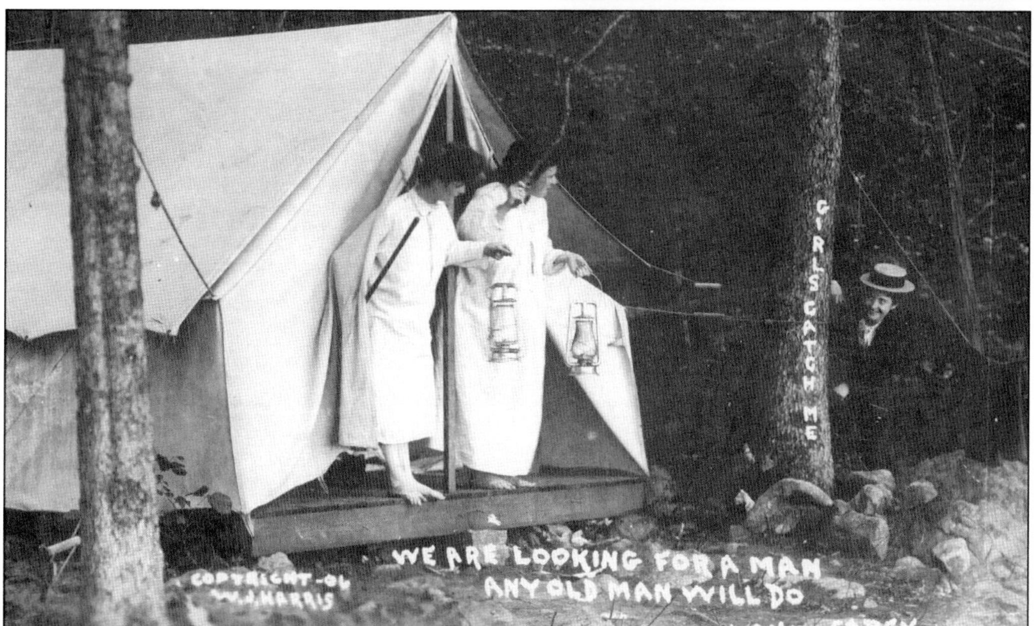

Summer romance was eagerly sought by many young people. In this real-photo postcard, two girls appear ready to settle for a woman dressed as a man. This Harris card's 1909 buyer wrote from Summer Rest cottage, "I had a lovely ride in a canoe . . . with a man [underlining original], they are not so scarce here. We have two in our party of nine and lots over at the picnic grounds where we go everyday." (Russell collection.)

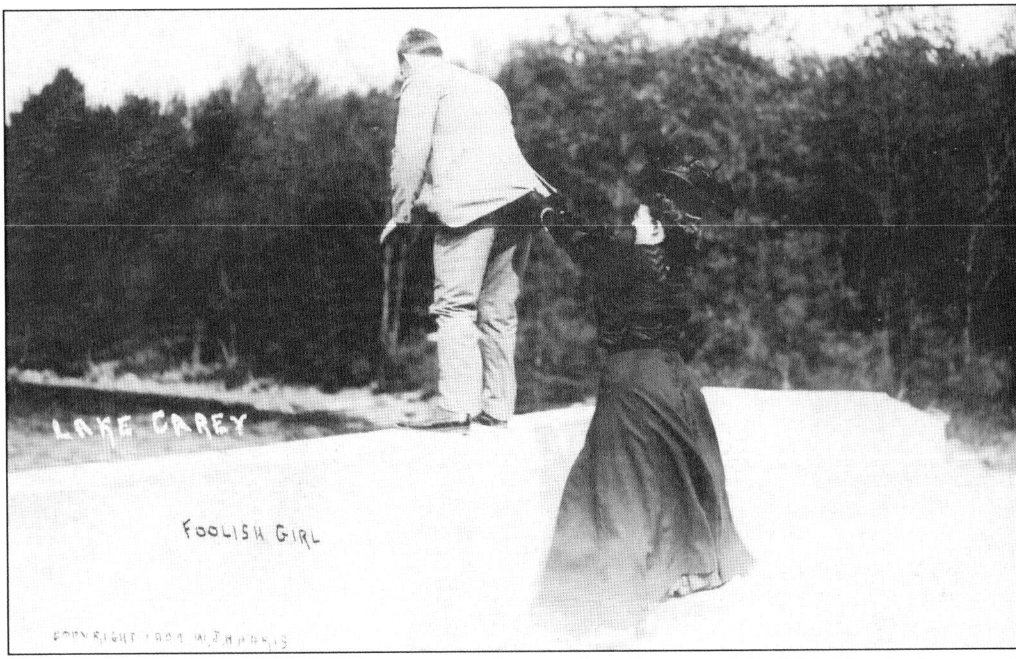

High drama on the causeway bridge is portrayed in another photograph by W. J. Harris. Apparently the real-photo postcard is intended as a humorous comment on the "worth" of the stronger sex to the weaker—most postcards were purchased and mailed by women. (Russell collection.)

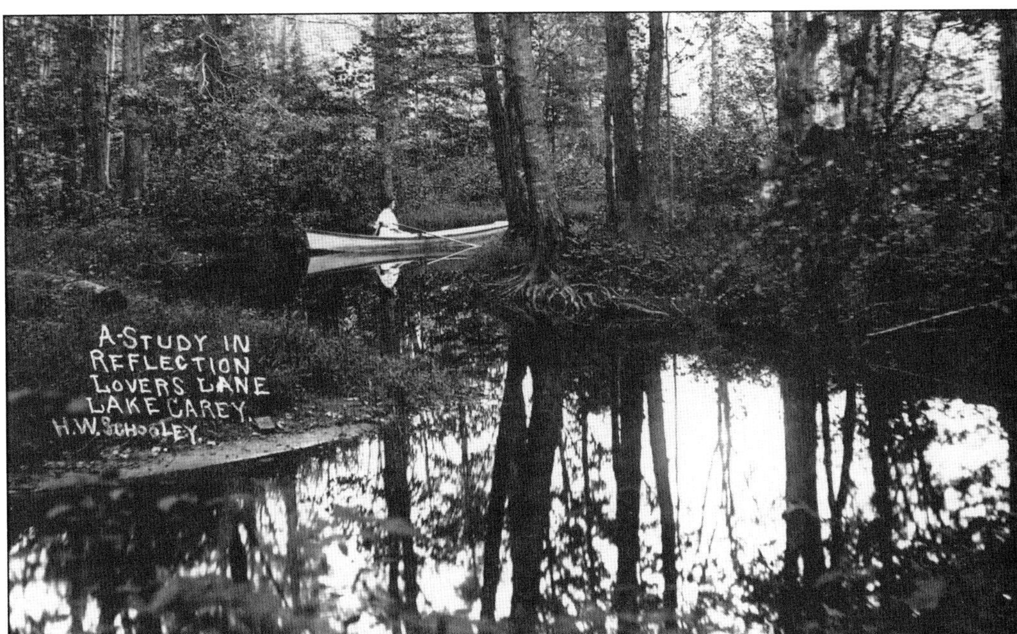

"Lovers lane" was located at the lake's inlet, a wetland where Mead Brook winds its way into the lake. This photograph by Harold W. Schooley of West Pittston sold well judging by the number of surviving copies of this real-photo postcard. (Weaver collection.)

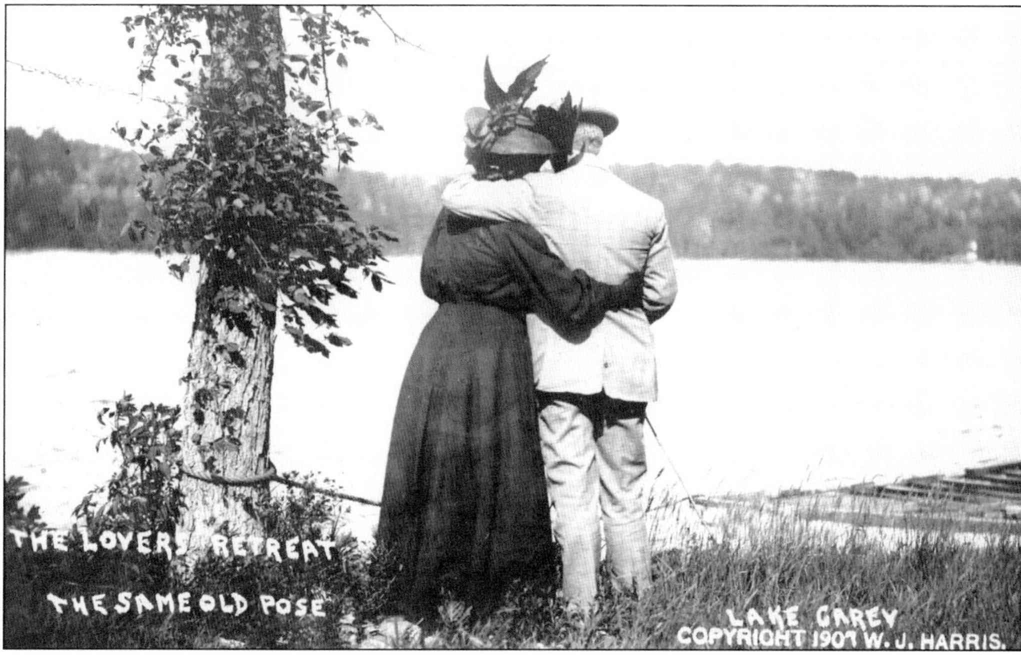

Romance must have been on the minds of some older couples visiting the lake or W. J. Harris would have not produced this real-photo postcard. Harris was a master of marketing; his cards typically sold well (and were often imitated). (Russell collection.)

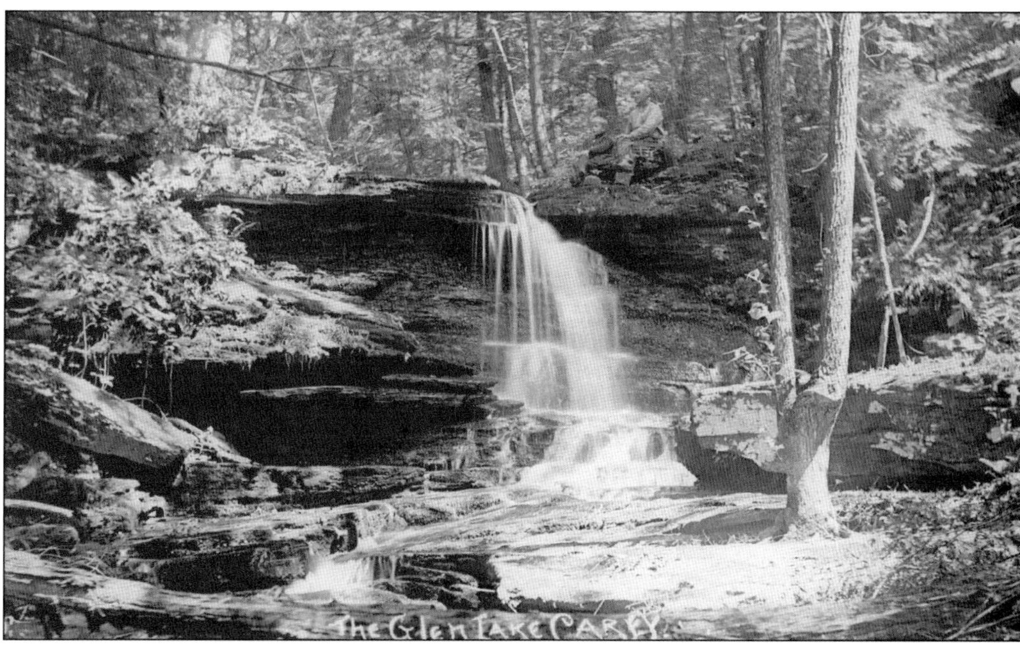

The glen on Billings Mill Brook, located below the mills at the lake's outlet, was a popular spot for picnics and for quiet contemplation, judging from the pose of the boy and his older companion at upper right in this real-photo postcard. (Robinson collection.)

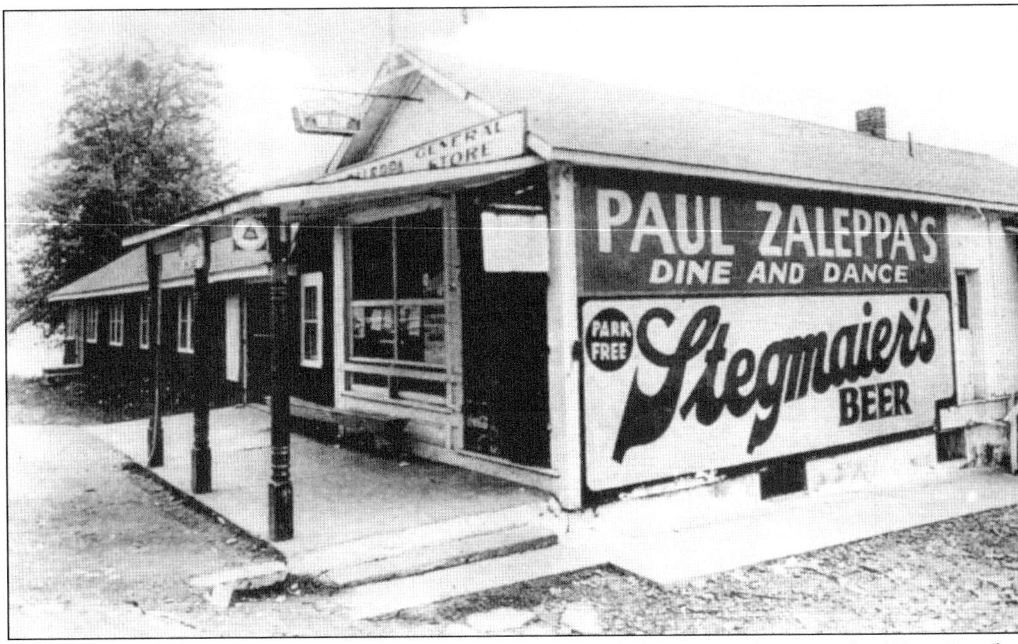

Paul and Mary Zaleppa purchased this general store and dance pavilion on the Flow Pond in 1935 from Evelyn Cooper (who kept her piano). Before the Cooper family purchase in 1914, this three-to-four-acre property had several owners. It was part of the George Washington Stark farm until Stark sold it in 1886. (Weaver collection.)

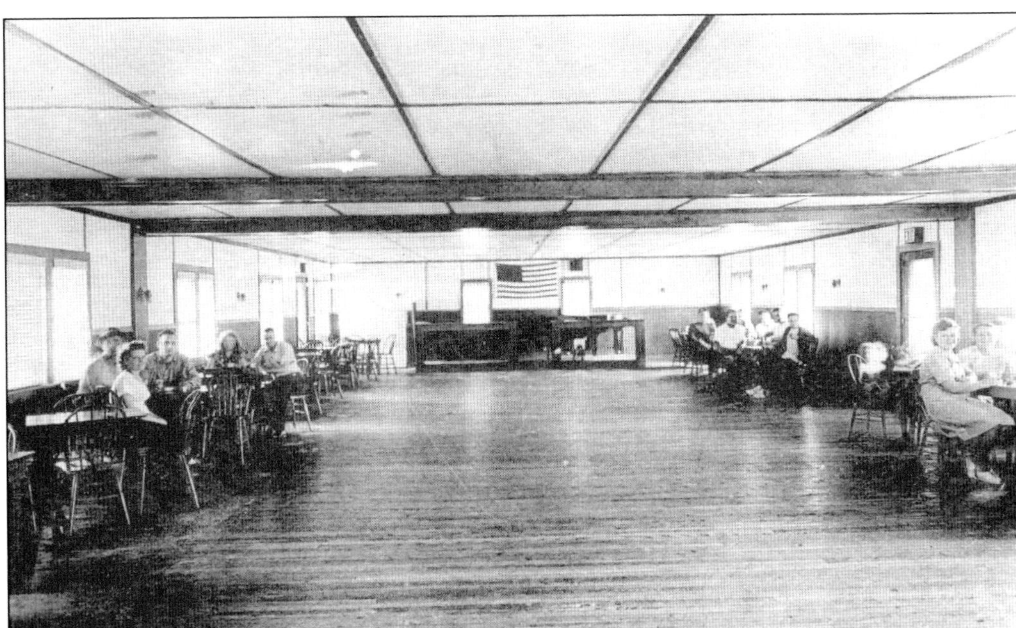

The Zaleppas enclosed the pavilion (seen in this postcard), a popular dance hall for decades. It featured square dancing on Wednesday evenings and local dance bands on Saturday nights, among them Jimmy Welch and the Aristo-Cats. On Sunday, mass was held here, until a Roman Catholic chapel was constructed on the west shore of the Flow Pond. (Author's collection.)

Three

The Camps of Lake Carey

As adolescence became an identifiable stage in life, child psychologists fretted at the prospects of teenagers raised by unprepared and untutored parents. A movement began around 1900 to provide institutions led by skilled and knowledgeable adults who could usher youth from childhood into adulthood with a minimum of trauma. They included settlement houses, the Boy Scouts and Camp Fire Girls, YMCAs and YWCAs, junior and senior high schools, and, of interest here, summer camps.

The typical camp of the early 20th century was owned and operated by a couple, frequently trained as teachers. Such was the case with Camp Pokanoket on Lake Carey's western shore. Named after the tribe that greeted the Pilgrims at Plymouth Rock, this boys' camp was probably the inspiration of Joseph W. Oliver and the financial responsibility of his wife, Elizabeth Bunnell Oliver. The Olivers met in the first decade of the 20th century at Columbia Teachers College. Joseph was completing a degree, and Elizabeth, the daughter of a Tunkhannock banker, was teaching. Together they opened the camp in a building Oliver and his staff constructed on one of four Diefenderfer lots his wife purchased. (Curiously, the camp appears to have opened one year before the property was purchased in August 1911.)

The camp drew heavily on the German Jewish population of Brooklyn, where Joseph was teaching in a manual arts high school. To staff it, he drew on his high school colleague Charles Collins. It was a sophisticated and very successful operation, complete with illustrated brochures. The boys' first- or second-generation American parents probably viewed the camp as a fine opportunity to escape the heat and crowding of Brooklyn and to master with other Jewish boys the subtleties of American middle-class culture. The Olivers, on the other hand, apparently hoped to help shape adolescent boys—who happened to be Jewish—into healthy and responsible young men.

In addition to the usual round of supervised camp activities popular with boys, Camp Pokanoket included photography, manual arts, tutoring, a camp magazine, and the production of a play at Piatt's Opera House in Tunkhannock. Composer Aaron Copland, who attended the camp's first four seasons, apparently was not called upon in these productions, nor does he recall any musical activities there in his autobiography. The wail of the Lehigh Valley freight train whistle when he camped overnight along the Susquehanna, however, remained a vivid memory (as did his swimming lessons at the camp).

By 1919, the Olivers had sold Camp Pokanoket to a Jewish couple from Brooklyn who ran it until sometime in the Depression. Elizabeth Oliver, who held the mortgage, then reclaimed the property. Her granddaughter now summers there in the camp's main building. Charles Collins opened his own Camp Carey farther down the lake in 1917 or 1918. It apparently lasted into the mid-1920s.

Several other camps were opened for various durations in the 1920s. Perhaps the shortest lived was that of Reverend Knoll, who opened a camp behind his cottage, the Beeches, to the consternation of his east shore neighbors. More successful was the Methodist camp operated by the Nanticoke Methodist Episcopal Church on the former site of the Fern Cliffe Hotel. For many years between 1924 and 1944 it operated for several summer weeks as a Boy Scout camp and then for several more as a Girl Scout camp. Its camp building, now a cottage, still sits on the site of the former hotel.

It would be a mistake to conclude that the growth of a separate life stage in the teenage years alone changed the patterns of resort life. The automobile, which played no small role in changing courtship, also independently affected patterns of summer vacations. When the railroad was king, Americans went for a day's outing or a week's stay at a resort hotel or boardinghouse where the railroad could take them. As standards of living rose, more and more families could afford an automobile and an extended vacation wherever it might take them. The hotel gave way to cabins on concrete highways, which in turn were supplanted by motels on interstates. The crowds that once flocked to picnic grounds for a day now had the means to vacation for a week at the shore, in the mountains, or with family in another state.

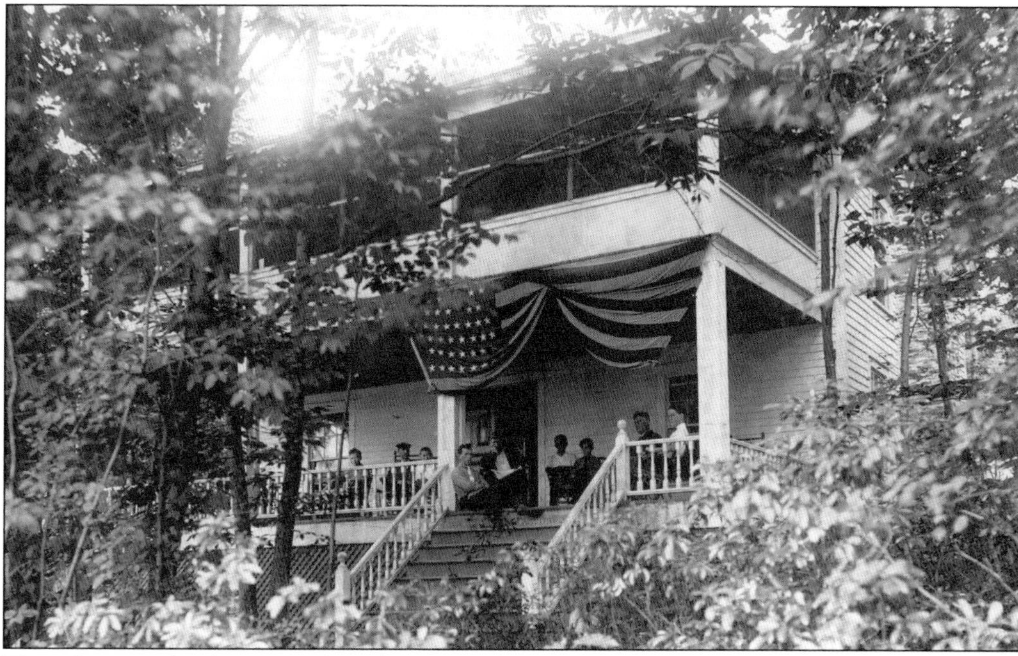

This photograph of Camp Pokanoket's main building on the lake's west shore includes owner Joseph W. Oliver, second from right. A graduate of East Stroudsburg and Columbia Teachers College, Oliver taught in Brooklyn's Manual Training High School. The first floor contained a living room, dining room, and kitchen. The second housed five bedrooms and a bath. The youngest campers, "Midgets," slept on the screened, second-story porch. (Redding collection.)

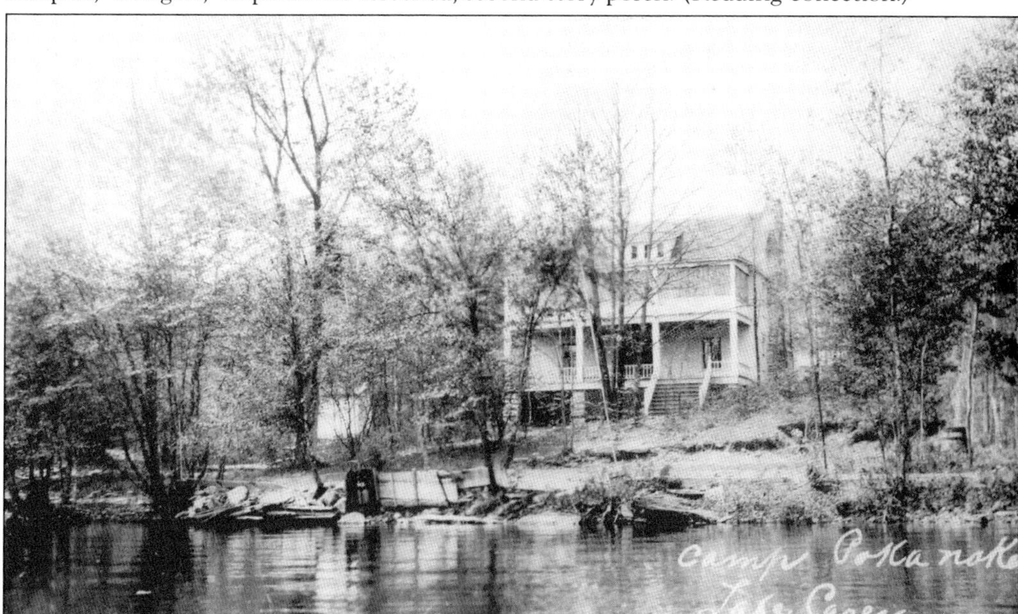

The message on this real-photo postcard, postmarked 1913, reveals that not every boy was a happy camper: "Don't think I will stay seven weeks. Walked alone, rowed alone, swam alone, slept alone, and even talked to myself. . . . Best part of the entire business was traveling. Would like to continue this pastime." (Russell collection.)

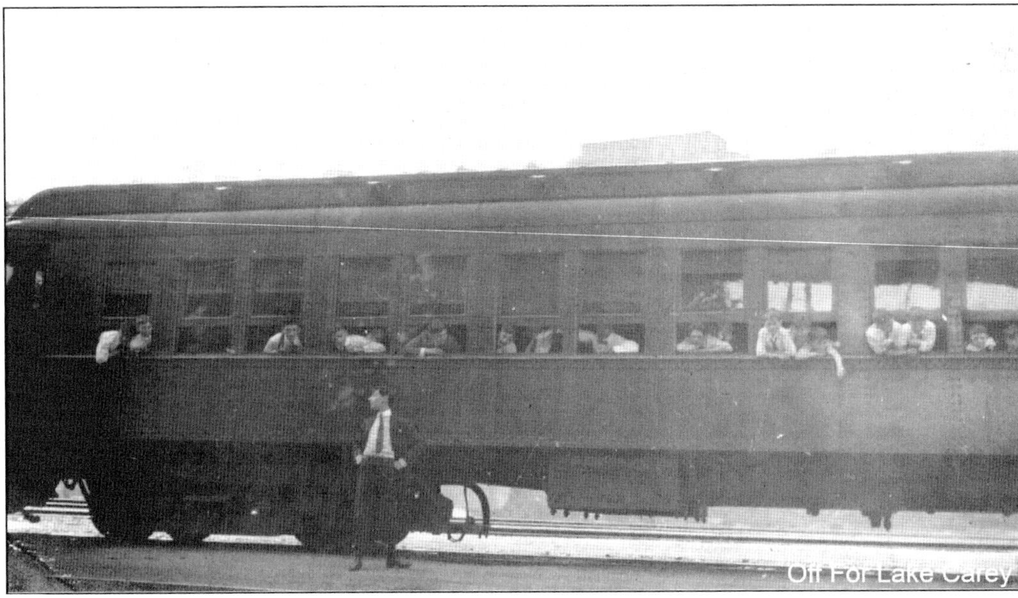

Joseph W. Oliver drew most of his clientele from Brooklyn where he taught. Here campers in a Lehigh Valley Railroad car prepare to leave Jersey City for the six-hour journey to Lake Carey. Charles Collins, the owner's colleague at the Manual Training High School and the camp, often accompanied the boys. (Russell collection.)

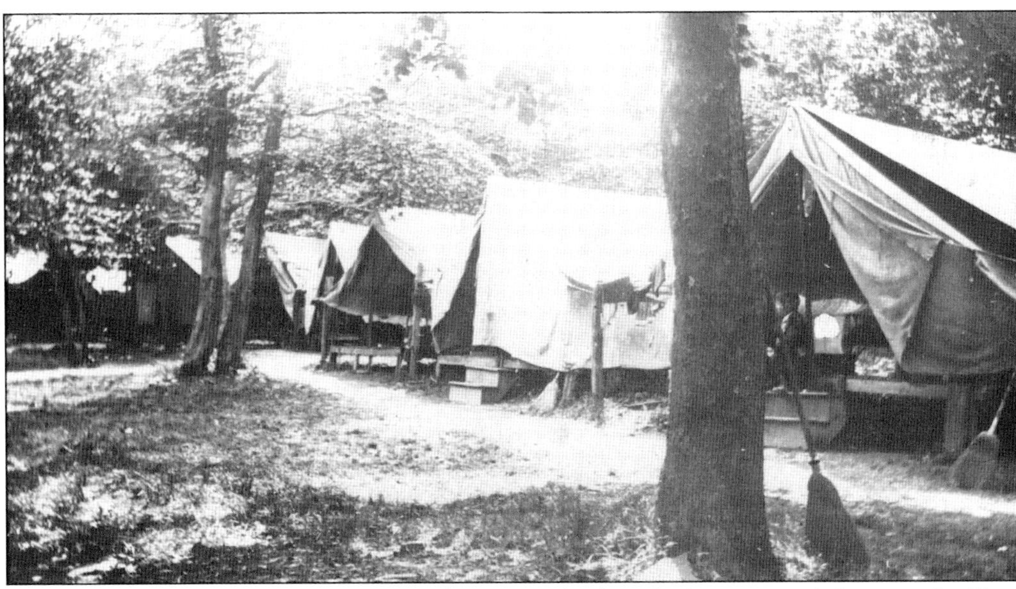

Most boys were housed in 12 platform-wall tents pitched on the lawn around the camp building. This photograph is from the scrapbook of 1918 camper Albert Kane, whose photography that year won a camp award. (Weaver collection.)

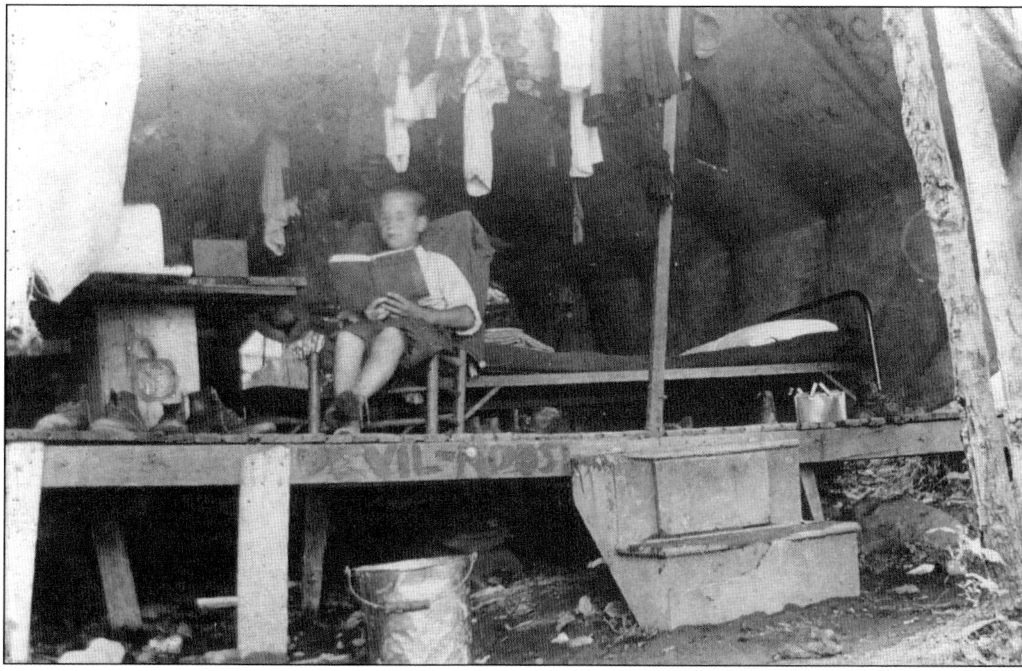

The tents were named. Here a resident of Devil-Roost reads amid boyish clutter in a Kane scrapbook photograph. Ninety minutes were reserved at 8:00 a.m. for reading and tutoring every day. The tutoring in "Regents subjects" cost $25, which was not included in the camp's eight-week fee of $125. (Weaver collection.)

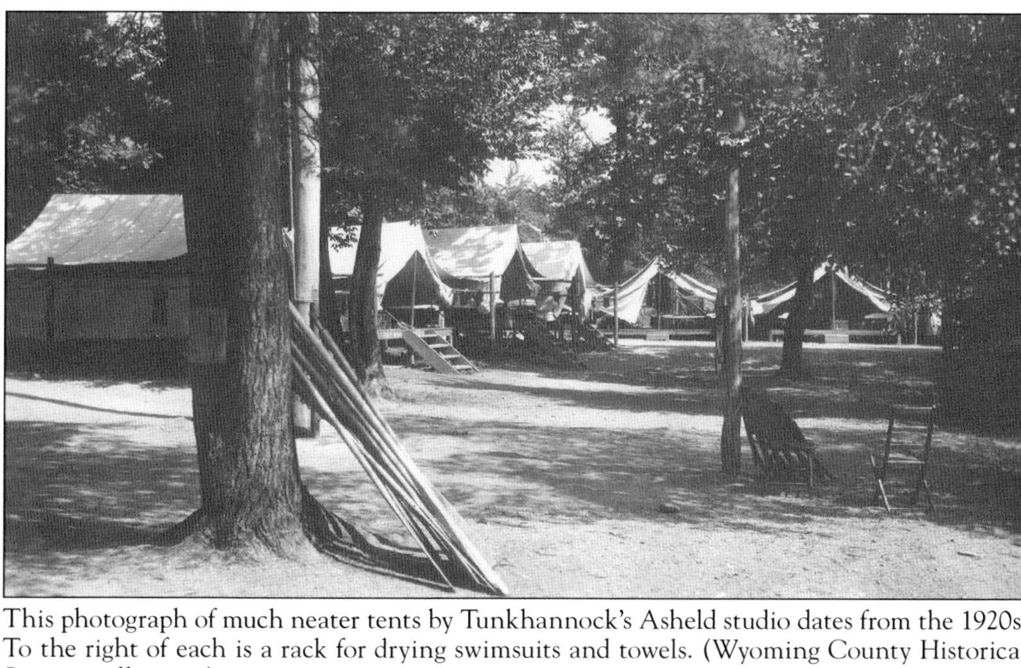

This photograph of much neater tents by Tunkhannock's Asheld studio dates from the 1920s. To the right of each is a rack for drying swimsuits and towels. (Wyoming County Historical Society collection.)

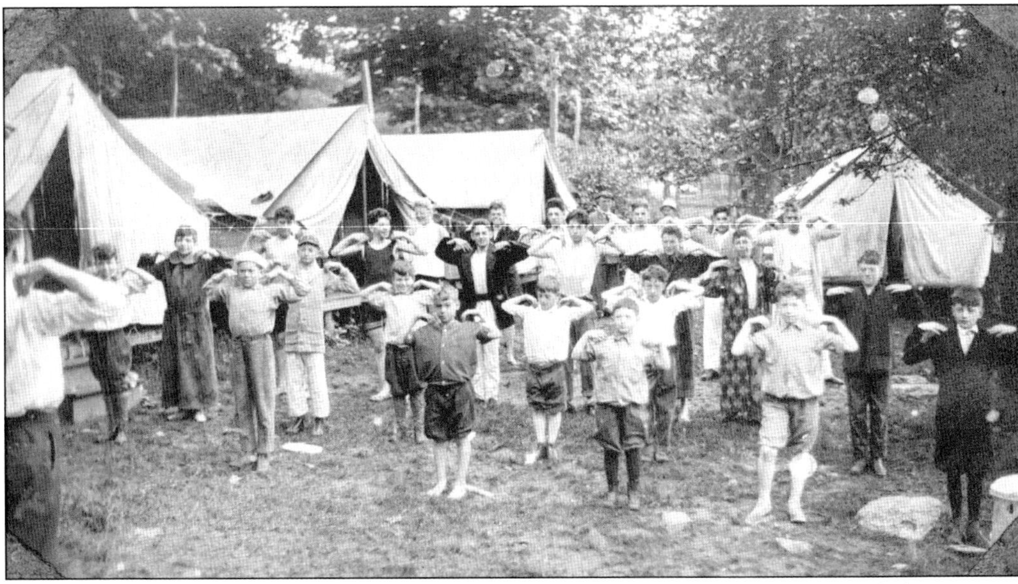

Psychological theories of the day emphasized the developmental importance of play—not to be confused with morally suspect loafing. The activities of the camp day were many and fully regimented. Reveille was at 7:00 a.m., the calisthenics photographed here by camper Albert Kane followed at 7:10. Next came a quick swim at 7:20 and breakfast at 7:30. (Robinson collection.)

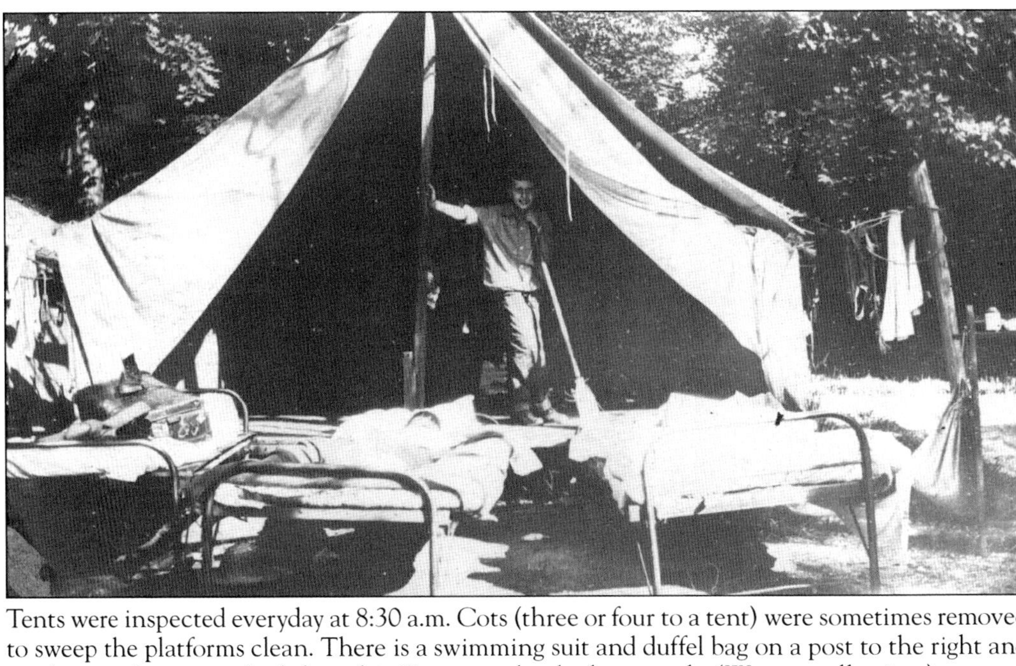

Tents were inspected everyday at 8:30 a.m. Cots (three or four to a tent) were sometimes removed to sweep the platforms clean. There is a swimming suit and duffel bag on a post to the right and a valise on the cot to the left in this Kane scrapbook photograph. (Weaver collection.)

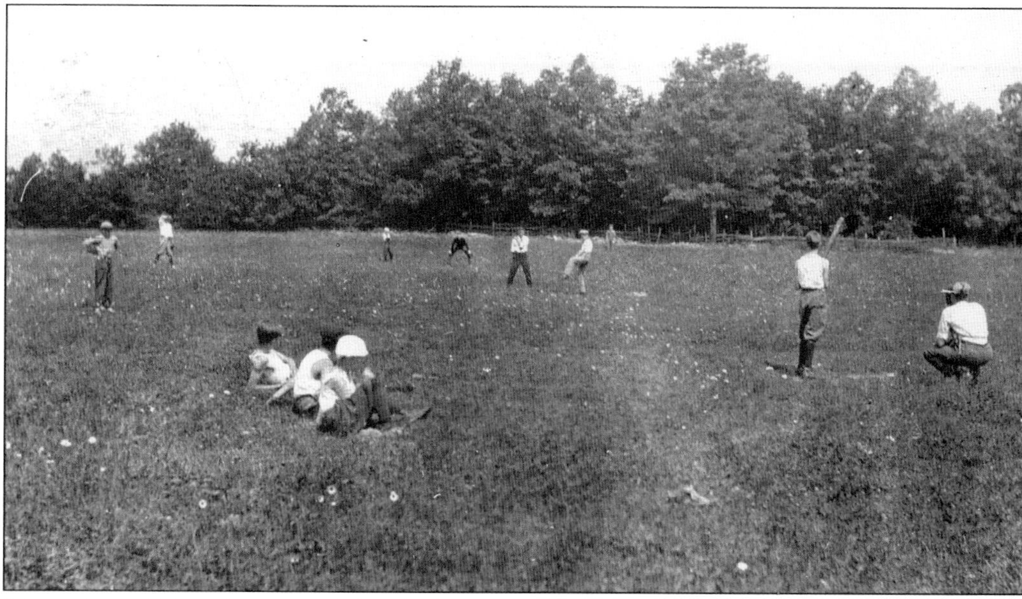

When Camp Pokanoket opened, baseball was already very popular. Ball games were scheduled for 10:00 a.m. The camp also fielded a team with cottagers Bill Quin in right field and his brother Robert on second base, among others, as ringers. Together they "swamped" Lemon and "slaughtered" Tunkhannock in 1915. Note the use of an open field in this Kane scrapbook photograph; regulation diamonds did not become common until the 1920s. (Weaver collection.)

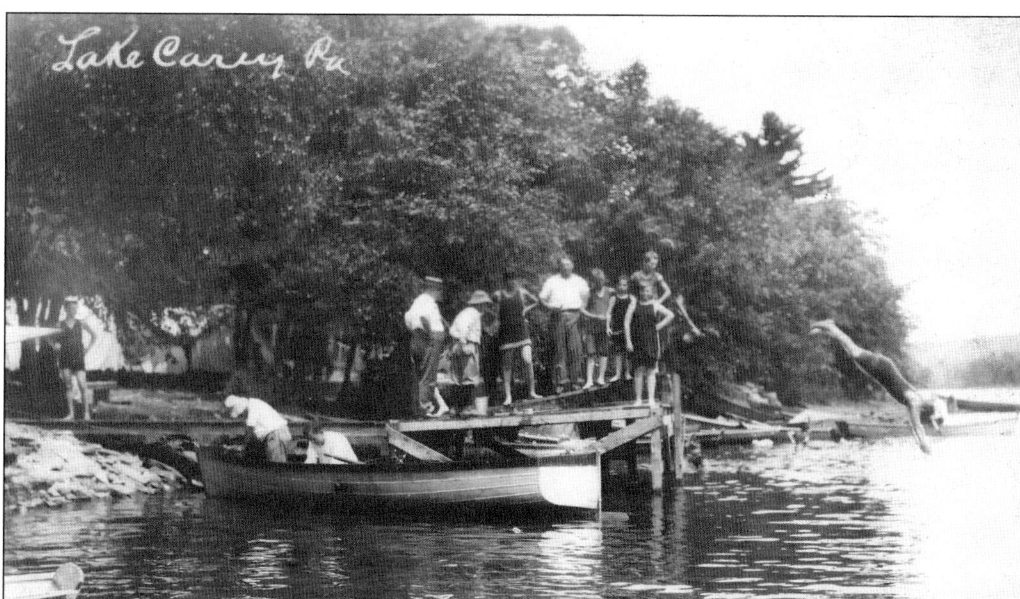

Swimming followed at 11:00 a.m. Here Joseph W. Oliver oversees swimming at the dock (the diver in this real-photo postcard has been superimposed on the image by the photographer). (Author's collection.)

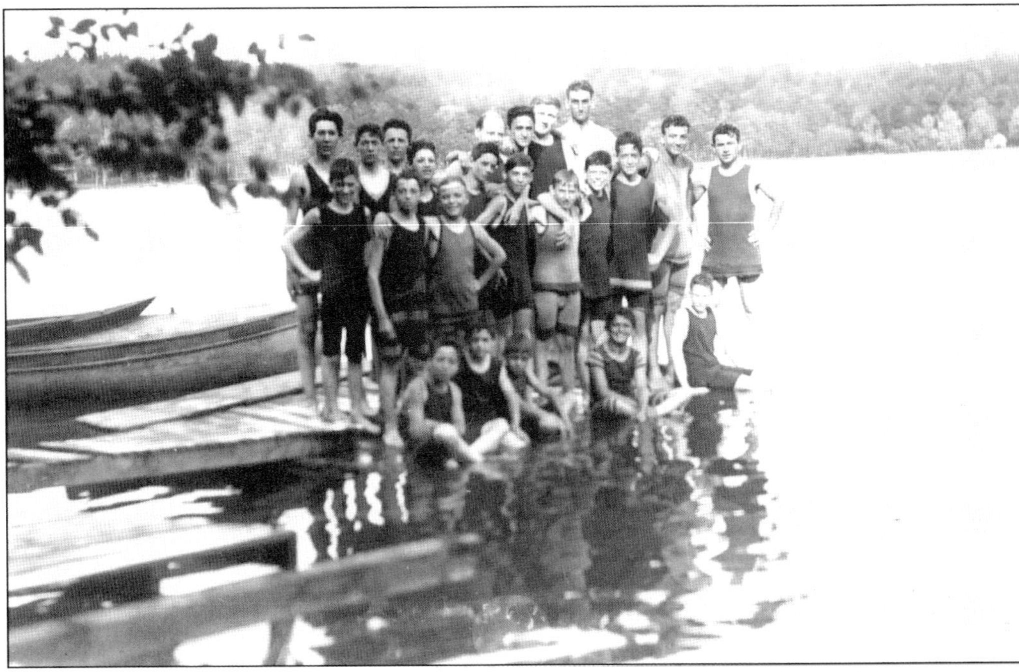

Camp Pokanoket's most famous camper, Aaron Copland (second row, first on left with friend's arm over his shoulder in this real-photo postcard), attended the camp from 1910 through 1913. Copland recalls learning to swim from an instructor who tossed him into the water from this dock and shouted, "Swim you son of a gun, swim!" In his brochure, Joseph W. Oliver described his swimming instructors as "competent." (Russell collection.)

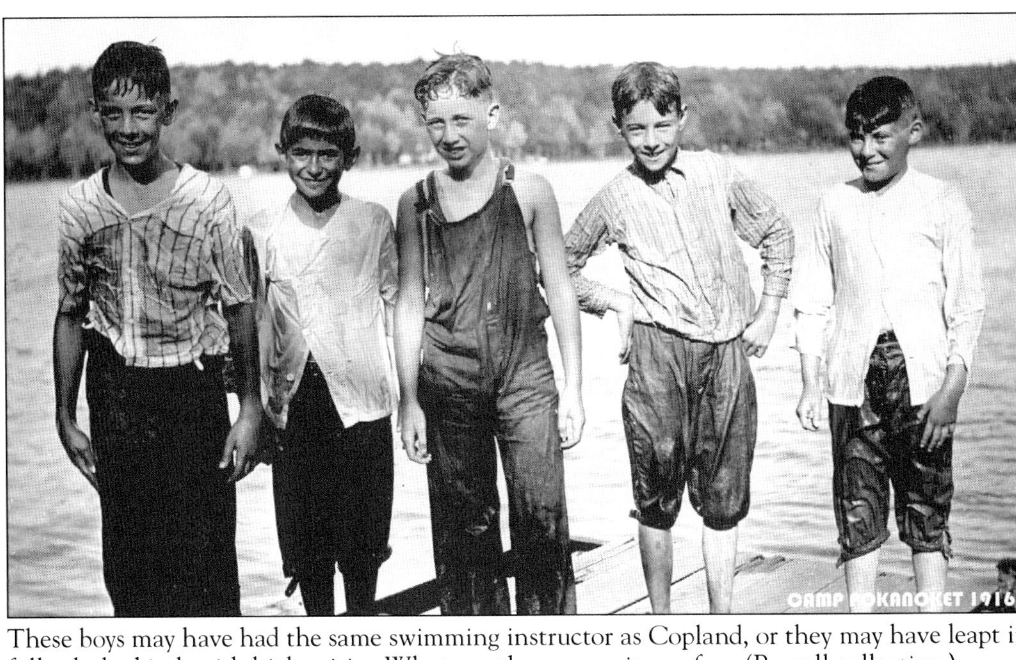

These boys may have had the same swimming instructor as Copland, or they may have leapt in fully clothed in boyish high spirits. Whatever the reason, it was fun. (Russell collection.)

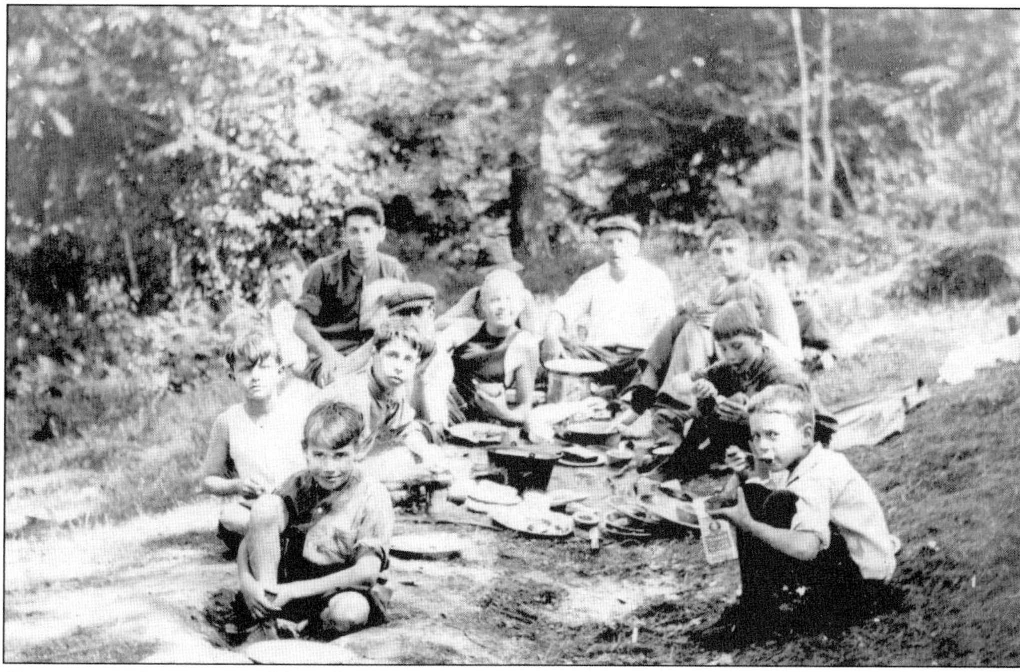

Camp was fun; no problem keeping one's elbows off the table when there is no table. (Robinson collection.)

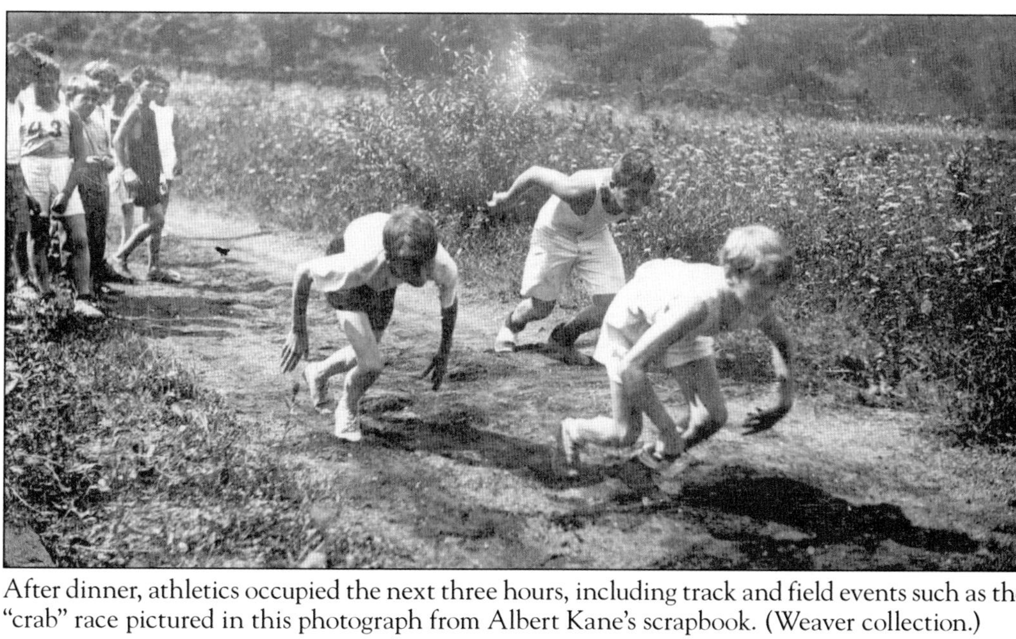

After dinner, athletics occupied the next three hours, including track and field events such as the "crab" race pictured in this photograph from Albert Kane's scrapbook. (Weaver collection.)

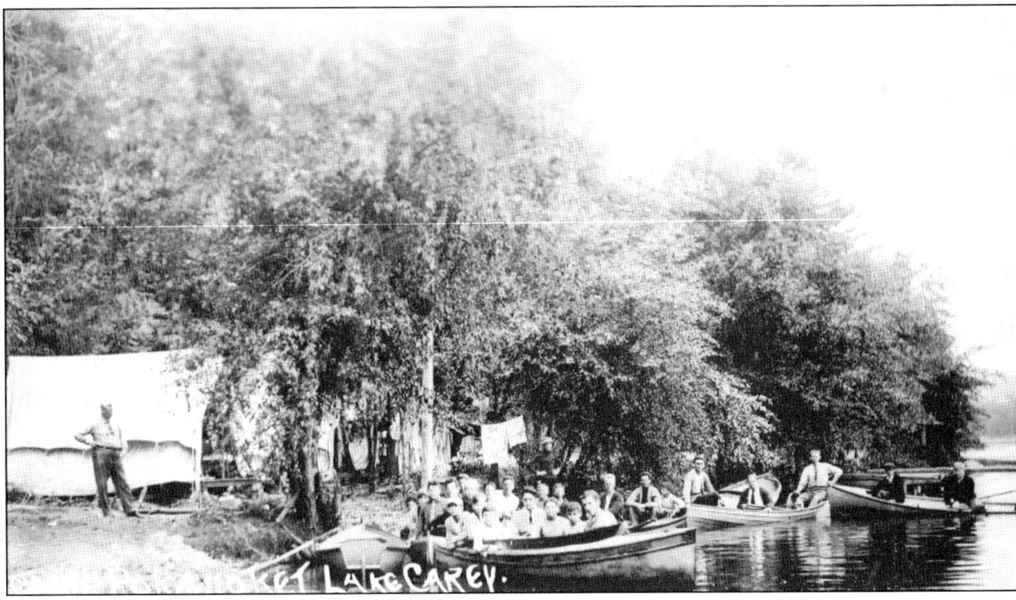

Joseph W. Oliver is photographed again keeping a watchful eye on waterfront activities. At this time, the tents were pitched at water's edge. Note the dense growth of river birch and the towels hung out to dry among them. The image on this real-photo postcard appears in the 1914 camp brochure and seems to be one of several taken, possibly by Oliver's friend F. C. Shook, to publicize the camp. (Russell collection.)

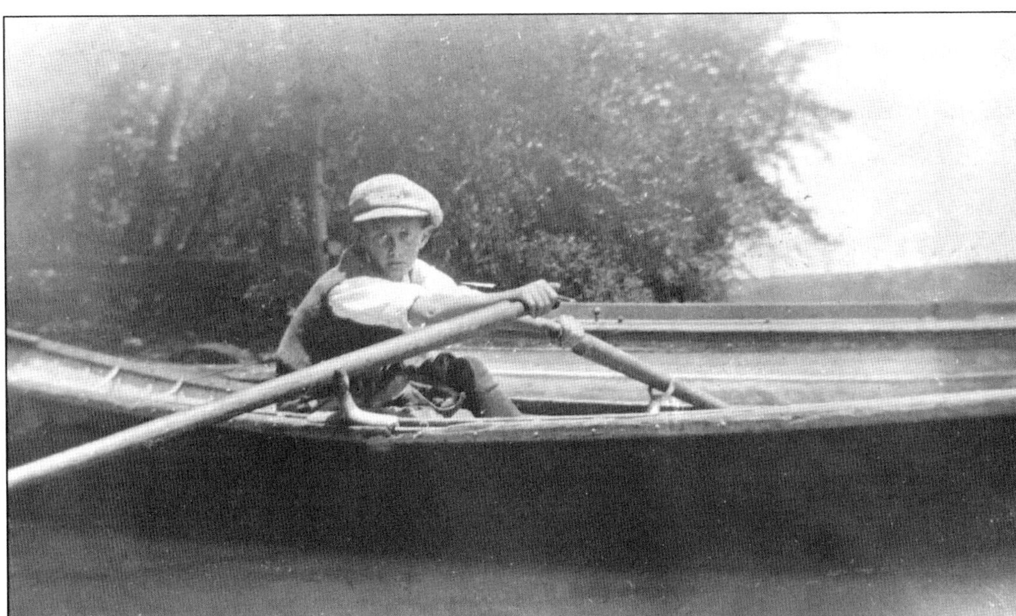

Boating was an important part of life at the camp. Aaron Copland notes in his autobiography that he also learned to row. (Russell collection.)

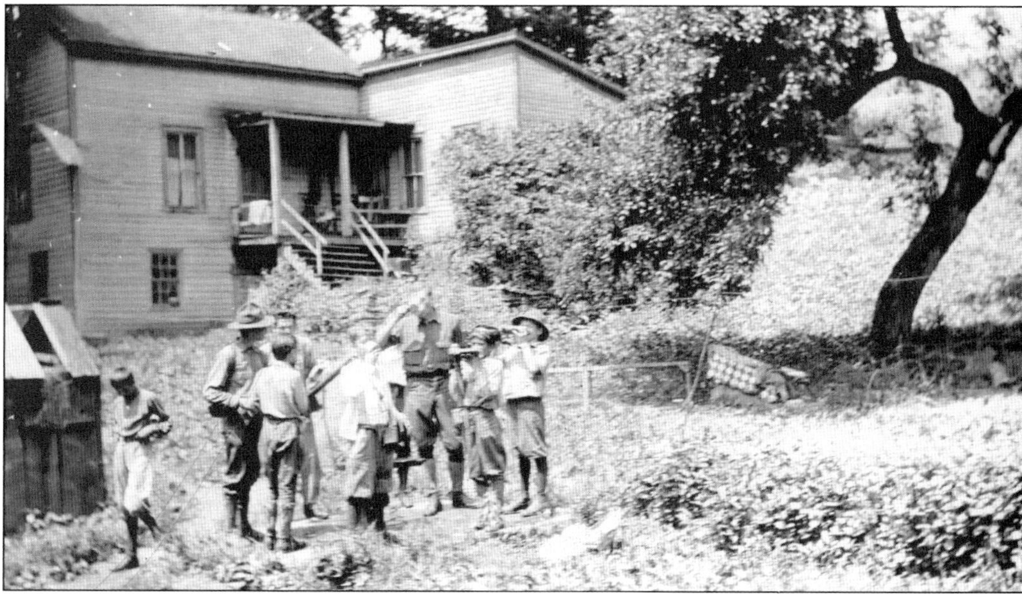

"Tramps" to Lemon, the mills at the outlet, or in the hills above the lake were a regular part of camp life. In this real-photo postcard, a group of boys with two counselors pauses near an old apple tree, canteens raised to their mouths. As in many camps of that era, however, the object was healthy exercise, not the study of the area's natural environment. (Robinson collection.)

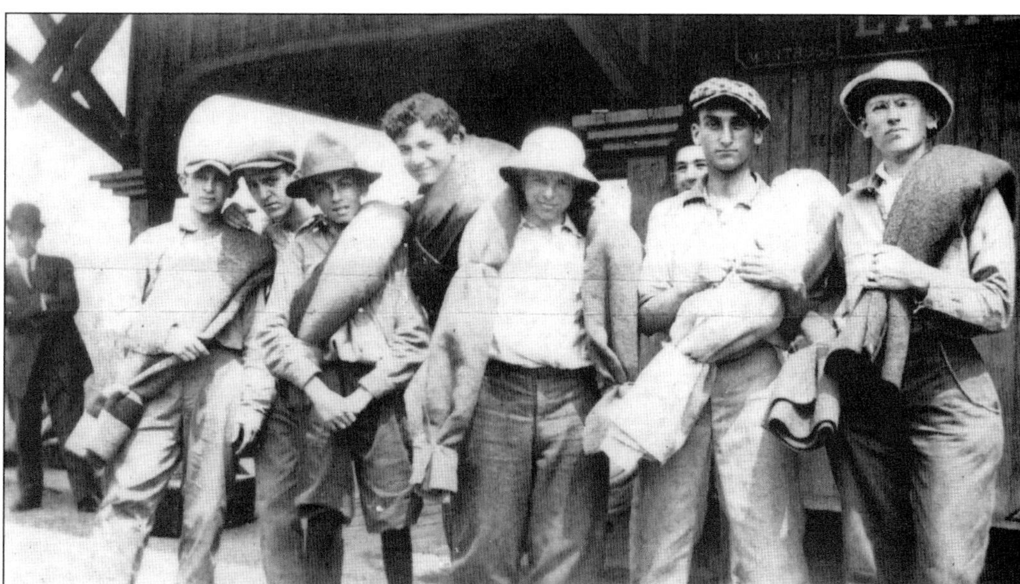

Every summer included a long-distance trip (Niagara Falls for several years) as well as overnights on an island in the Susquehanna. Here six campers and a counselor, bedrolls over their shoulders, prepare to leave from the railroad station across the road from the camp. (Redding collection.)

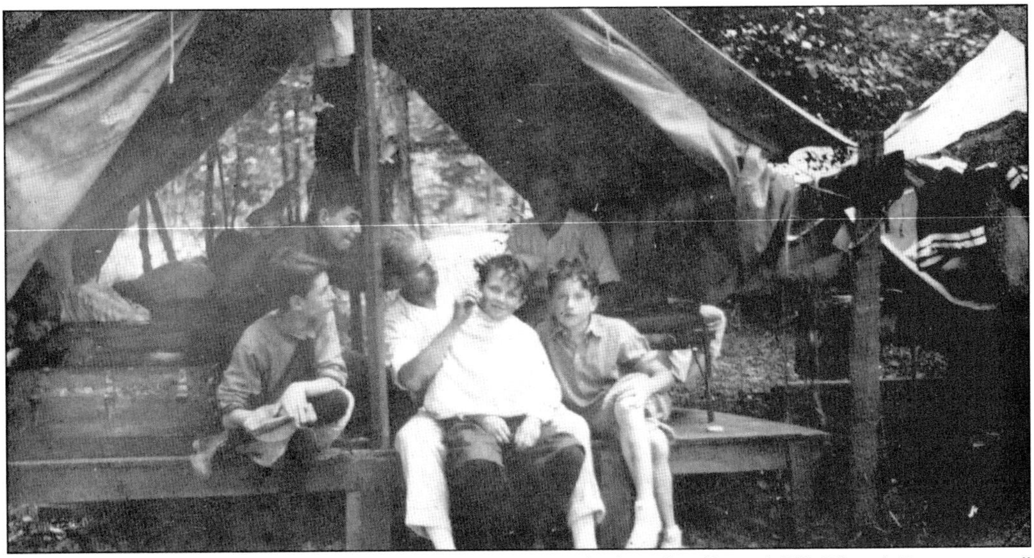

Amid all this activity, there was also time for haircuts at the hands of Joseph W. Oliver's "competent" counselors. The efforts of this counselor have attracted the amused attention of several of Albert Kane's fellow campers in this photograph from his scrapbook. (Weaver collection.)

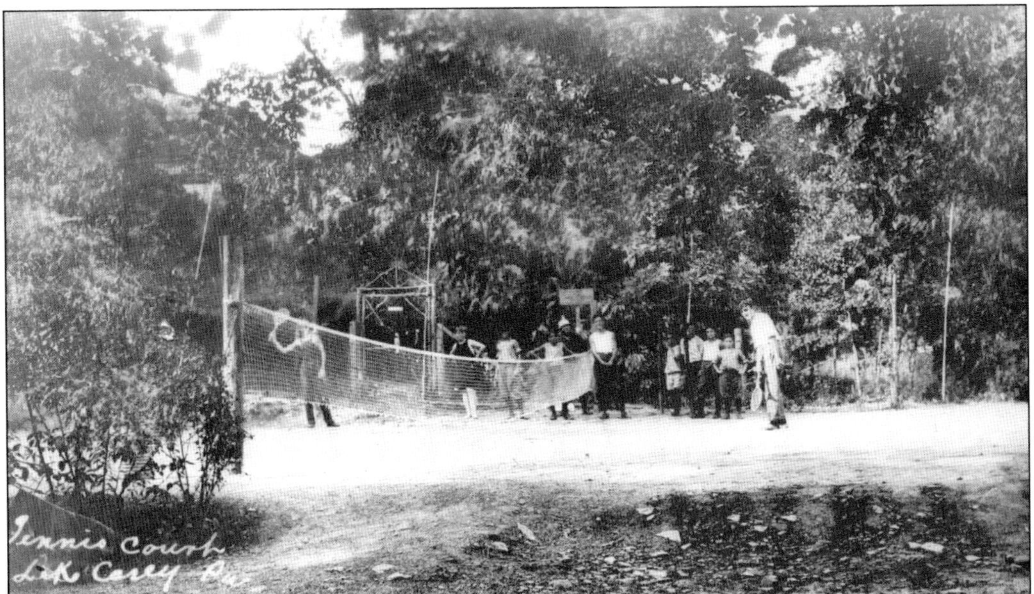

The camp also featured a tennis court (seen in this real-photo postcard) it shared with the Spring Grove Inn after the Olivers purchased the hotel. Aaron Copland acknowledges that he also learned to play tennis here, a pastime he continued in adulthood. (Russell collection.)

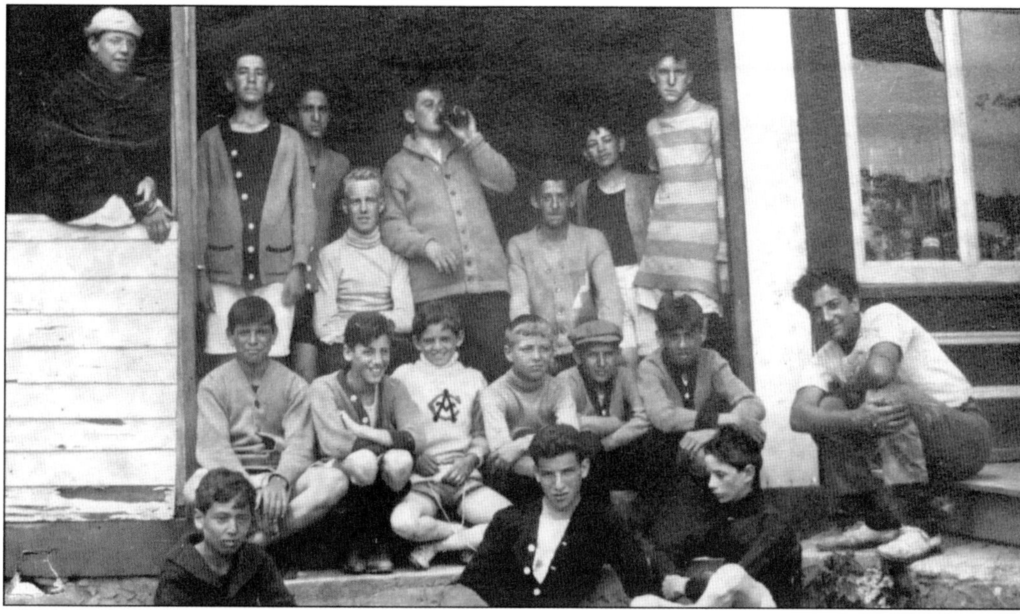

While loafing was not approved, hanging out at Cassedy's store across the street from the camp was permitted. Whitman's candy, soda pop, and Harrington's ice cream were all sold there. (Redding collection.)

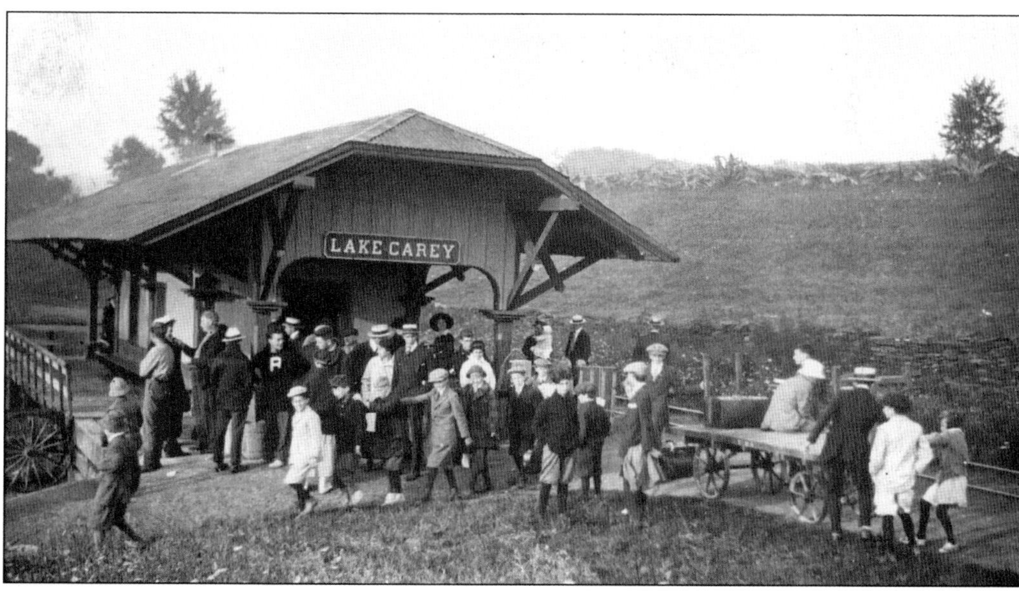

At the end of August it was time to return to Brooklyn and to family, as well as to another year of school. Note the older boy with the *P* on his shirt standing by the station's front pier on the left in this photograph from the Kane scrapbook. (Tinner collection.)

Farewell Banquet

Wednesday, the Twenty-Seventh of August

Nineteen Hundred Thirteen

Menu

"Now good digestion wait on appetite,
And health on both. —***Macbeth.***

FRUIT MELANGE

WAFERS

PICKLES OLIVES CURRANT JELLY

BROILED SPRING CHICKEN ON TOAST

COLD ROAST LAMB

POKANOKET SANDWICHES PIMENTO SANDWICHES

SWEET POTATOES WITH NUT DRESSING

TOMATO SALAD

CHEESE SALTINES

ICE CREAM IN CANTALOUPE ANGEL FOOD

SUNSHINE CAKE BLACK CHOCOLATE CAKE

AFTER-DINNER MINTS BLANCHED PEANUTS

COFFEE

The summer ended with a farewell banquet. This is the meal that was served Aaron Copland and his fellow campers in August 1913. (Copland later wrote to his parents from Paris that the food at Lake Carey did not compare well to the food he was then enjoying.) (Weaver collection.)

Toasts

"A merry heart goes all the day,
Your sad tires in a mile-a." —*Winter's Tale.*

Toastmaster—J. W. Oliver.

CAMP KODAKS . . . . R. L. MASSONNEAU

"And this our life, exempt from public haunt,
Finds tongues in trees, books in the running brooks,
Sermons in stones, and good in everything." —As You Like It.

THE CRAFTSMAN . . . . M. W. SCHULER

"Light boats sail swift, though greater hulks draw deep."
—Troilus and Cressida.

ATHLETICS . . . . H. O. SMITH

"Pleasure and action make the hours seem short." —Othello.

THE HIKE . . . . S. HEIMANN

"To climb steep hills requires slow pace at first." —Henry VIII.

DRAMATICS . . . . C. R. COLLINS

"The play's the thing,
Wherein I'll catch the conscience of the king." —Hamlet.

BILLY AND PRINCE . . . . I. FRIEDMAN

"I am not of the feather to shake off
My friend when he must need me." —Timon of Athens.

ACCIDENTS . . . . M. B. KUNSTLER, M. D.

"He jests at scars that never felt a wound." —Romeo and Juliet.

OUR OUTLOOK . . . . M. G. MICHAELS

"Heaven give you many, many merry days."—Merry Wives of Windsor.

Presentation of the P's.
Presentation of the Prizes.
Presentation of the Medals.

"Parting is such sweet sorrow."—Romeo and Juliet.

After dinner, prizes were awarded. They included a triangular medal depicting a tent, and the camp's monogram, to be displayed on a shirt or sweater. Points were awarded "in a spirit of friendly rivalry" throughout the summer for excellence in each activity. The highest numbers merited a medal and second and third places camp letters. (Weaver collection.)

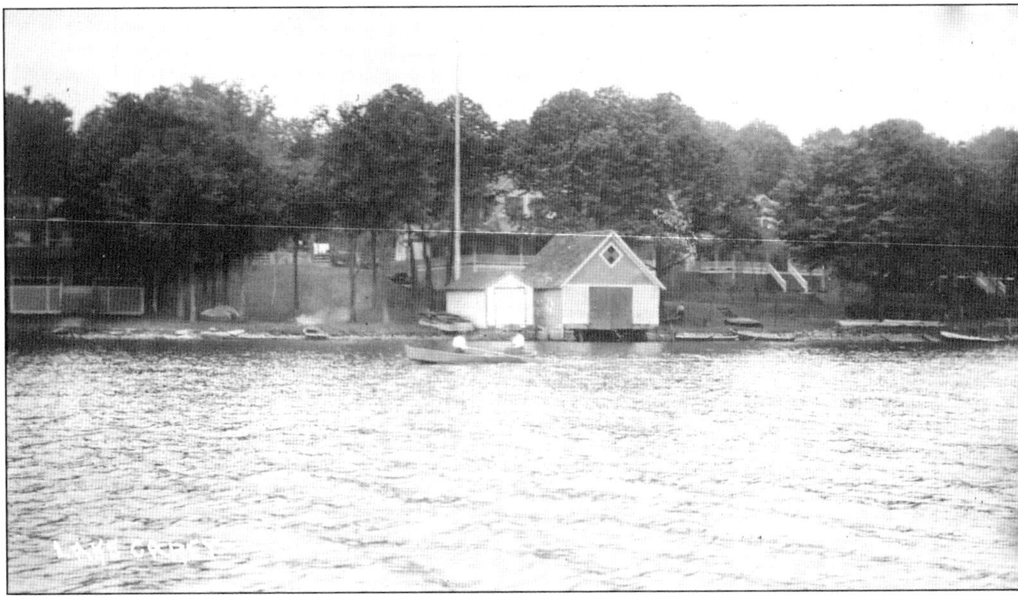

In August 1918, Joseph W. Oliver's colleague Charles Collins purchased a west shore cottage—seen in this real-photo postcard in 1907 behind the boathouses—and three vacant lots where he operated Camp Carey for several years. Within a year of his purchase, the Olivers sold Camp Pokanoket to Maxwell and Lydia Croohe of Brooklyn for $6,625. The Croohes operated it, restricting its clientele to Jewish boys, until it failed during the Depression. (Author's collection.)

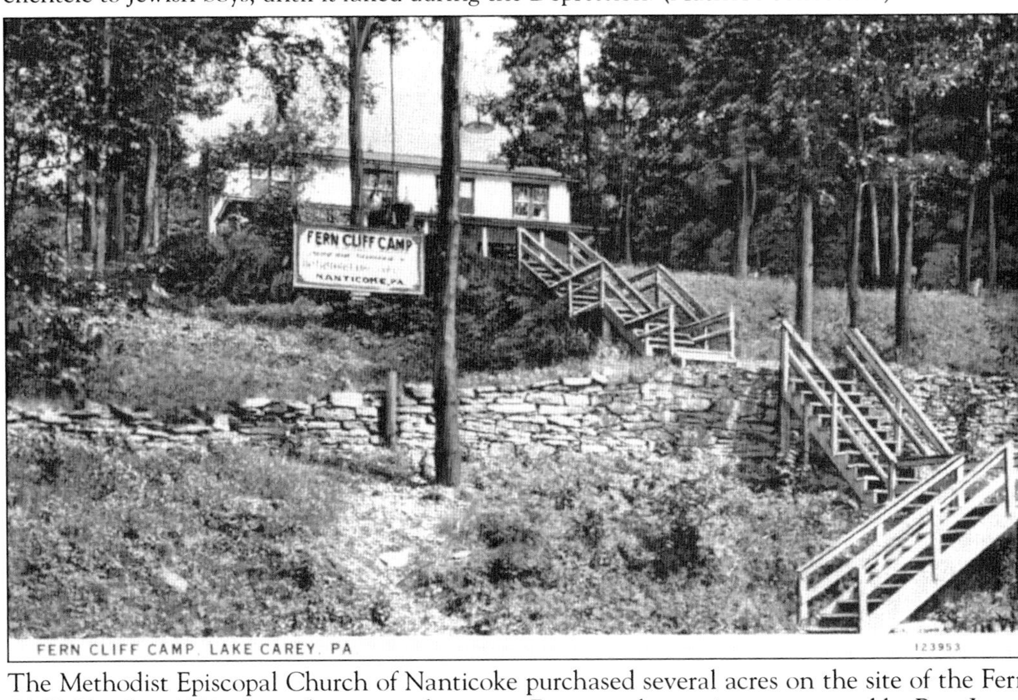

The Methodist Episcopal Church of Nanticoke purchased several acres on the site of the Fern Cliffe Hotel in 1924 where they opened a camp. For several years it was operated by Rev. James Lawson, who also preached summer sermons at Union Chapel. In 1927, a grateful congregation awarded Boy Scout and camper Guy Leinthall a watch for his rescue of a drowning woman. (Author's collection.)

Four

A Commodious Cottage at the Lake

The emerging resort at Lake Carey did not escape the attention of John and Alvin Day's rival Republican paper. Its editor visited this "beautiful, healthful and invigorating summer resort," in 1881 to report on the new cottage community. He was clearly impressed, especially by the Wheaton's Beech Grove Camp.

> Here we find a commodious cottage, the rooms in the main part of which are wainscoted and ceiled with hard wood, while the bedrooms are furnished with regular chamber suits [*sic*], and everything conducive to comfort abounds. The . . . main part is 12 by 16 feet, with one wing 12 by 28 and two 8 by 10, besides a dining platform, consisting of a floor and canvass roof, 12 by 16 feet. There are also two large tents used for sleeping apartments, an ice house . . . and a large store-house for odds and ends. The grounds are supplied with easy chairs, hammocks, a twelve-foot umbrella, croquet, etc. A substantial stone wharf has been built all along the front of the camp, and landing is consequently easy.

Cottages began to spring up, as if overnight, as local developers platted and sold their lots. Few were as elaborate as Beech Grove Camp, but the comforts of middle-class life were seldom neglected. Most of them were built in a modified stick style then popular with the middle classes at summer resorts. They were two stories high, with an open-front gable and porches on both stories. Decorative shingles might be added to the gable, and elaborate brackets, turned posts, and railings to the porches. They were painted in two or three complementary colors with the often dark, natural hues favored by the Victorians. (After the Colonial Revival became popular, they were repainted white with dark green trim.)

At Lake Carey many early cottages were of single-plank construction. Two-story-high, vertical planking was attached to two-by-eight beams, which ran along the bottom, middle, and top of what would become the cottage walls. If the planks were butt jointed, battens were nailed later across the joints; if the planks were milled with a tongue on one side and a groove on the other—into which the adjacent plank's tongue could be inserted—battens were unneeded. After the walls had been raised, the beams were nailed together at the corners, and floor joists notched into and hung from the beams on the sidewalls to support the floors and to tie these two walls to one another. The rafters for the roof were then erected upon the tops of these long sidewalls. There were no corner posts, nor braces. Because these frameless structures often bulged from the weight of the roof, cables with turnbuckles were sometimes run from side to side at the attic floor and cellar ceiling. These dwellings were cheap, quickly constructed, and drew on a widespread building tradition in the region. (Many farmhouses were built of double, vertical planking and even more sheds and outbuildings with single planking.) More affluent families built balloon-frame structures.

Wood was inexpensive and readily available. Some of it was probably milled at the lake's outlet from trees on the site. Despite their greater fire resistance, brick and stone were not used. Most cottages included a chimney, usually with a fireplace. Solid shutters were often attached to one side of the windows to be closed in the fall, protecting the cottage from mischievous boys and the occasional vandal.

More affluent families would add an icehouse behind the dwelling, others might include a root or ice cellar in one wall of the basement. Only a very few included a carriage house or barn; the lake enjoyed regular train service. And, of course, every cottage included an outhouse or necessary in the back.

The downstairs often contained a front parlor, an all-purpose room for dining and informal living, and a kitchen. Three or more small bedrooms were present on the second floor. Boys usually shared one, girls another, and their parents slept in the front bedroom with a lake view. Walls were thin and privacy at a minimum, especially when filled with a typical summer crowd of 8 to 12 family and friends. In time, these cottages were filled with cast-off furniture from the family's year-round home.

Until Roosevelt's rural electrification program wired the lake, oil lamps and kerosene stoves provided light, heat for cooking, and warmth to take the chill off the damp morning air. One or two cottages had their own electric generator, and some of the stores, picnic grounds, and camps relied on Delco battery plants. Fire was a real hazard. One hotel, a store, the toy factory, and six or more cottages were destroyed in accidental fires before 1930. Despite fire and a 1998 tornado, the lake's built environment is remarkably intact. Most of its original cottages have survived. (Unless a caption otherwise notes, the cottages pictured are still standing and in use.)

In this section, the images are ordered in a virtual, clockwise tour around the lake. It begins with Beech Grove Camp, an iconic cottage and arguably the lake's first. Throughout the text, cottages are referred to by the name their original or subsequent owners bestowed. These cottagers were fond of winningly bad puns—Auto Rest, Isle of View—or names they hoped would reflect the quality of their lives at the lake—Idle Hours, Summer Rest—or those they thought descriptive—Point Breeze, Buena Vista. Whenever possible, the original owner of the lot (presumably the individual or family for whom the cottage was constructed) has been identified, as well as the lot's plat number and the date of its purchase (after which the cottage was presumably built).

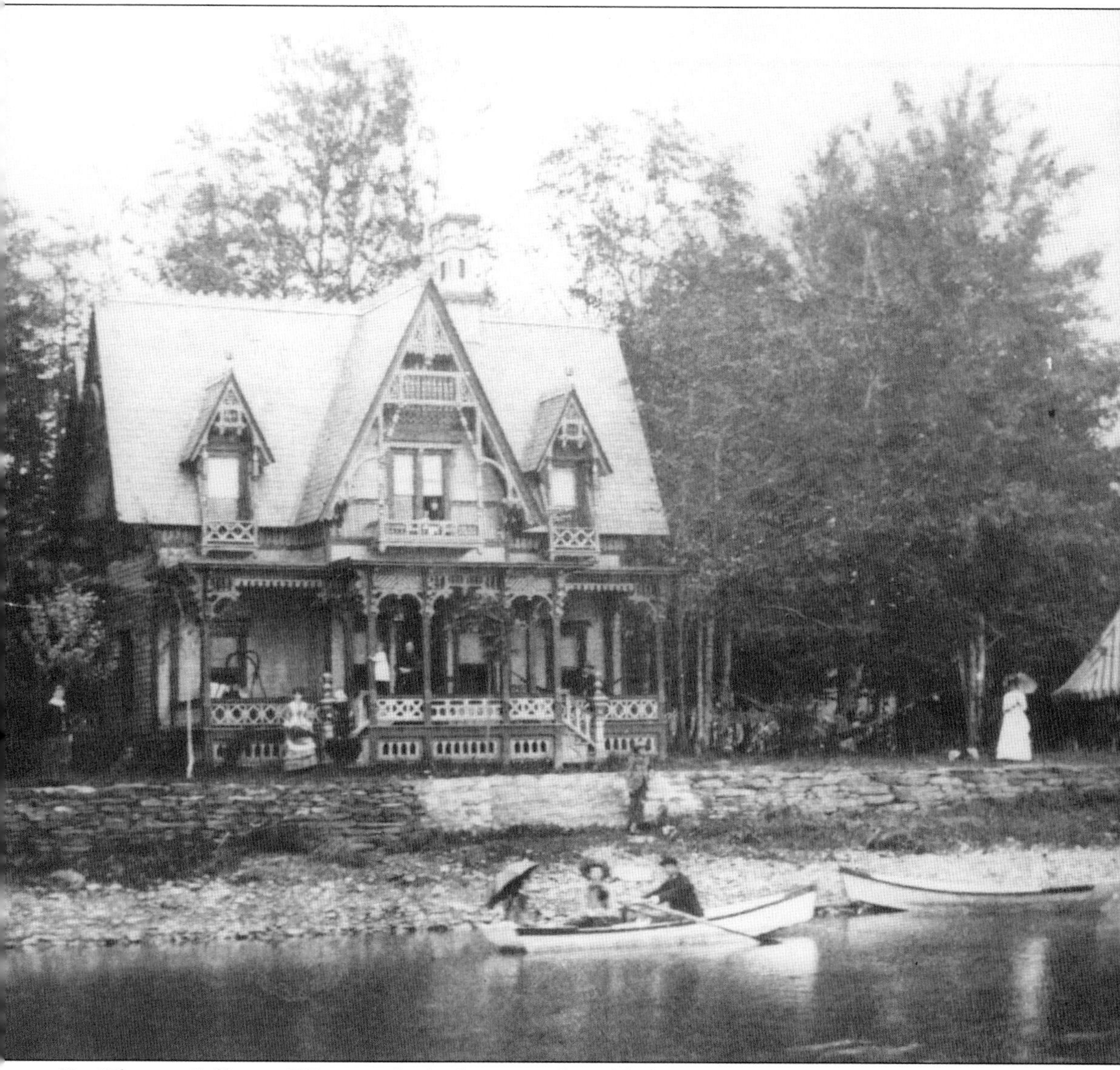

Dr. Thomas Jefferson Wheaton built this gingerbread-laden cottage with a commanding view of the lake on the one-acre point he purchased from Asa Stevens in 1880. The Wheatons had camped here in 1879. They continued to use tents to house visitors and for outdoor dining for many years. Altogether Beech Grove Camp could accommodate 27 people (there are 12 photographed here), and it frequently did so. (Fellows collection.)

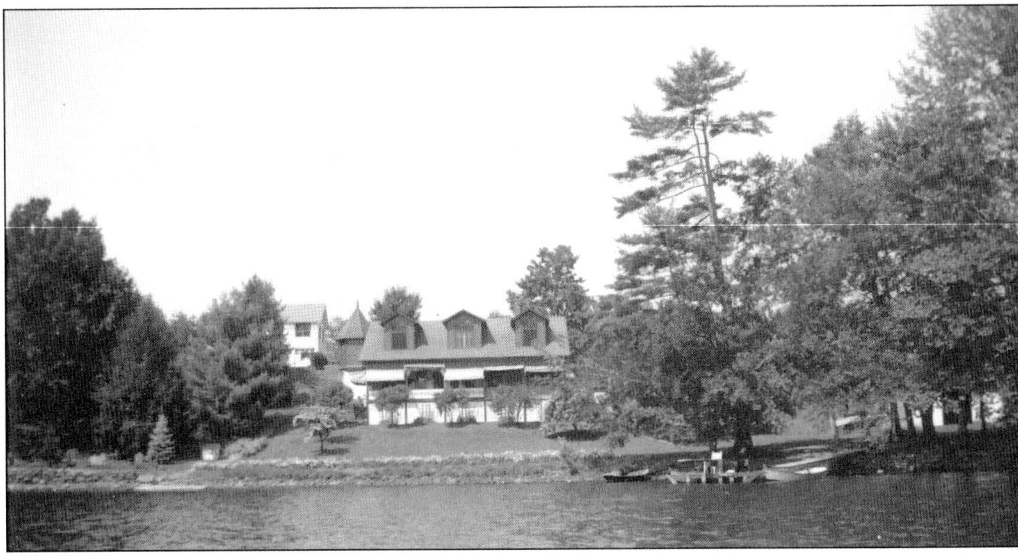

Jessie Rhodes Sherman, Thomas Jefferson Wheaton's daughter, built this cottage adjacent to that of her father. Adm. Harold R. Stark purchased it from her in 1924 after he married her daughter, Katherine Rhodes. The admiral added a summer kitchen, and the four-car garage and oak water tank visible on the left in this real-photo postcard, and enlarged the dormers. (Tinner collection.)

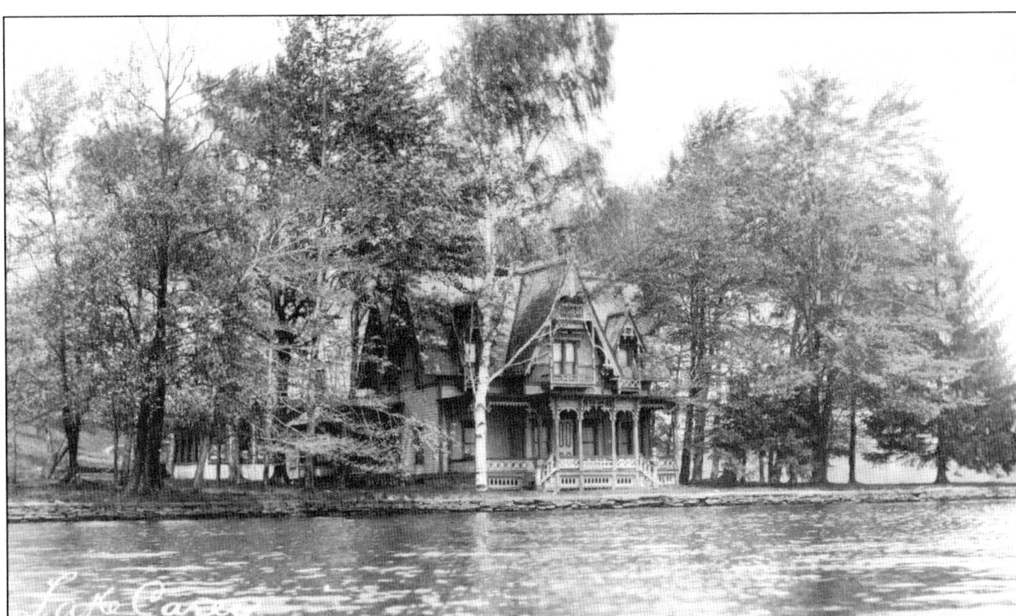

In this real-photo postcard, Beech Grove Camp awaits the Wheatons' arrival in the springtime around 1910. The cottage is virtually unchanged today, save for the loss of the balconies beneath the second-story windows and spiked metal trim on the roof's ridge. (Petrillo collection.)

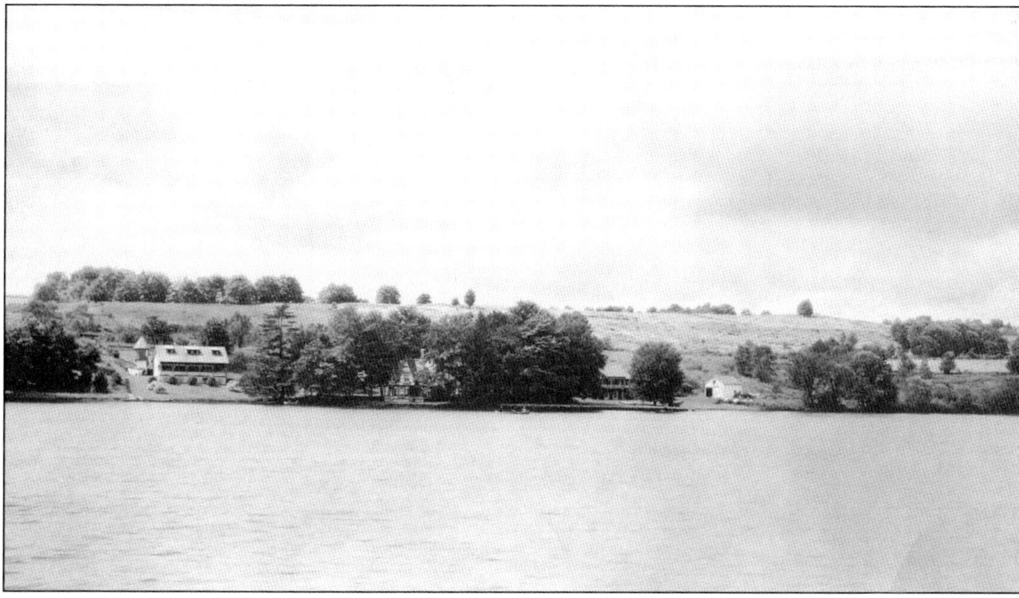

Over the next several years, Wheaton acquired another seven acres on which he constructed an icehouse, carriage house with a second-story theater (now Kilkenny cottage, second from right), and other outbuildings. This photograph includes the cottage (left) built by Wheaton's daughter, Jessie Rhodes Sherman. (This photograph was taken before Admiral Stark enlarged the dormers.) (Kelly collection.)

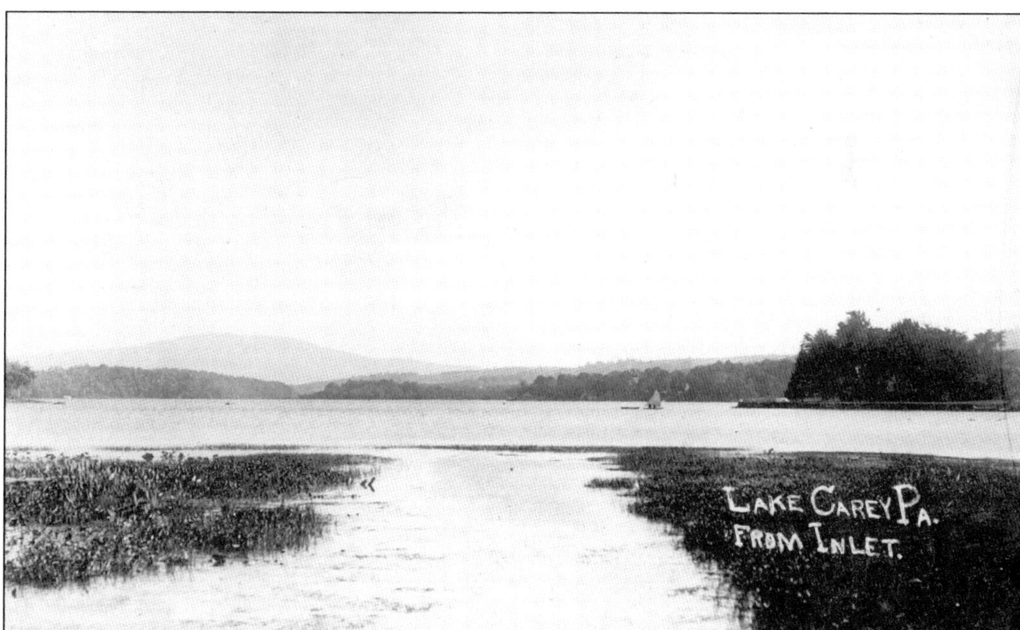

On this rare real-photo postcard, the view from the lake's inlet to the causeway includes Osterhout Mountain in the distance. Wheaton Point is heavily wooded—presumably with beeches—on the right. (Butler collection.)

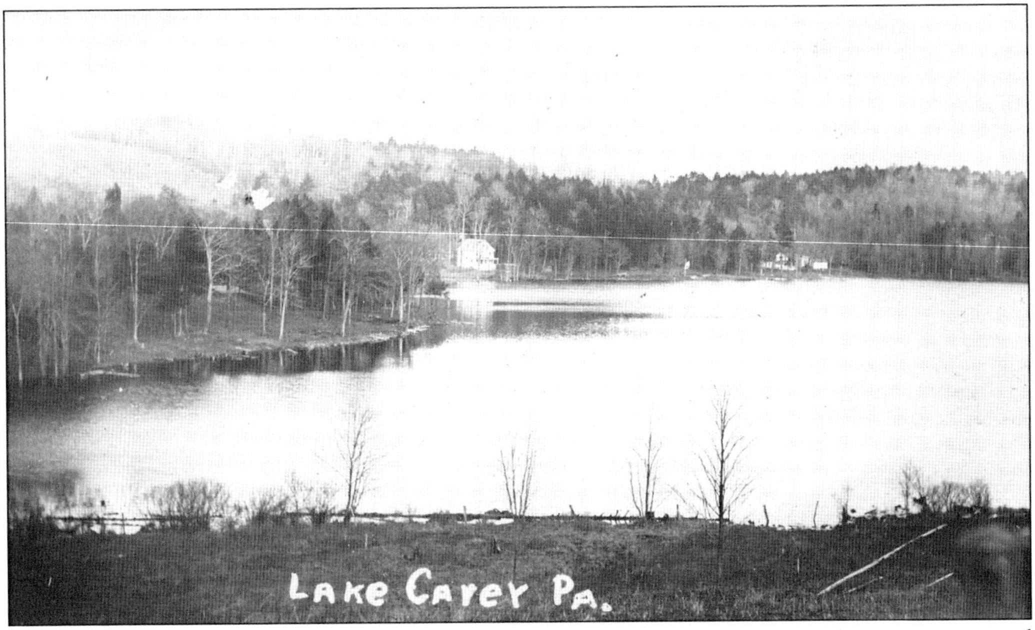

In this real-photo postcard, the view of the lake's northern end shows the farmhouse constructed by Frank and Cora Cooper, who purchased the 236-acre Wrigley farm after John Wrigley's death in 1907. The Coopers sold the Wrigley farmhouse, just visible to the right through the trees, to Elizabeth A. Carmody in 1924. She named it Dan-Dee after her husband, Dan. It is owned by her descendants today. (Author's collection.)

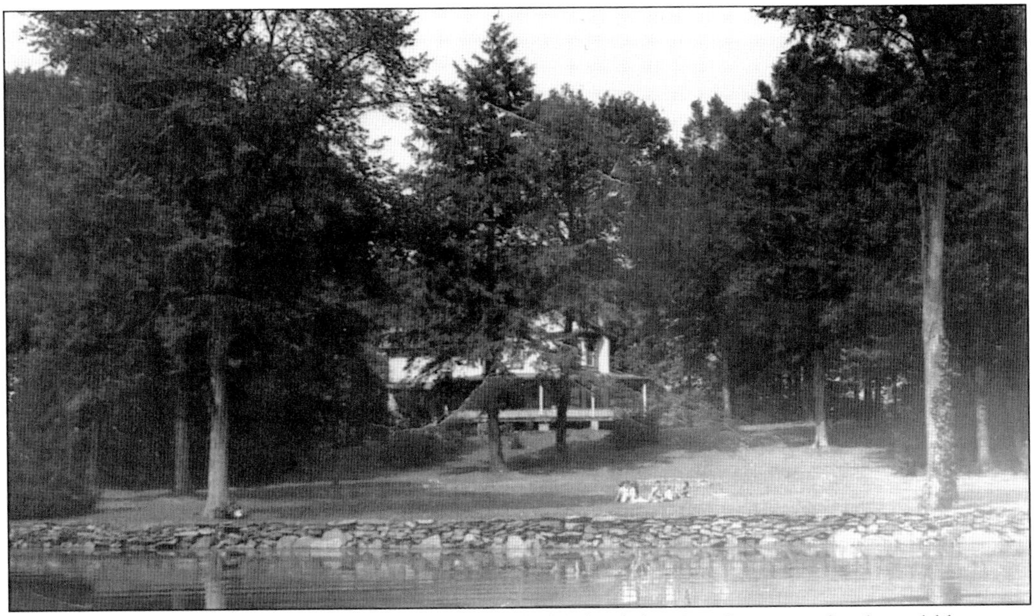

This east shore farmhouse near the inlet was probably built by Asa Stevens after he sold his west shore home to E. L. Diefenderfer in 1882. In addition to farming, Stevens rented fishing rafts and boats and operated a steamboat, the *Empress of the Lake*. Felix W. Bolowicz, a prominent Wilkes-Barre attorney, acquired the 80-acre farm from Stevens's son Arthur in 1924, fifteen years before this photograph was taken. (Robic collection.)

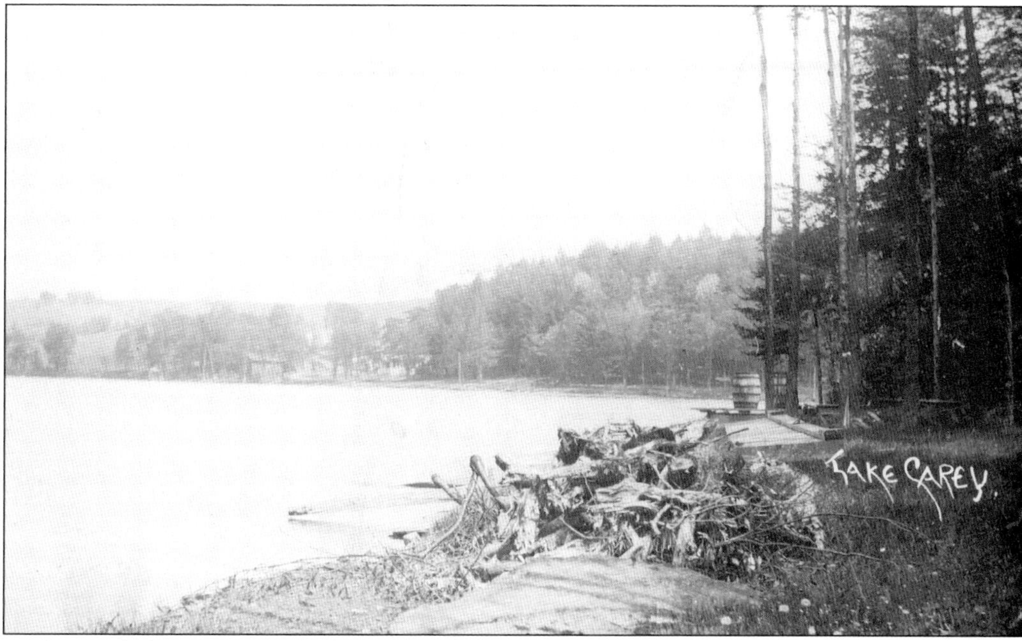

In this real-photo postcard, the view up the lake appears to have been shot from the point across the road from Tarnden. The Frank and Cora Cooper farmhouse and its lakeside icehouse are just visible beyond the curve of the bay on the right, in which Wrigley's Grove once sat. (Butler collection.)

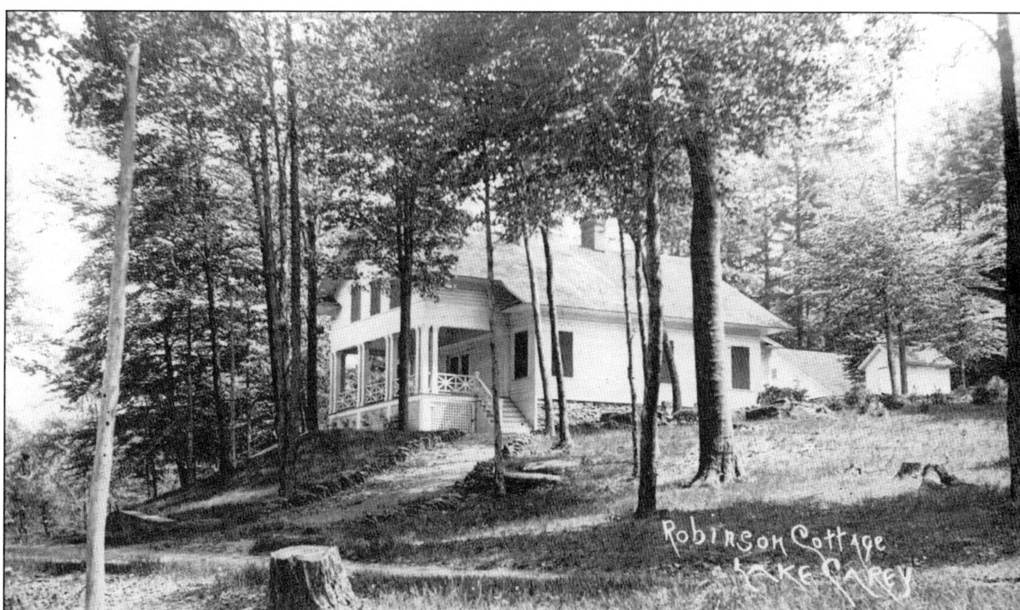

The handsome cottage in this real-photo postcard was designed and built in 1891 by John Robertson (not Robinson), a Scottish immigrant and colliery owner, using carpenters from his mine. Tarnden, Gaelic for "small mountain lake lair," was furnished with Gustav Stickley furniture, Tiffany lamps, and three paintings by Scranton plein air painter John Willard Raught. One oil, *The Gorse Gatherers*, was painted in Scotland on commission from Robertson. (Weaver collection.)

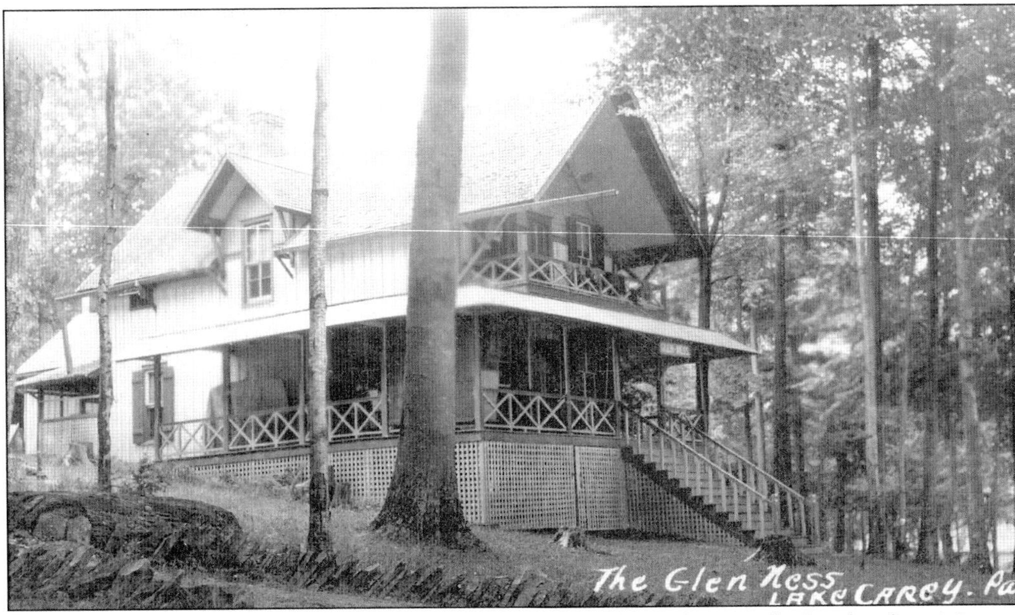

Glen Ness, seen in this real-photo postcard, was built by John Robertson for his daughter Marjorie and her husband, Joseph Jennings, a civil engineer. Their daughter, Jean Jennings Hennings, inherited her grandfather's cottage, Tarnden, where she summered every year until recently. (Author's collection.)

Penn Grove, seen in this real-photo postcard, was owned by J. S. Prestzman in 1928 when the Lake Carey Park Association was resurveyed before its dissolution as a corporation. At this time, covenants were placed in many of the deeds prohibiting the construction of structures between the road and the lakefront. (Russell collection.)

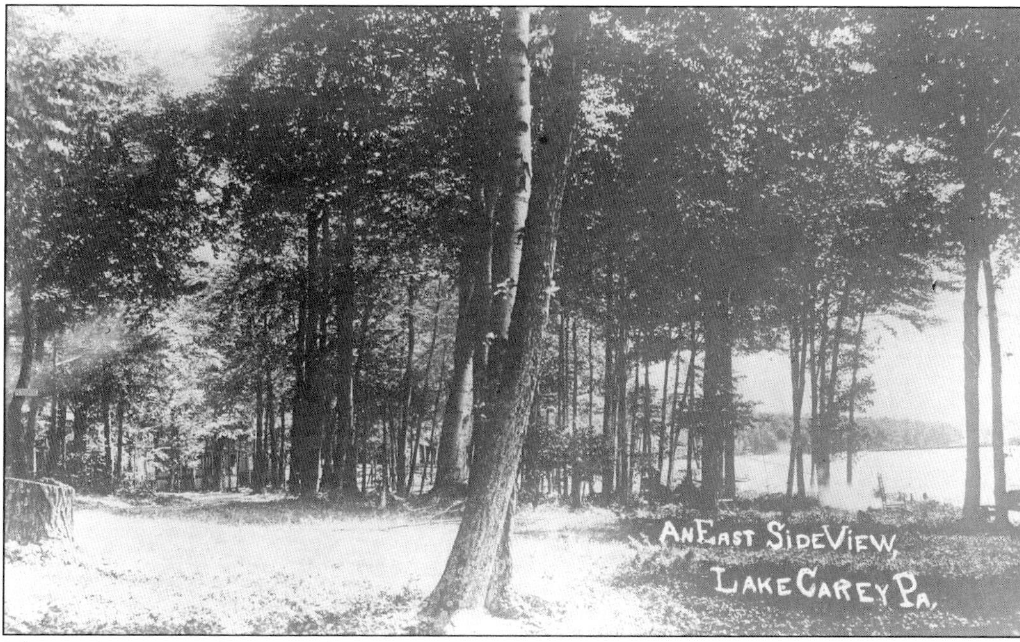

This is the postcard view looking south from the shoreline across the road from Glen Ness. The porch of Point Breeze is just visible to the left through the thick stand of trees. The card's troubled sender writes, "S is better but still in bed . . . Dr. thinks it a good change . . . I am OK again." (Author's collection.)

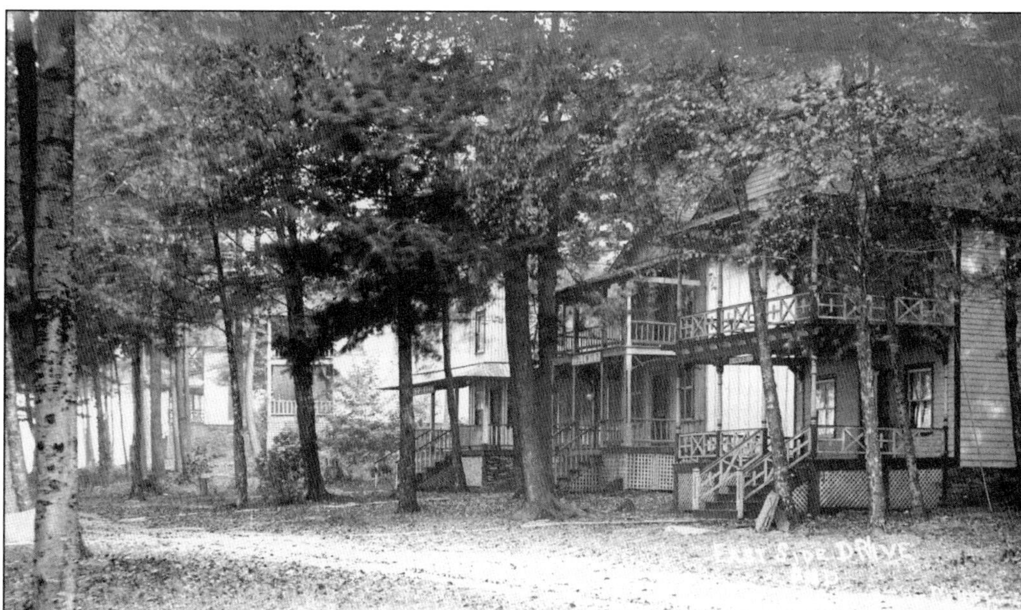

The photograph in this real-photo postcard of Billings City features three early cottages (from right to left), Summer Rest, Idlewild, Point Breeze, as well as the later Penn Grove and Glen Ness. The Albert Townsend family, which occupied Idlewild, sometimes brought the family cow to summer with them. Point Breeze was shared by S. Judson Stark, his brother-in-law John Day (the *Wyoming Democrat's* publisher), and John's brother Alvin (the paper's editor). (Russell collection.)

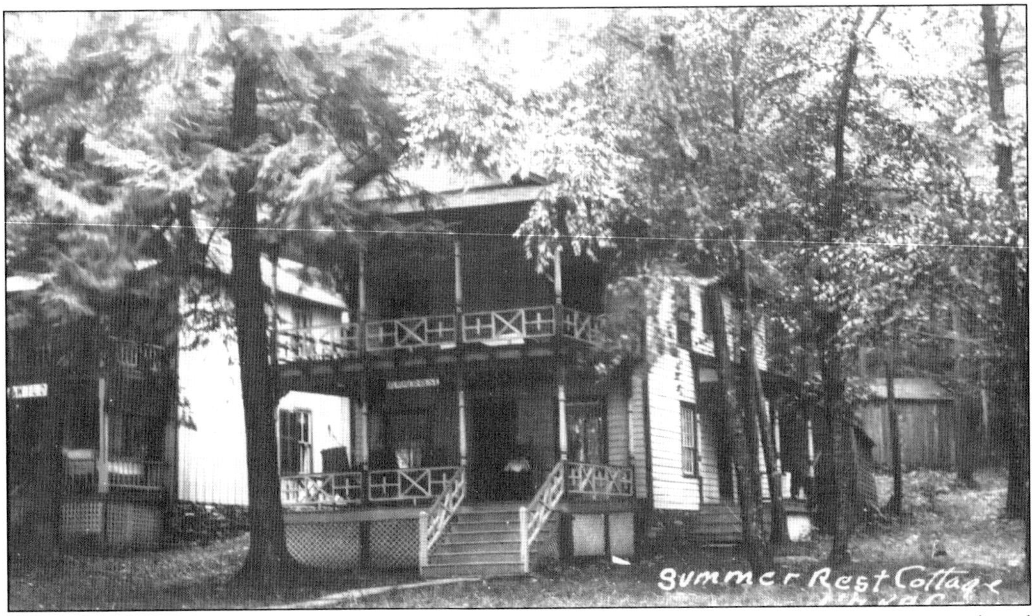

Summer Rest, seen in this real-photo postcard, was shared by the families of brothers Paul and Perry Billings. According to family lore, their Tunkhannock home was moved on logs up the back road to become Summer Rest. Paul was a wholesaler of hay and grain, owner of a Tunkhannock hardware store, and a director of the Montrose Railroad. His daughter would row him across the lake to catch the morning train on his weekday commutes. (Russell collection.)

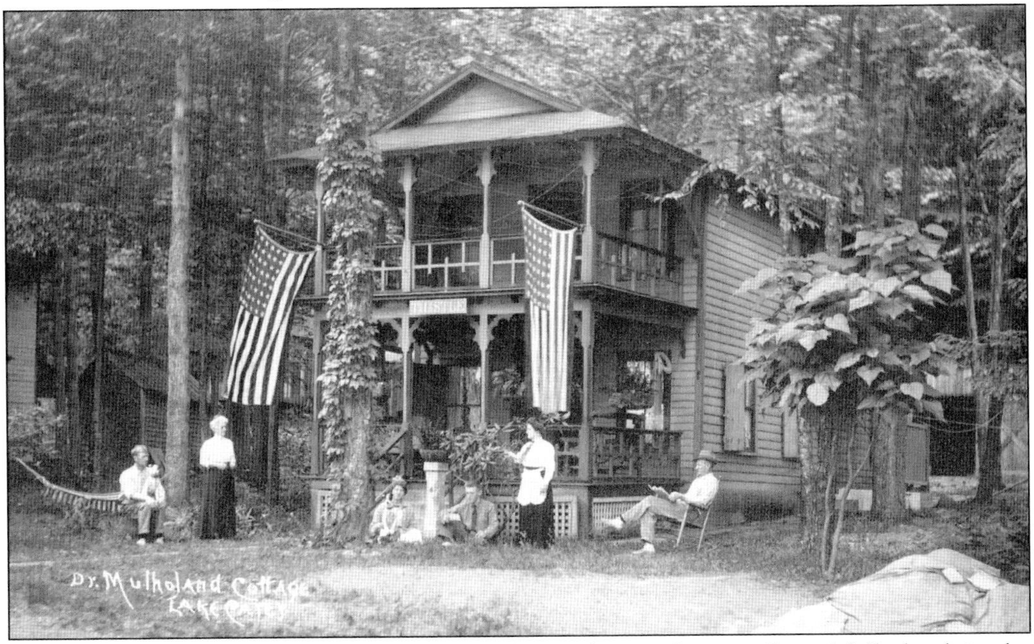

Dr. John M. Mulholand's Thistle cottage stood next door to Summer Rest. Mulholand, in the rocker, was an 1875 graduate of the Cincinnati Eclectic Medical School and a partner of A. B. Woodward, M.D. In this real-photo postcard, to his right is Eva Driesbach Mulholand (his second wife), her brother Albert, her sister Ester, her mother, and on the far left their neighbor Jack Townsend, all presumably celebrating the Fourth of July. (Bell collection.)

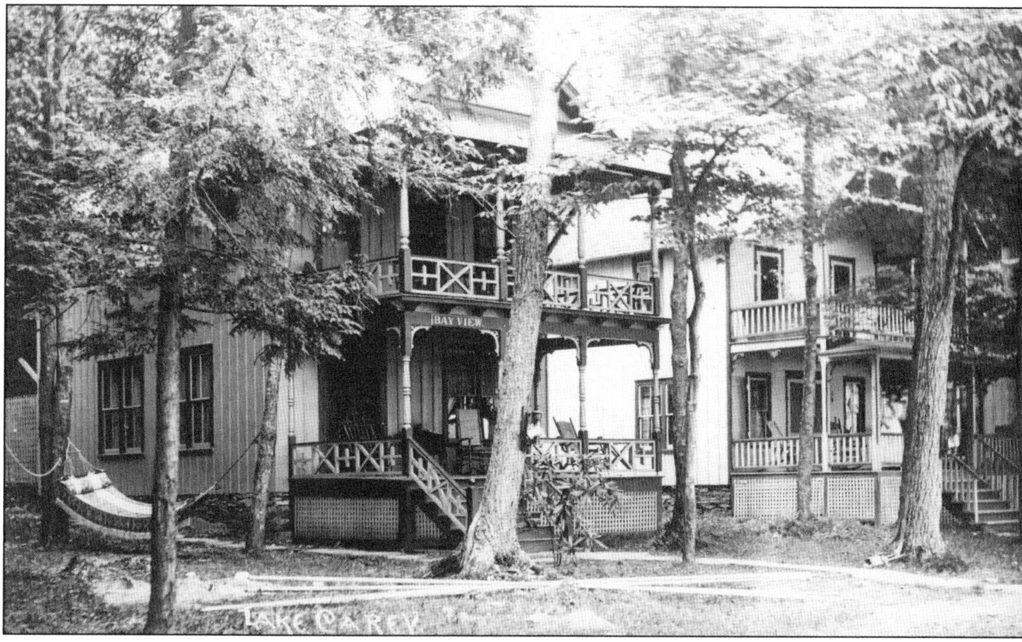

Bayview, seen in this real-photo postcard, was built by Lake Carey Park developer Draper Billings (another Billings brother) across the park from Thistle cottage. Bayview was later owned by Walter Tewksbury, 1900 Olympic gold medalist in the 200 meters and 400-meter hurdles. The future dentist is said to have learned his technique leaping tombstones in a Tunkhannock cemetery. (Weaver collection.)

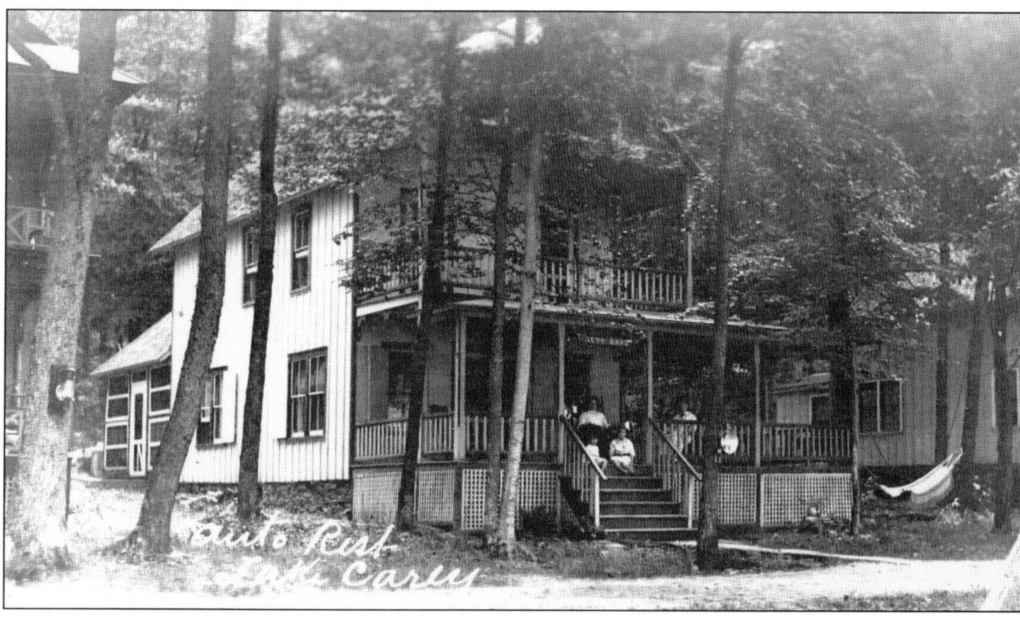

Auto Rest was built by Dr. A. B. Woodward, a prominent physician and owner of a witch hazel factory and Tunkhannock pharmacy. An eclectic physician like his partner Dr. Mulholand, he was a founder of the Susquehanna medical society and a president of the state medical society. Bayview is just visible on the left in this real-photo postcard. Auto Rest was demolished in the 1980s. (Russell collection.)

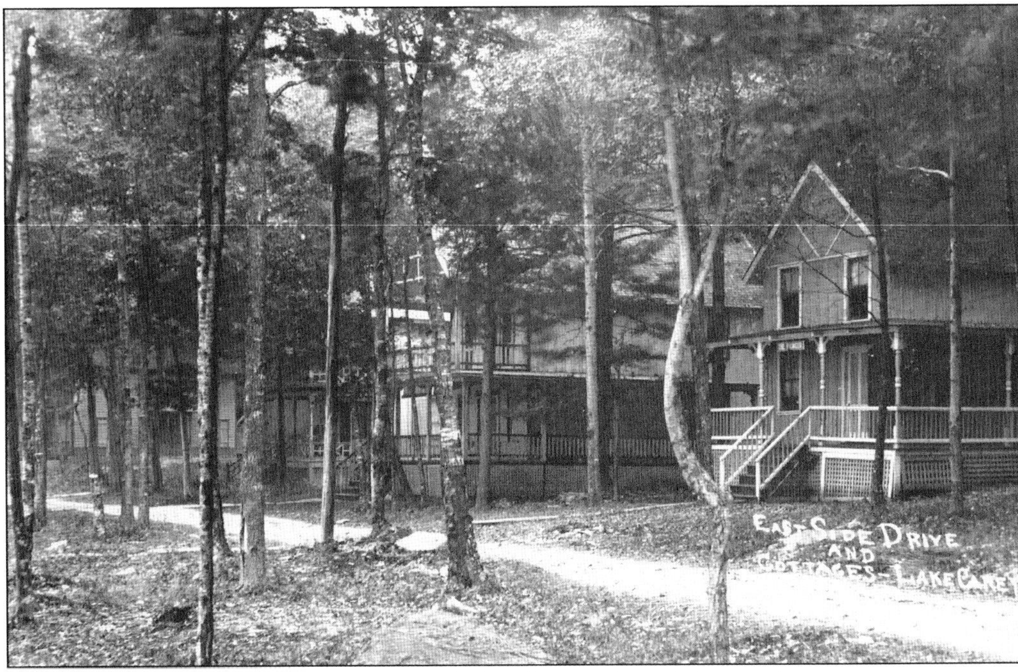

The view in this real-photo postcard includes, from right to left, the Pioneer as well as Auto Rest, Bay View, Thistle, and Summer Rest cottages. Note the many small trees among which the cottages are set; the lake's hemlocks, beeches, and maples were valued by the first cottagers because they created a rustic retreat. (Russell collection.)

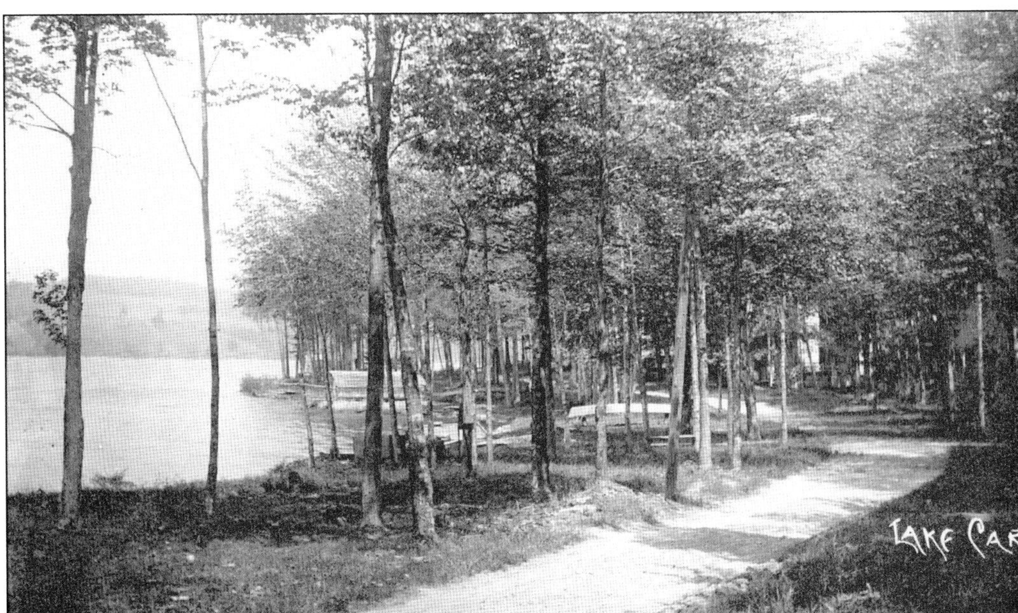

The view in this real-photo postcard is from the front of the Pioneer looking north along the one-lane dirt road toward the point across from Tarnden. The early cottages of Billings City front a shallow bay with views of the west shore. Note the one-story boathouse visible through the trees. (Weaver collection.)

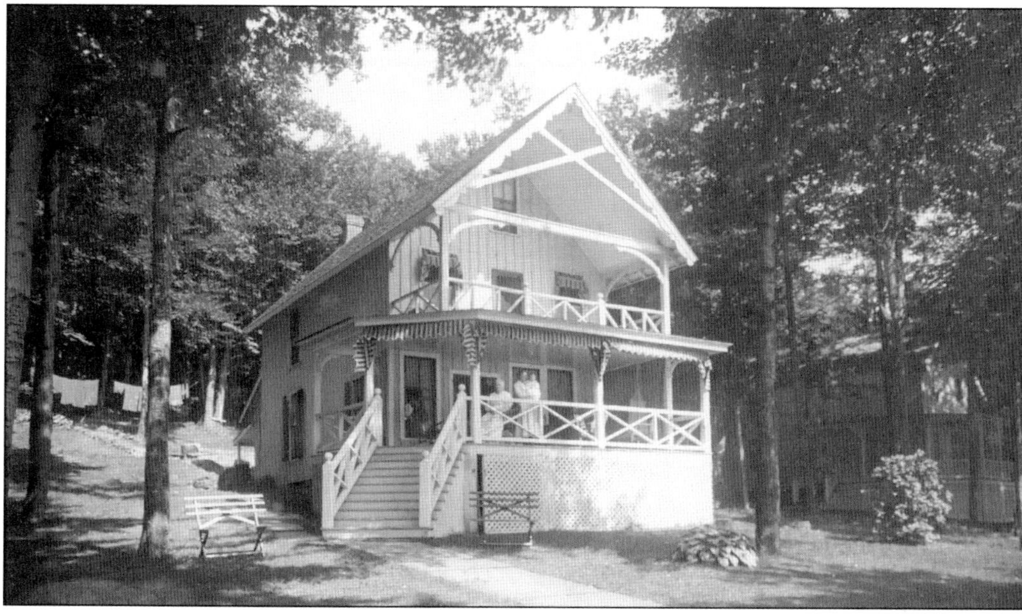

This cottage with its elegant striped awnings was built by John and Isabel Scrimgeour, Scottish immigrants who owned plumbing stores in Pittston and West Pittston. Isabel, daughter Margaret Morris, and granddaughter Isabel Morris Fellows pose on the porch. The cottage was destroyed by a fire about 1930, begun when the then owner's children played with matches. (Fellows collection.)

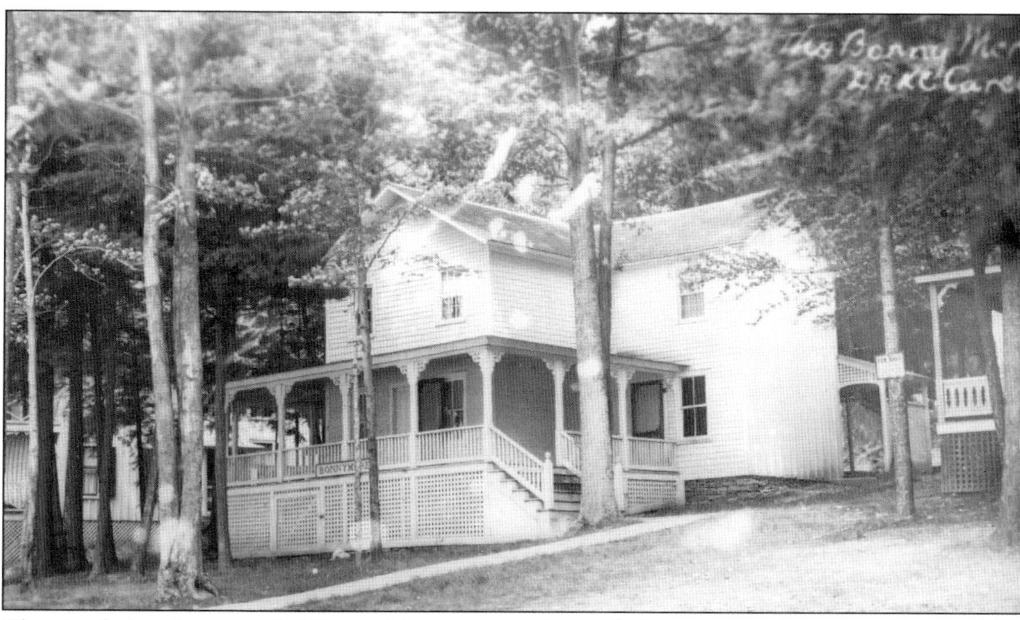

The simple farmhouse-styled Bonny Mere, seen in this real-photo postcard, was saved by neighbor Raymond Fellows when the Scrimgeour cottage next door caught fire. Fellows organized a bucket brigade to wet down the roof and walls. (Robinson collection.)

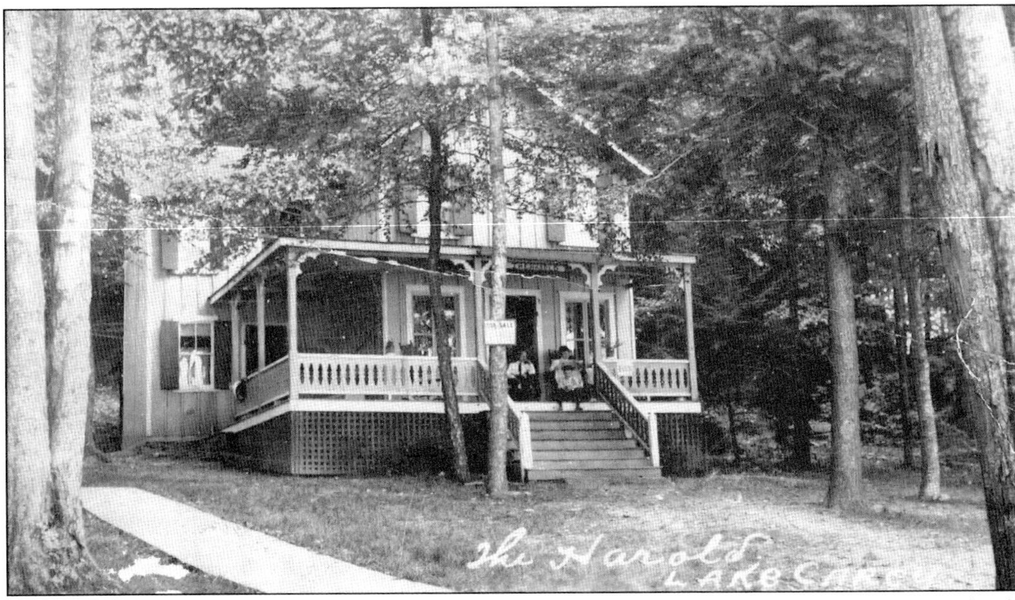

Evidently the Harold is for sale in this real-photo postcard. (The sign is also visible on the far right in the previous photograph.) Sara J. Brown, its owner for many years, is thought to have named it after her son, Harold Brown. (Author's collection.)

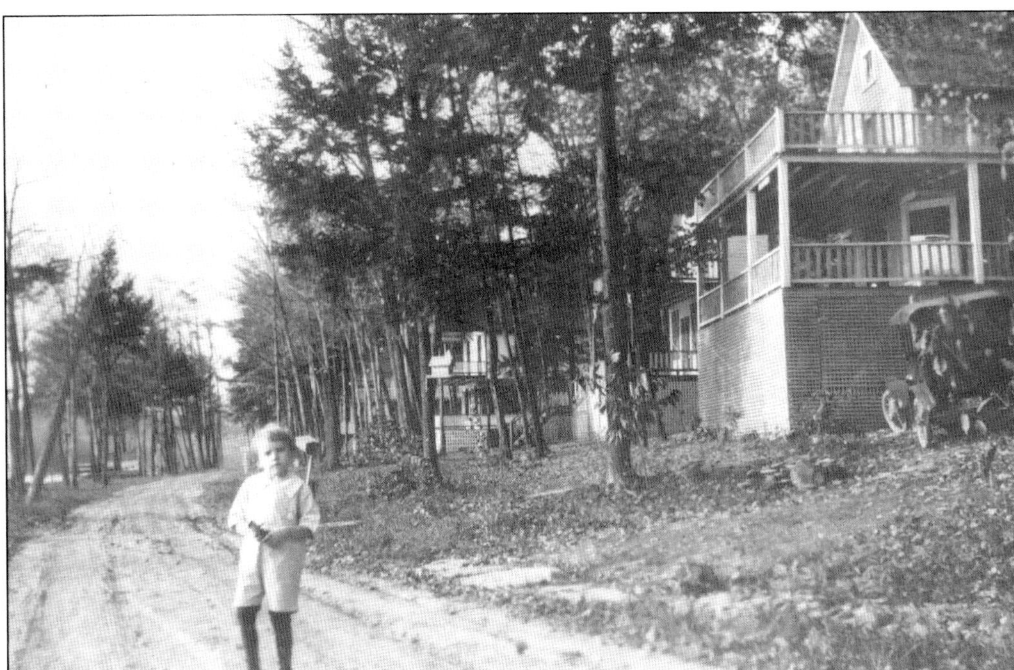

Isle of View is the third cottage built by Emma Martin (than Mrs. Frank Diament). A young Rob Fellows, grandson of Annie Kellow, stands in the dirt road in front of the cottage several years after his grandmother's 1922 purchase. A 1923 Buick is parked beside the porch awaiting better roads, but they were not paved until after World War II. (Fellows collection.)

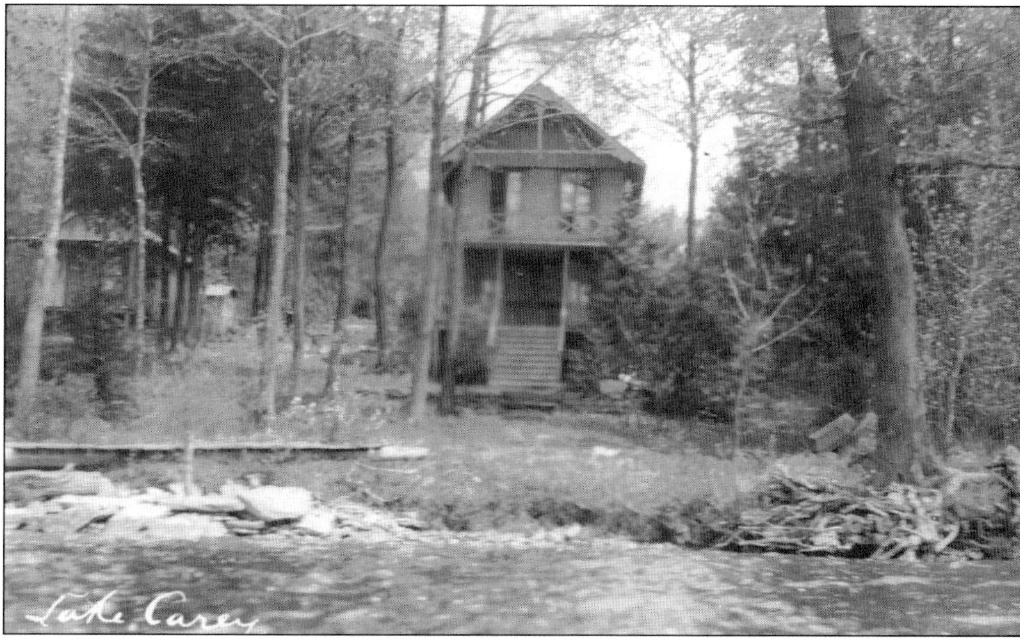

Emma Martin, sister of Fern Cliffe's Eugene Martin, had this cottage, her first, built in 1880 by carpenter A. E. Buck. The editor of a local paper described it as "commodious and attractive," possessing an "artistically finished" gable. Emma must have liked it too; she married A. E. Buck soon thereafter. Emma sold the cottage to Katie Lutton in 1919. Note Emma's modest rental cabin, Top-o'-the-Walk, to the left. (Lumi collection.)

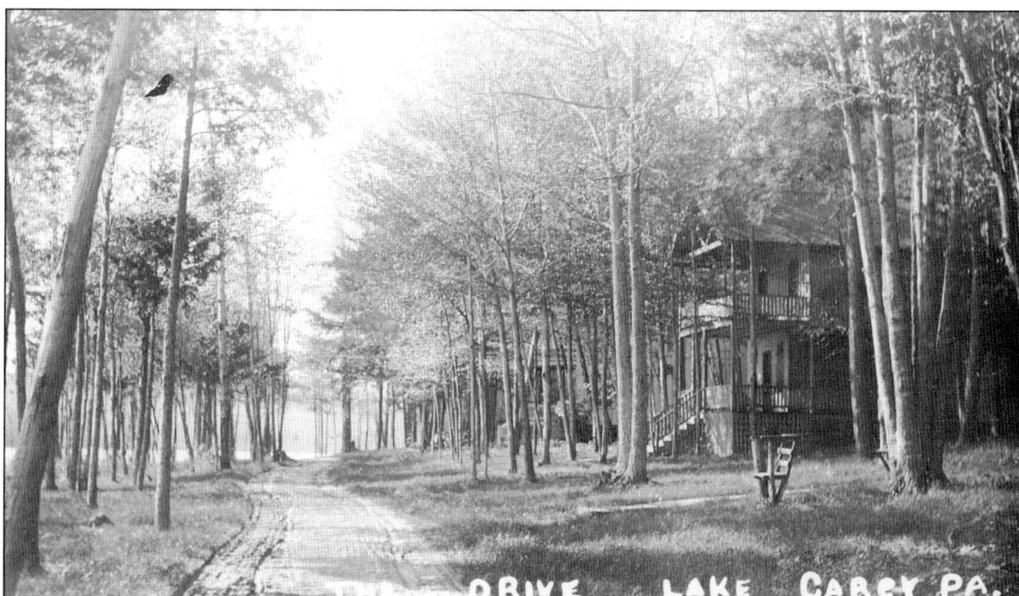

This inviting path passes by two east shore cottages demolished in the 1920s. Quinton Stemler, president of a Mauch Chunk bank, was first to build a then-fashionable, shingled bungalow here; Dr. Rebhorn, a Scranton physician, so admired it he built one too. The first cottage pictured here, probably demolished by Rebhorn, was one of two nearly identical structures; its twin—Careyview, out of view to the right—survived. (Author's collection.)

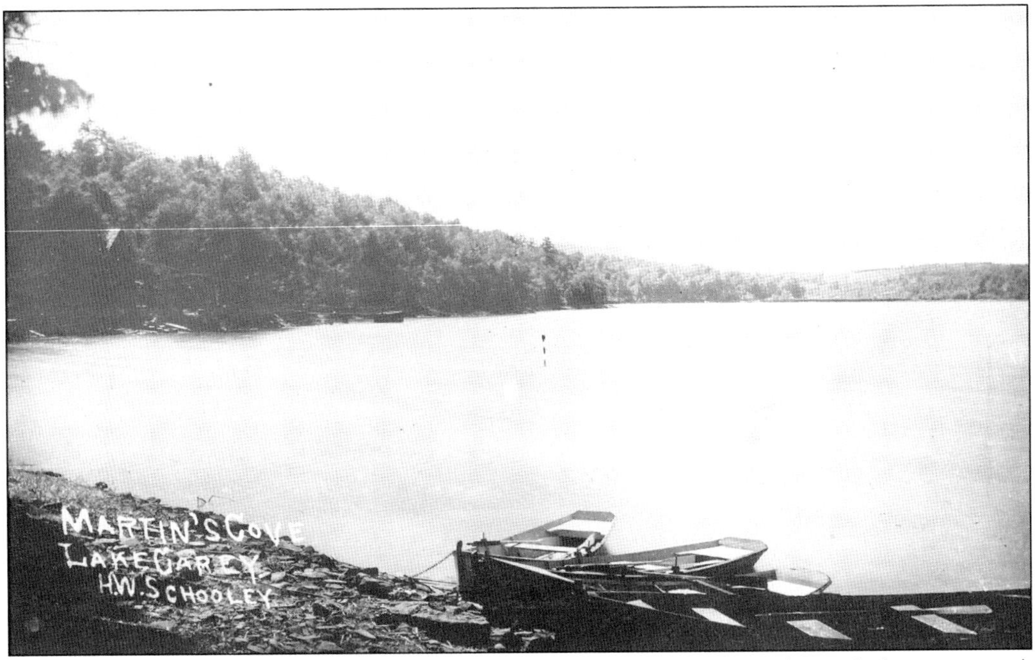

Turning 190 degrees, a fine east shore view appears from Martin's Cove in this real-photo postcard. To the left, just visible in the trees, is the gable of the store Eugene and Jennie Martin operated after their hotel failed. Beyond is the rock that once ended the hotel's dock. The store, long an east shore fixture, was sold to LeRoy Chambers in 1923. Chambers also rented cottages, camping sites, boats, and canoes. (Author's collection.)

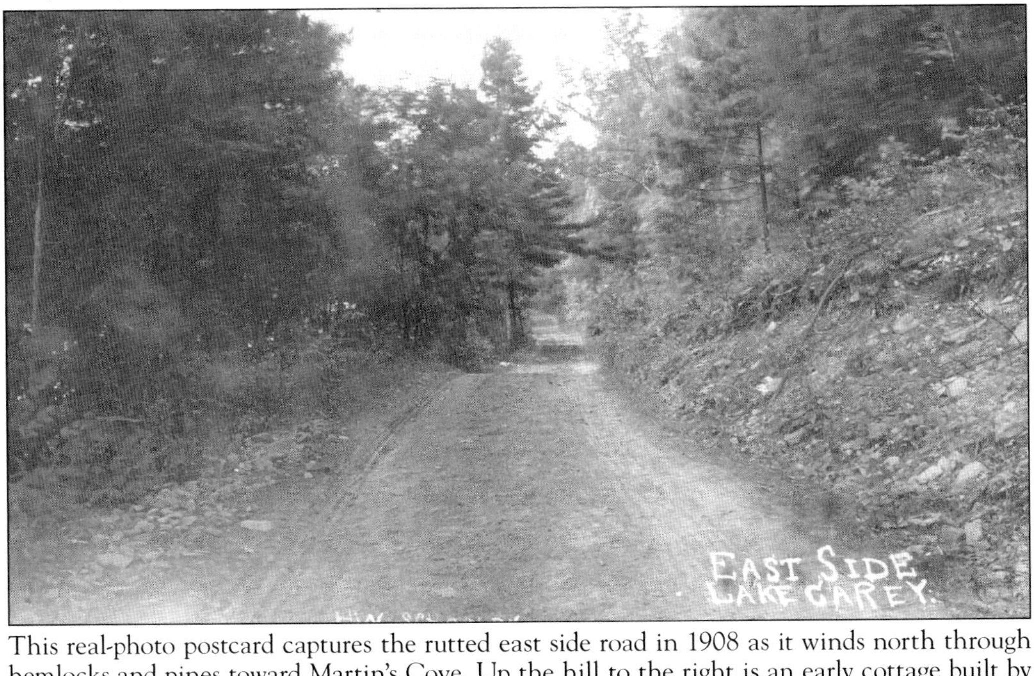

This real-photo postcard captures the rutted east side road in 1908 as it winds north through hemlocks and pines toward Martin's Cove. Up the hill to the right is an early cottage built by Methodist minister J. L. Race in 1881—as well as the charred ruins of the Fern Cliffe Hotel. (Weaver collection.)

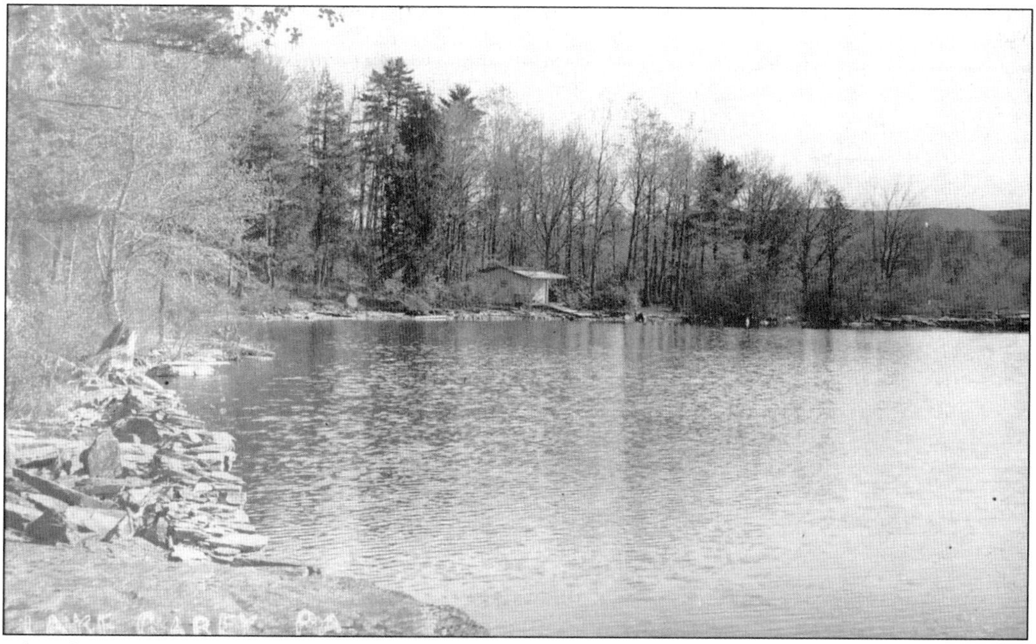

This photograph of "Jonesy's shack" was taken from the east shore rocks, themselves a prominent landmark. The causeway can be seen to the right. (Weaver collection.)

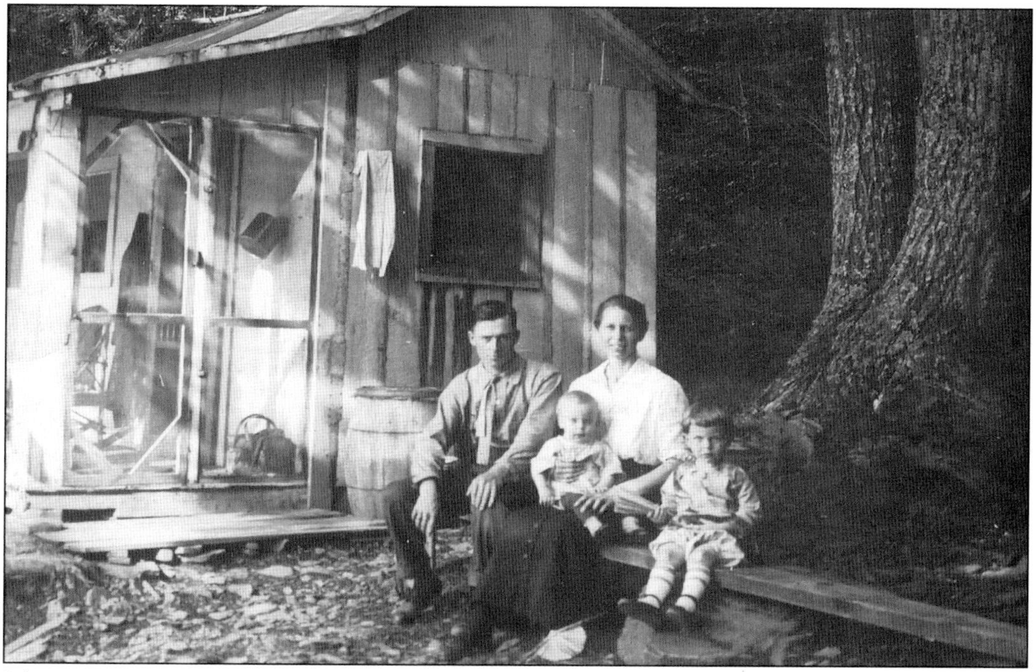

John Jones's one-room cottage with a screened porch stood for years at the other end of the lake from Dr. Thomas Jefferson Wheaton's Beech Grove Camp. In this real-photo postcard, Jones's neighbors Perry and Jessie Buckworth Dickinson pose around 1915 with their children Bob and Dorothy beside Jonesy's shack. The Dickinsons journeyed to the lake on a free Lehigh Valley Railroad pass where Perry worked as a locomotive engineer. (Weaver collection.)

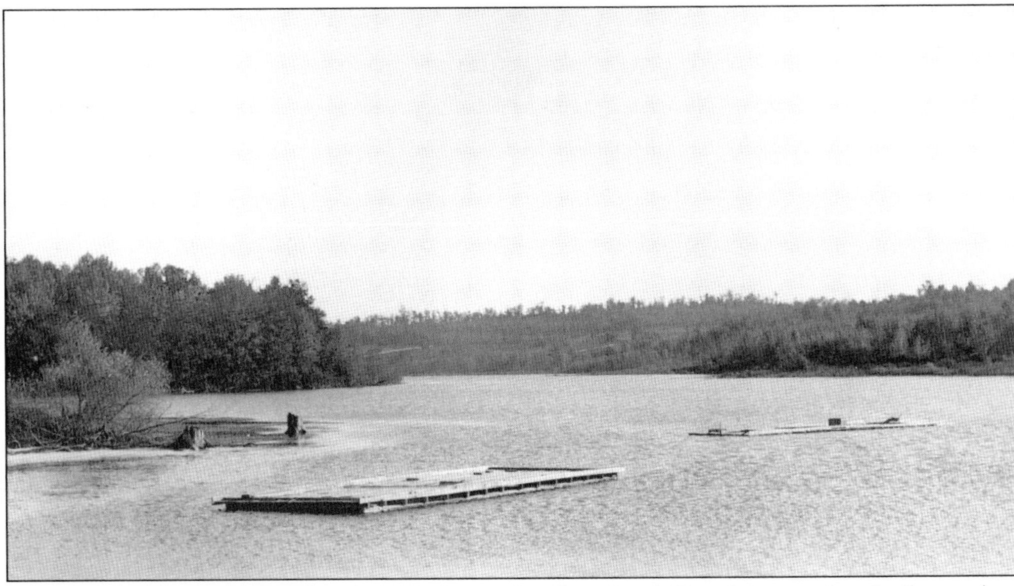

This photograph dated October 6, 1898, shows the Flow Pond. Two fishing rafts, similar to those once for rent from Dan Carey or Asa Stevens, float in the foreground. The level of the lake, here at its present height, had been raised in 1876 when the dam at the outlet was strengthened and raised to accommodate the Tunkhannock Toy Company, newly located there. (Daniels collection.)

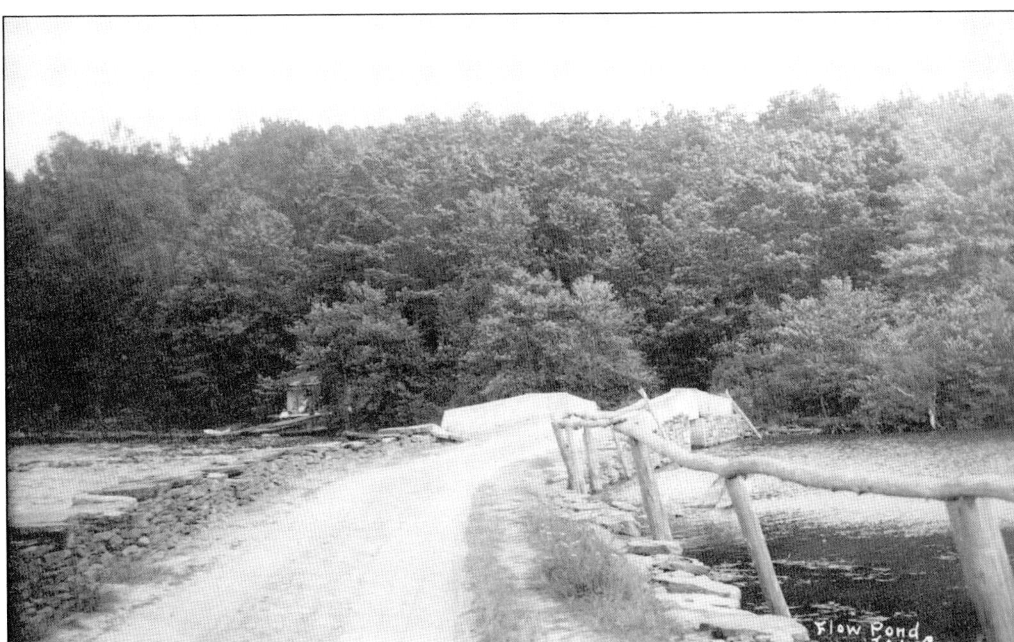

The east shore was still densely wooded at Coopers Corners when this real-photo postcard of the causeway bridge was made around 1910. Cooper's store (later Zaleppa's) is shrouded in trees on the right, but Jonesy's shack is clearly visible on the left. Note the none-too-sturdy wooden guardrails. (Russell collection.)

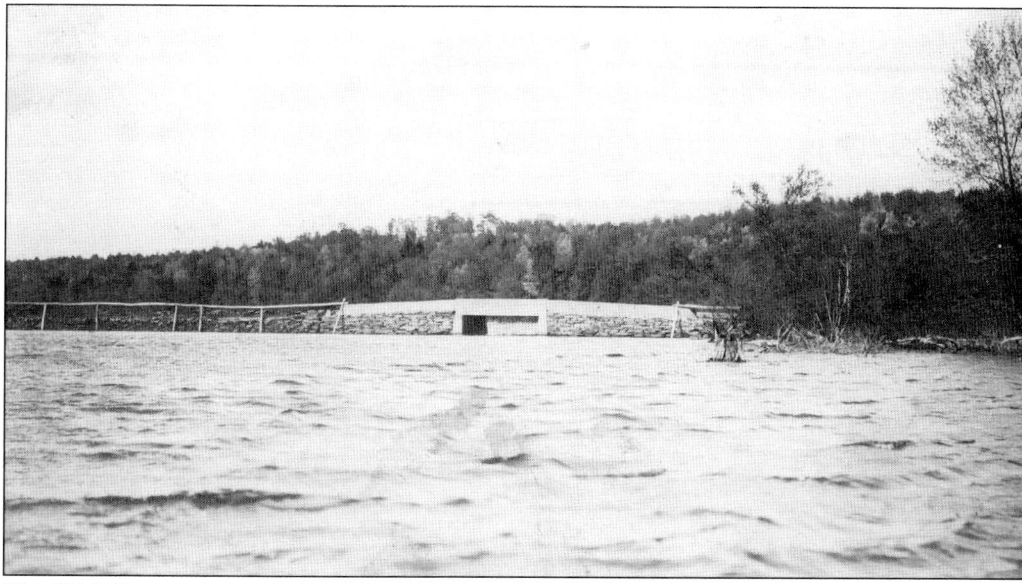

The W. J. Harris photograph in this real-photo postcard captures the causeway bridge from the Flow Pond. Cooper's store is out of view on the right. (Robinson collection.)

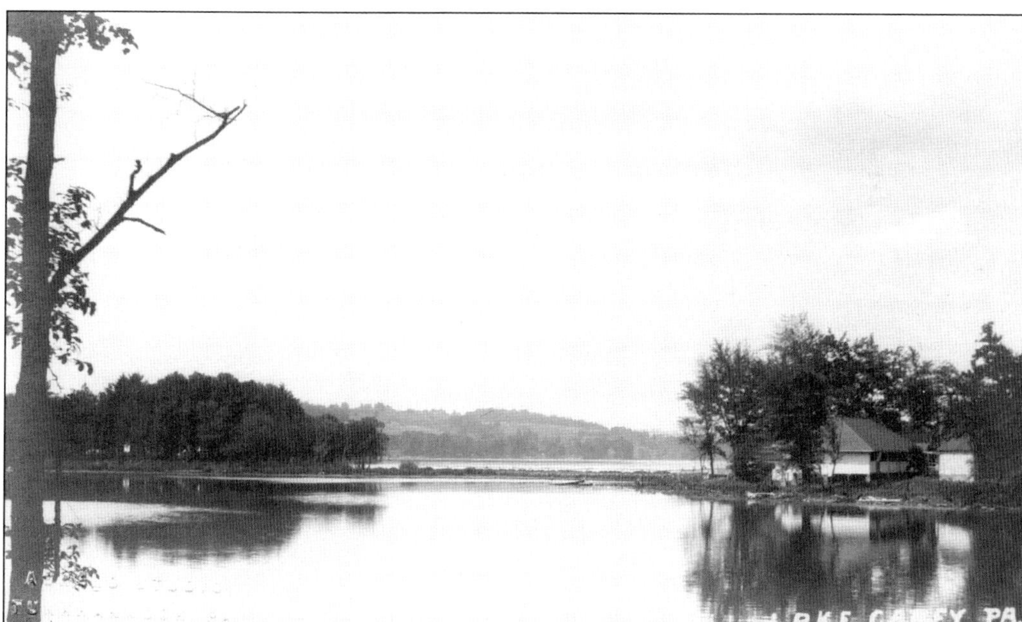

This photograph by Tunkhannock's Asheld studio includes the dance pavilion at Coopers Corners before it was enclosed by the Zaleppa's. The structure to its right may be an icehouse (there were two) or the Delco battery plant. (Russell collection.)

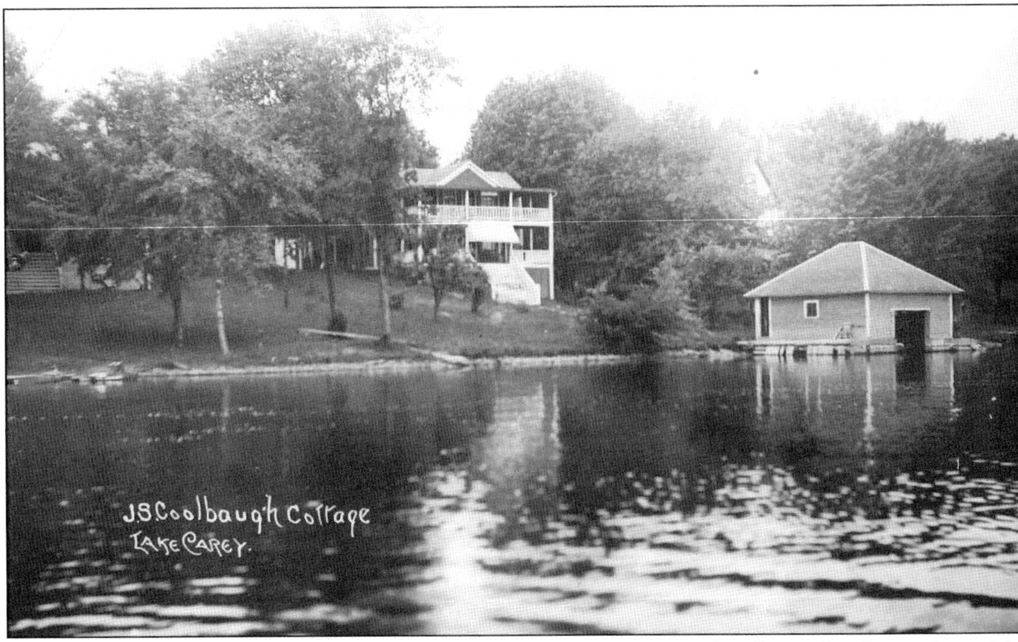

In this real-photo postcard, Buena Vista stands on Ansart and Billings lot 3 purchased by Henrietta Farnham in 1884. Moses and Harriet Stark Coolbaugh acquired it in 1894 and willed it to their son, John Stark Coolbaugh. For six years John managed the Spring Grove House for E. L. Diefenderfer's widow. After the Diefenderfers sold the hotel, John and his wife boarded visitors in Buena Vista. (Author's collection.)

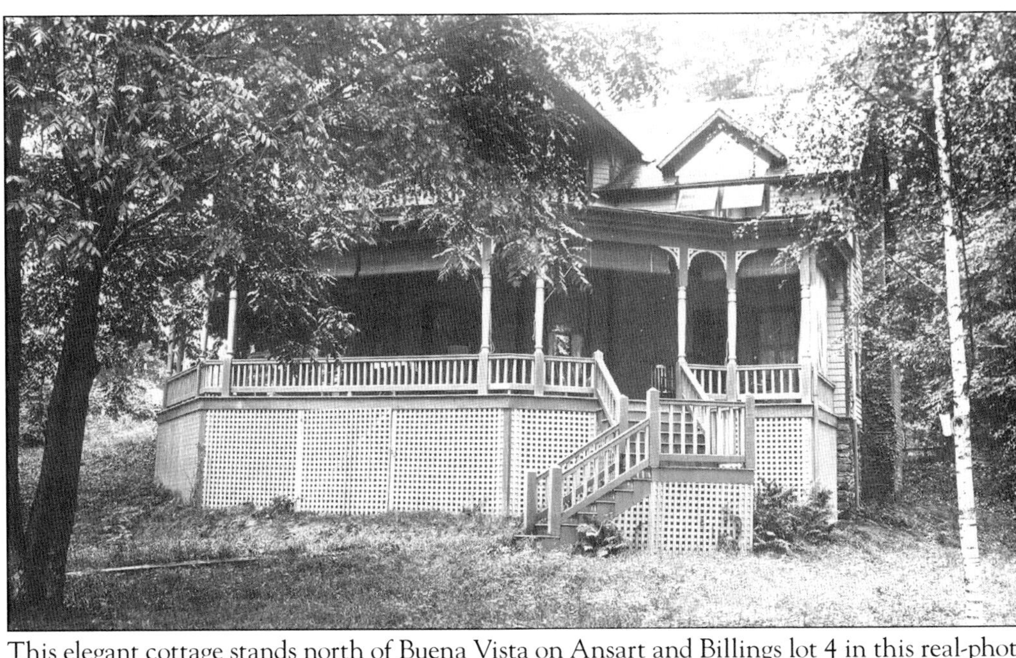

This elegant cottage stands north of Buena Vista on Ansart and Billings lot 4 in this real-photo postcard. Note the bow in the porch below the cottage's projecting second-story porch and the shuttered dormer to the right. The lot was purchased by A. W. Schlingman in 1884. The cottage was later owned by the Stevens/Herrick family. (Tidball/Davis collection.)

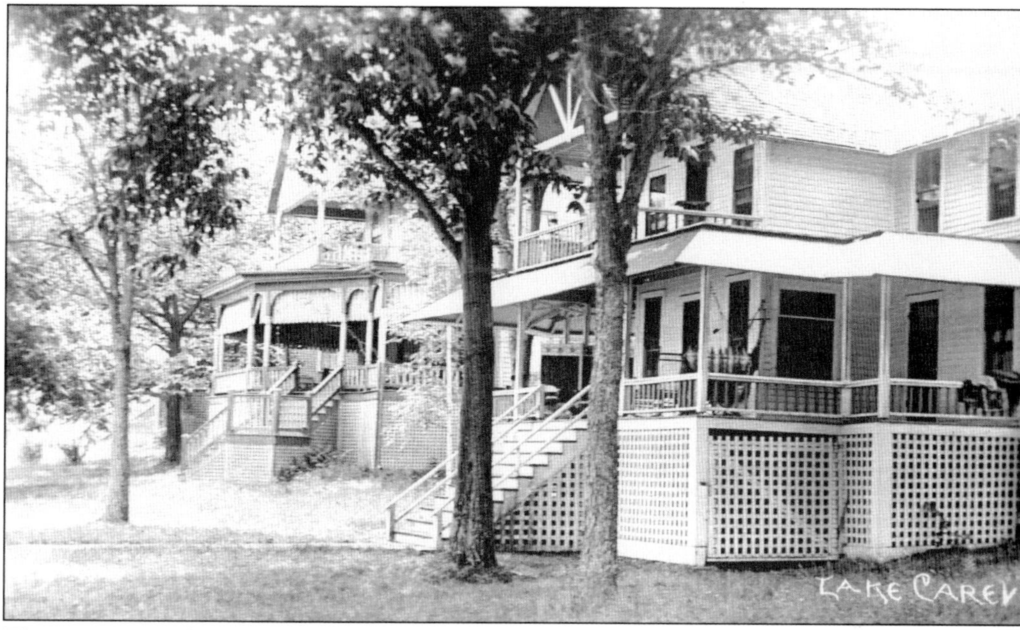

The cottage in this real-photo postcard was probably constructed by S. Judson Stark after he purchased its lot in 1884 (after three summers with the Days in Point Breeze). It displays several common cottage features: a second-story porch with an open gable above, a wooden awning on the lower porch, and a projecting one-room-wide ell providing the parlor and master bedroom with better lake views and ventilation. (Russell collection.)

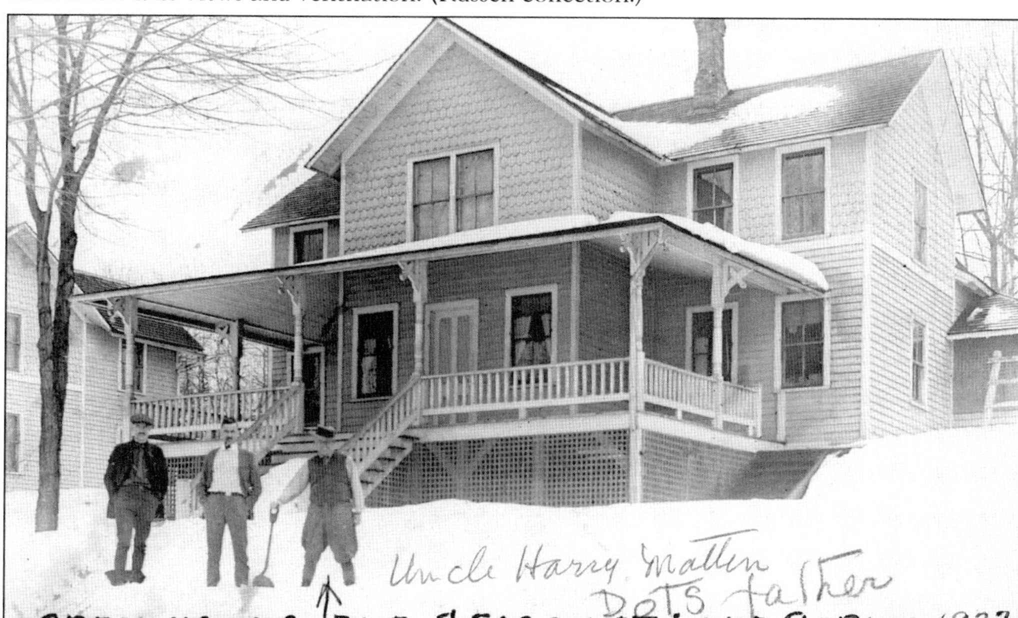

Susan Stone Marcy bought two Ansart and Billings lots in 1884. She built a cottage for her son and daughter-in-law and another for herself and her husband. In this real-photo postcard, Dr. Matten, a Wilkes-Barre dentist, is opening the cottage his wife, Cora, inherited from her mother, Susan. Six to eight cottages in this design, several with identical porch brackets, were built on the west shore, presumably by the same carpenter. (Pitkin collection.)

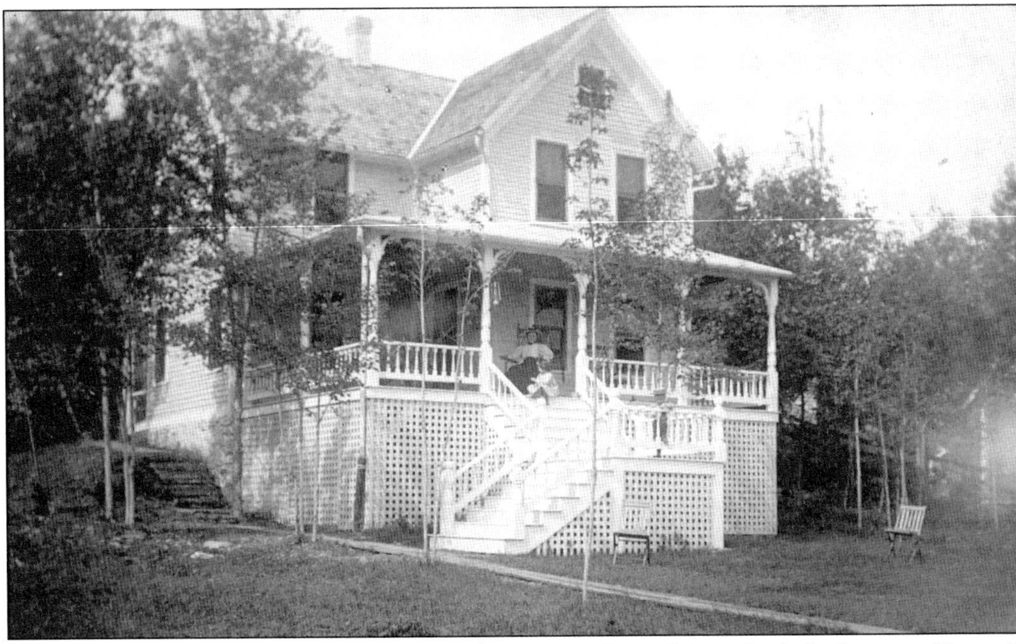

This photograph, dated July 1896, pictures the cottage Susan Marcy built for her son, Harry G. Marcy, and his wife, Mary, who sits on the porch. This branch of the Marcy family was distant cousins of Abel Marcy, whose family owned much of Lake Carey when it was known as Marcy's Pond. (Pitkin collection.)

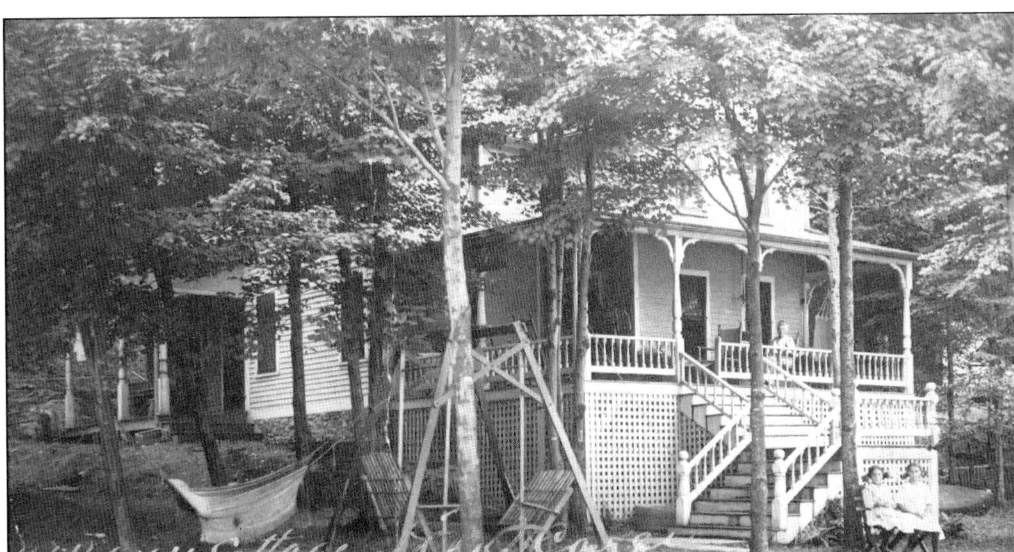

Helen and Ruth Marcy, two of Harry G. and Mary Marcy's five children, sit demurely at the foot of the stairs, while Mrs. Hawley looks on, in this real-photo postcard. At this time, about 1913, the Marcy children spent their summers at the lake, while their parents remained in Tunkhannock. (Pitkin collection.)

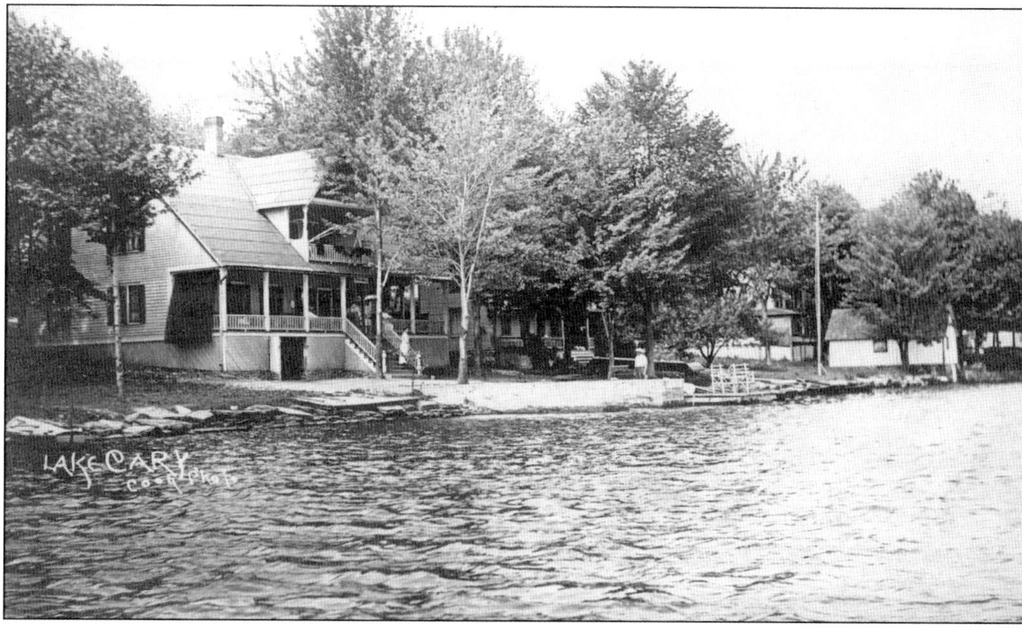

The distinctive cottage in this real-photo postcard with its broad, sheltering roof stands on Ansart and Billings lot 14 purchased by Agnes Parker in 1886. It was later owned by James W. Piatt, proprietor of Piatt's Opera House in Tunkhannock. Piatt shared an icehouse, water tank, and windmill with his neighbor on lot 15. (Weaver collection.)

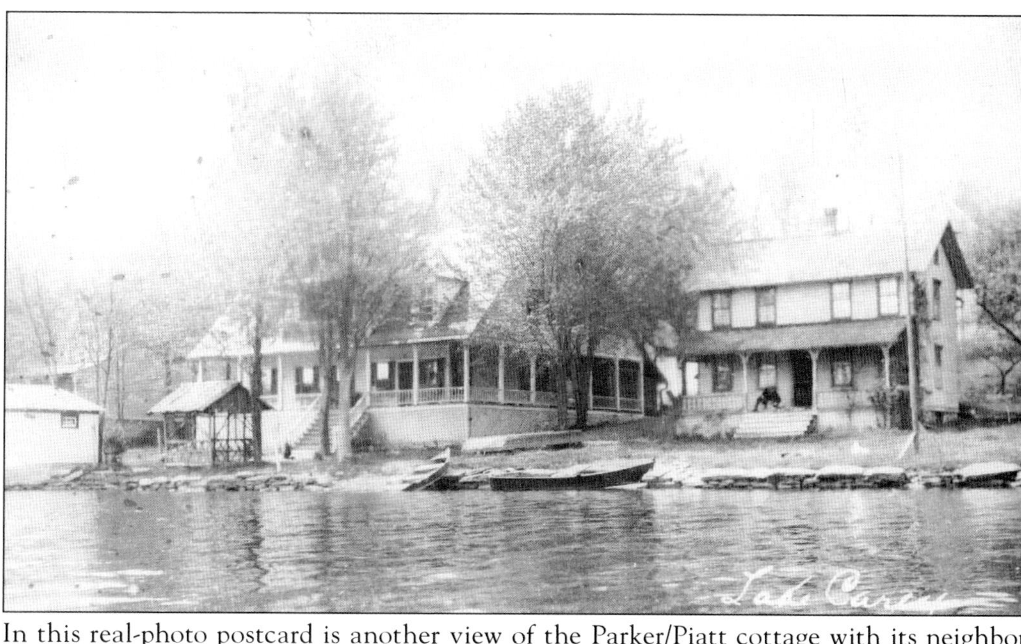

In this real-photo postcard is another view of the Parker/Piatt cottage with its neighbor on lot 15 to the right. Lot 15 was purchased in 1884 by Gertrude L. Blackman for $105. (Petrillo collection.)

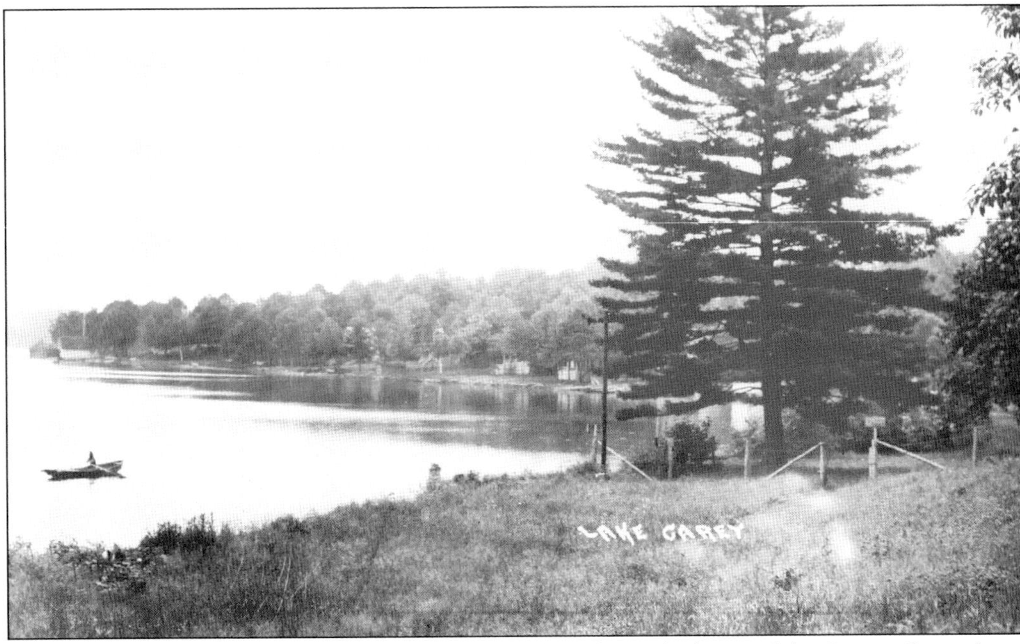

The view in this real-photo postcard of the west shore from the lawn of the Spring Grove hotel features a lone boater on a still and reflective lake. (Russell collection.)

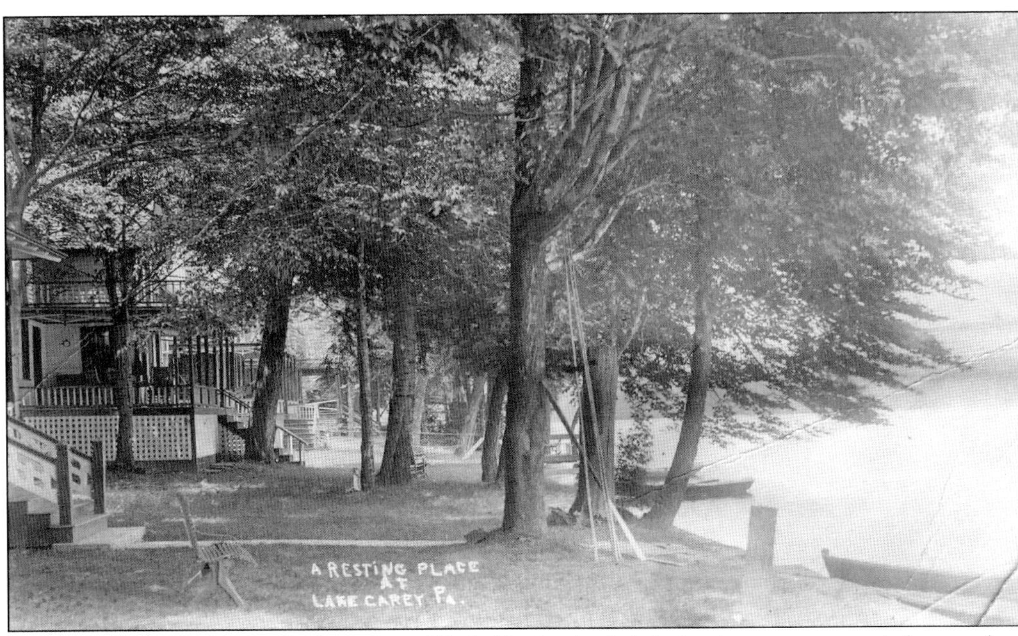

In this real-photo postcard, the steps of E. L. Diefenderfer's Lakeview cottage and the porch of A. B. Mott's Ingleside are visible in this west shore view. Ingleside was sold in time to Mary F. Stark; it was here that her son, Adm. Harold R. Stark, acquired his love of boating. (Ingleside survives, but Lakeview was demolished in 1993.) (Author's collection.)

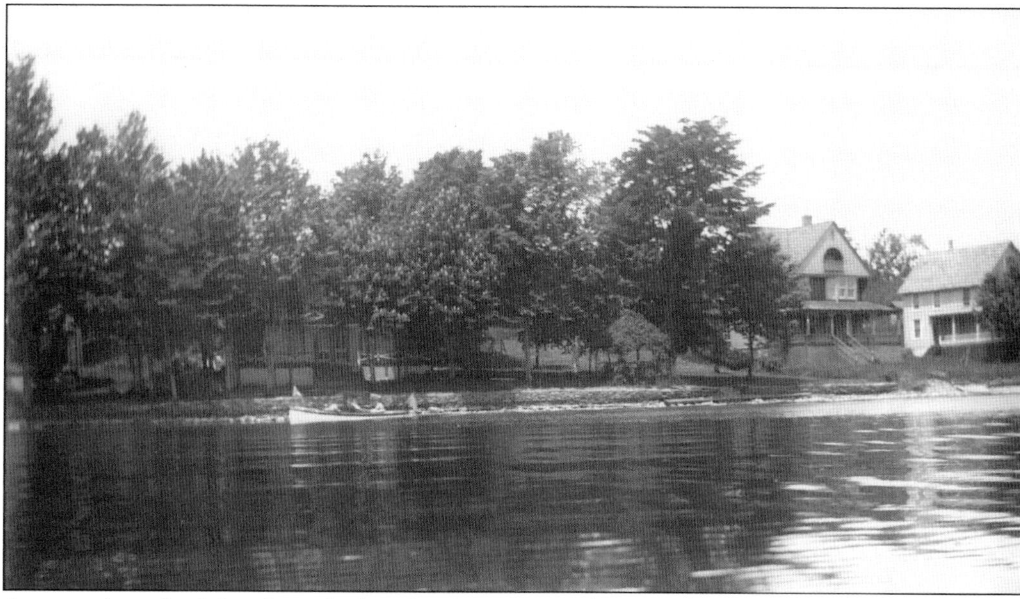

A motor launch glides through the placid waters on the west shore. In the trees behind it is a double cottage (to be demolished in 2008) built by L. E. Stearns on Diefenderfer's lot 2. To its right on lot 3 is Elsmere. Lot 3 was purchased by Emma Martin (then Mrs. A. E. Buck) in 1889. This is her second cottage at the lake. (F. C. Shook glass plate, Daniels collection.)

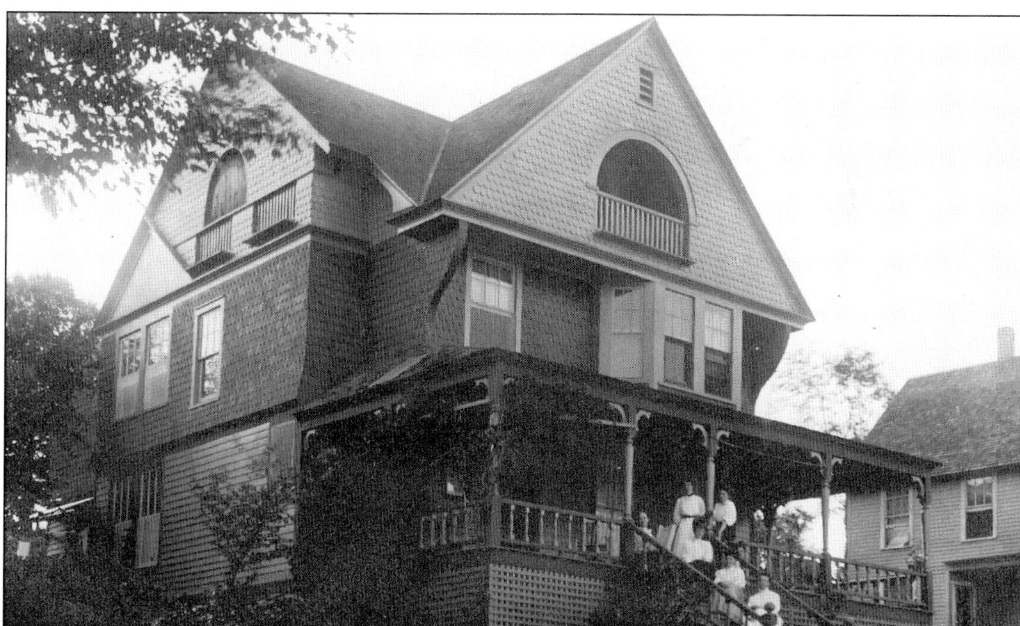

An elaborate Queen Anne with shingle-style elements, Elsmere also was likely built by A. E. Buck for Emma. As his wife, she may have insisted on something grander than the cottage he built for her on the east shore before they married. This real-photo postcard, signed by her in 1907, likely includes Emma among the women on the steps. (Author's collection.)

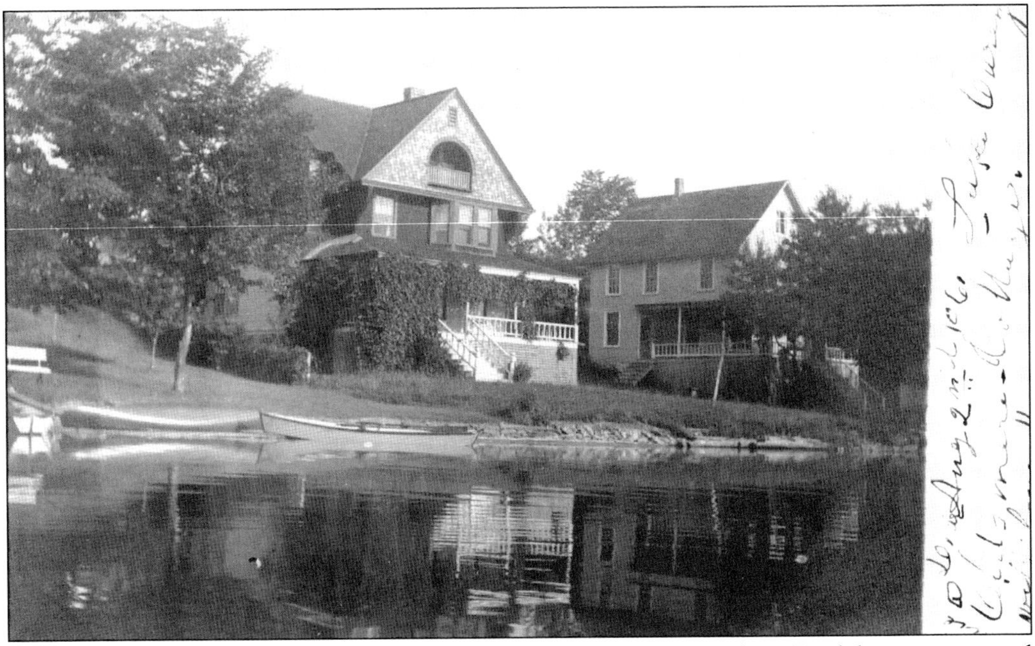

In this real-photo postcard, Elsemere is reflected in the waters before it; three Finch boats are moored on the left. Then owner Emma Martin Buck operated a popular variety store in Tunkhannock for many years. The cottage next door was built by the Ingrahams on the Diefenderfer lot they purchased from Emma. (Russell collection.)

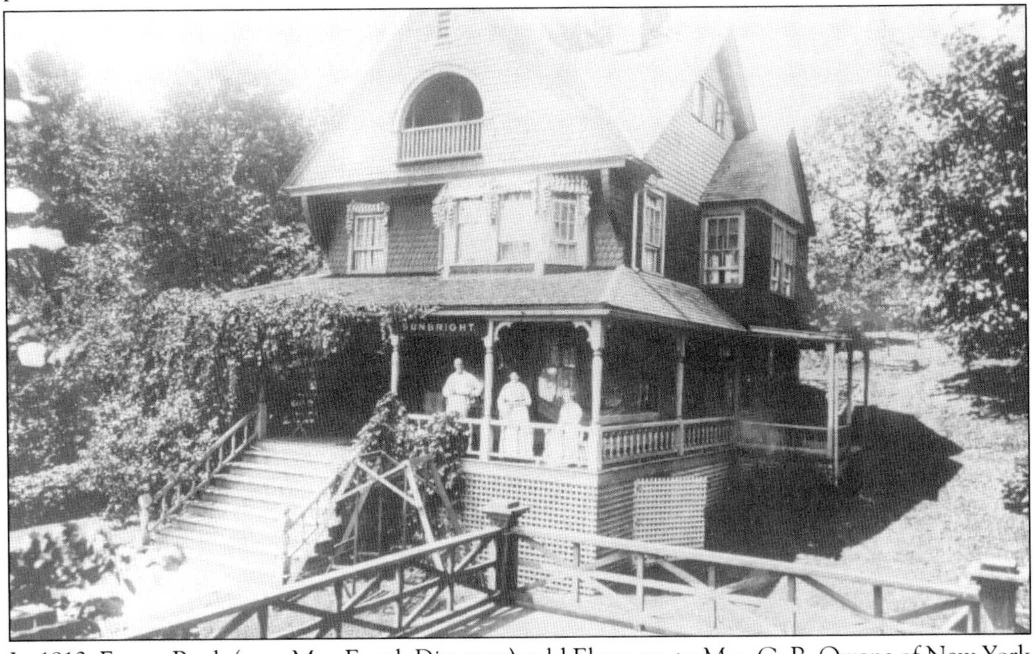

In 1913, Emma Buck (now Mrs. Frank Diament) sold Elsemere to Mrs. G. B. Owens of New York City who renamed it Sunbright. Married to the Lehigh Valley Railroad's chief engineer, Jean Owens traveled to and from the lake in a private railroad car—with her cats who occupied the cottage third floor. At this time, Sunbright had its own electric plant, a boathouse, and several servants. (Willoughby collection.)

Five

Cottage Life

Like Alvin Day, many early cottagers were drawn to Lake Carey by the romantic sight of its "Rembrandt-looking hemlocks, quivering aspen and melancholy pines." Many were the grandchildren or great-grandchildren of the region's pioneers. Family accounts of the early days in this "wilderness, [where] solitude reigned supreme, interrupted only by the hoot of the owl or the cry of the panther" would have made a deep impression on them as children. They were likely taught to admire the fortitude, self-reliance, and piety of their forebears who mastered such a world to create enduring communities. Here, in the tranquility of Lake Carey's still wild setting, the cottagers likely hoped they could transmit this heritage to their own children and grandchildren.

Although no longer a wilderness, the lake provided more exposure to nature than did small-town life. There are 1880s newspaper reports of bald eagles near Wheaton Point (one was shot by Dr. Thomas Jefferson Wheaton and stuffed by his "amiable" wife) and poisonous pilot snakes near Point Breeze cottage (they were killed). Kingfishers, great blue herons, and osprey fished its waters. Snapping turtles were common in the lake's shallow northern and southern waters. (Ponderous females still come ashore to lay their eggs at night.) Minks raised their young in stone walls along the shore, and muskrats could be spotted in the reeds at the northern inlet. Bobcats and black bears frequented the nearby woods. Purple martins filled the tiered birdhouses at water's edge, drawn by the swarming insects on the lake and in the adjacent fields.

There are very early accounts of superb fishing at Lake Carey. In its early resort years, the lake was particularly known for black bass, introduced by Susquehanna River fishermen when they dumped them as fry into the lake with other bait. Moses Coolbaugh seems to have caught the largest in 1896 at 6¼ pounds. By this time, the state fishery was also augmenting the lake's ample spawning grounds with fry they bred elsewhere. Most cottagers fished. Indeed, some cottages survived the hard years of the Depression and World War II as fishing camps.

Important too was the 19th-century belief in the healthful nature of rural life. (Death rates in urban places in the 19th century were in fact much higher.) An ailing Samuel Rhodes (Adm. Harold R. Stark's father-in-law), for example, was brought to the family's Beech Grove Camp in 1882 in hopes that he would there recover from kidney disease. Despite everything, including the ministrations of his father-in-law, Dr. Thomas Jefferson Wheaton, he died at Beech Grove at the age of 30.

Happily, life at the lake also offered more certain advantages. Chief among them must have been its slightly cooler temperatures and steady breezes. Opportunities to swim and to boat were others. And the community itself, once established, drew yet more people to join family, neighbors, friends, and business associates in the pleasures of summer pastimes at the lake.

The cottages were usually full with family and friends. Parties of young people frequently commandeered them. On one week in 1882, for example, A. B. Mott's Ingleside was occupied by Jessie and Nellie Carver, Anna Wheelock, Lizzie Bower, Stella Sickler, Addie Leighton, Carrie Leighton, Dora Ross, Belle Miller, and Mercy Brungess of Tunkhannock, as well as Henrietta Lyons of Williamsport and Nettie Stiles of Bloomsburg. Across the lake, a group of 9 young men were staying at Eugene Martin's Fern Cliffe cottage, and another 10 young men from Hyde Park in Scranton occupied a second east shore cottage. Such a week passed quickly in boating, swimming, fishing, taffy pulls, and dancing.

The lake offered recreational opportunities for every age. Children tented by the cottage, flew kites, picked berries, held wienie roasts, and learned to fish, swim, and boat. Their elders rocked on porches, greeting passing neighbors. Porches provided a place too for solitary reading, sociable gossip, or competitive games of poker, bridge, and hearts. Tennis, quoits, and ball games also filled their days. Local characters provided ample material for rich anecdotes—a fiercely independent Frank Cooper tossed his veteran's benefit dollars away rather than accept a government handout; an impish Walter Tewksbury persistently offered his neighbor, Adm. Harold R. Stark, a sailing lesson or two; a "sociable" Katie Lutton regularly dropped in on her east shore neighbors just as they sat down to supper.

Nothing, however, provided more enduring memories among cottagers than Admiral Stark and the Comet regatta he sponsored. As befitted an admiral—he became rear admiral in 1934 and chief of naval operation and admiral in 1938—his cottage household included a chauffeur and handyman (Jackson), two to three maids (Alice and Lena are remembered best), and a cook, all African Americans he brought with him from Washington. He and his wife dined formally on even the hottest summer evening, to the discomfort of his daughters and their cousins who had to change out of their swimsuits for the occasion.

Although sailboats were present on Lake Carey as early as 1881, racing apparently began in 1934. In that year, 11 boats, several built by their owners, raced on Labor Day weekend. In 1939, Stark offered a perpetual trophy to be awarded to the winner of what had become a three-race Labor Day regatta of Comet-class boats. By that time, the races were a popular pastime for many cottagers, including the Dunns, Quins, Coons, Bostons, Ridgways, Fassetts, and Stevens. Many were sailed by married couples. Peg Fassett recalled rushing home from church on Sundays to prepare lunch and wax the boat's bottom, before crewing for her husband, Alvah, in the afternoon's race. Luffing the jib or heading too close into the wind could cost a boat the race and skipper and crew their tempers. For a brief time, Alvah and Bill Quin swapped wives (as crew members), but the exchange brought no relief.

For the hardy few, the lake offered winter pastimes also. Ice fishing, iceboating, and skating were popular. Some even attempted skiing down the sloping shores onto the lake or driving automobiles on its frozen surface.

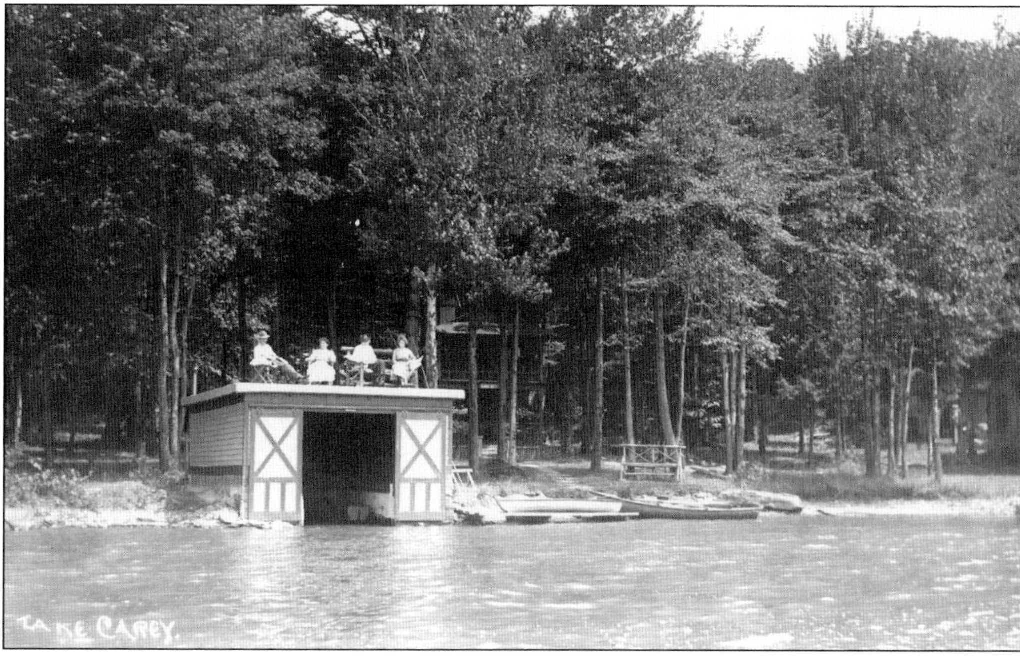

Relief from the heat before Carrier invented the air conditioner was a major attraction of lakeside life. In this real-photo postcard, a party of four at Summer Rest enjoy the breeze and the view from atop their boathouse on the east shore. (Russell collection.)

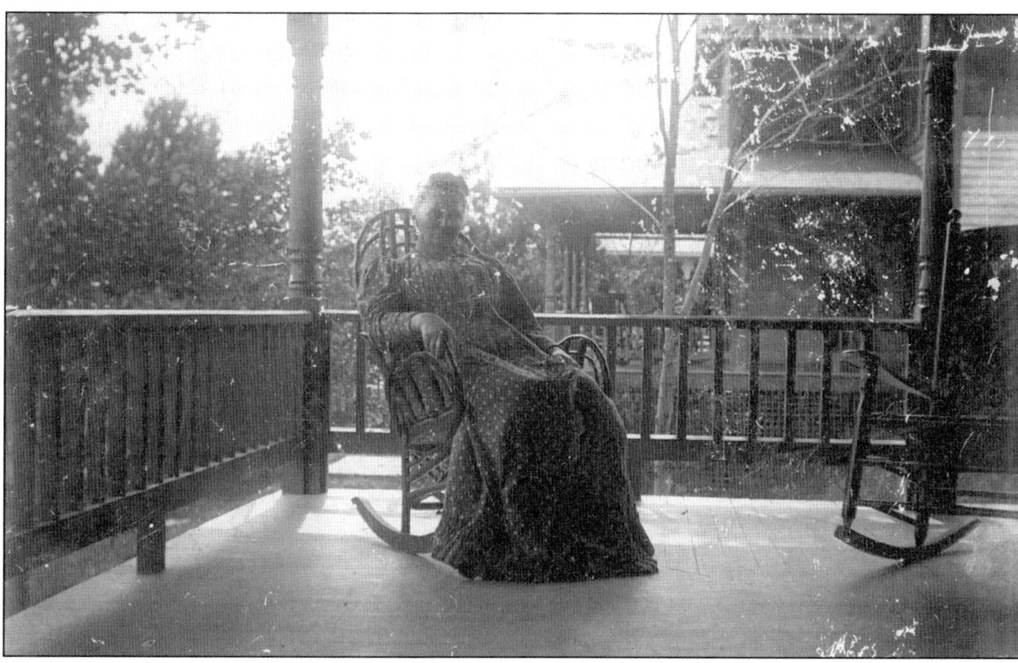

Rocking on the porch was cooling too. Susan Stone Marcy contemplates the photographer and his camera on her porch, probably in July 1896. (Pitkin collection.)

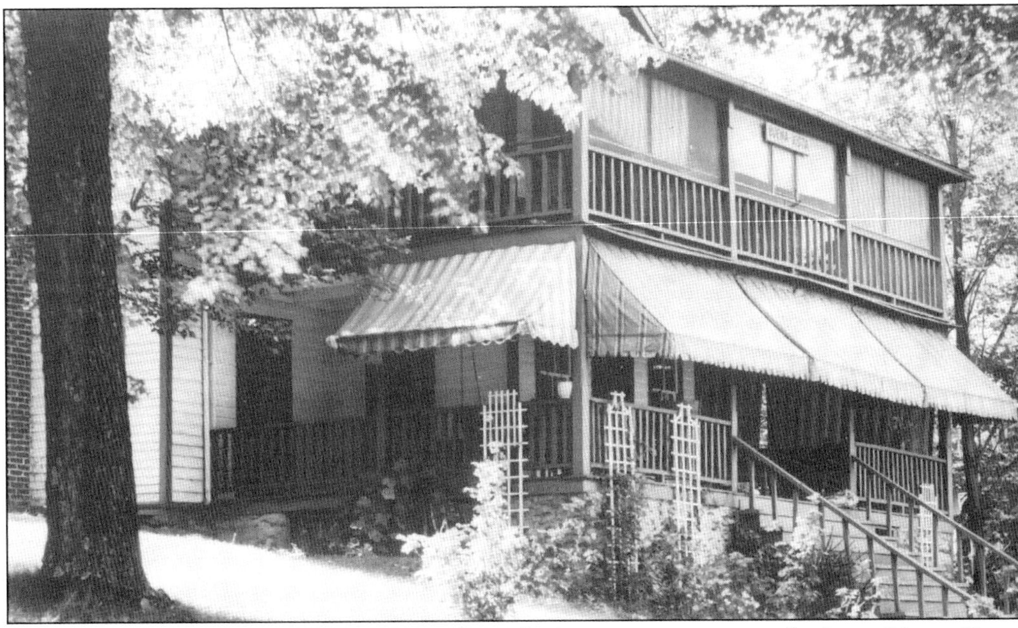

Just looking at a porch shaded by awnings from the hot morning sun is refreshing. This is Buena Vista in the 1930s. (Stevens collection.)

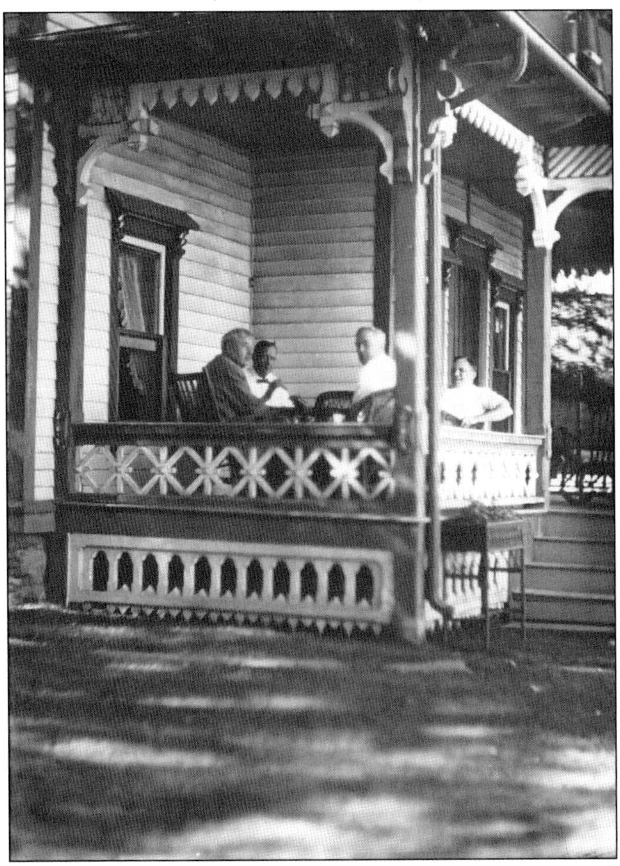

Porches were good for shooting the breeze as well. Here, on the porch of Beech Grove Camp, Frank Wheaton, William S. Kelly, Roscoe Moore, and Frank W. Kelly Sr. hash over the topics of the day—it was 1933 and that fellow Roosevelt might have been mentioned. (Kelly collection.)

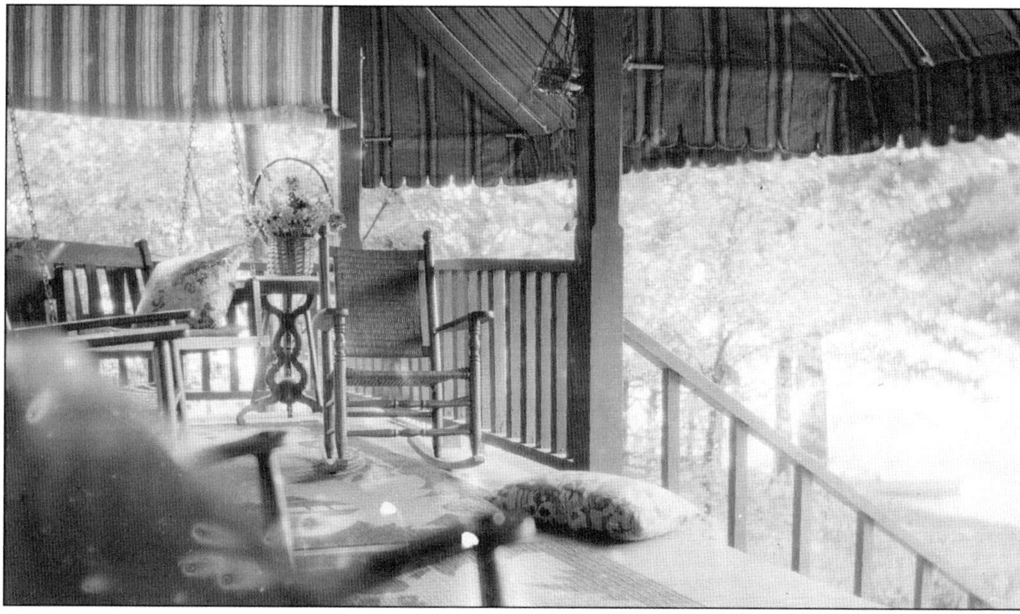

Three rockers, two pillows, and a wooden swing await the occupants of Buena Vista. There is probably a light onshore breeze at this hour of the day as well. (Stevens collection.)

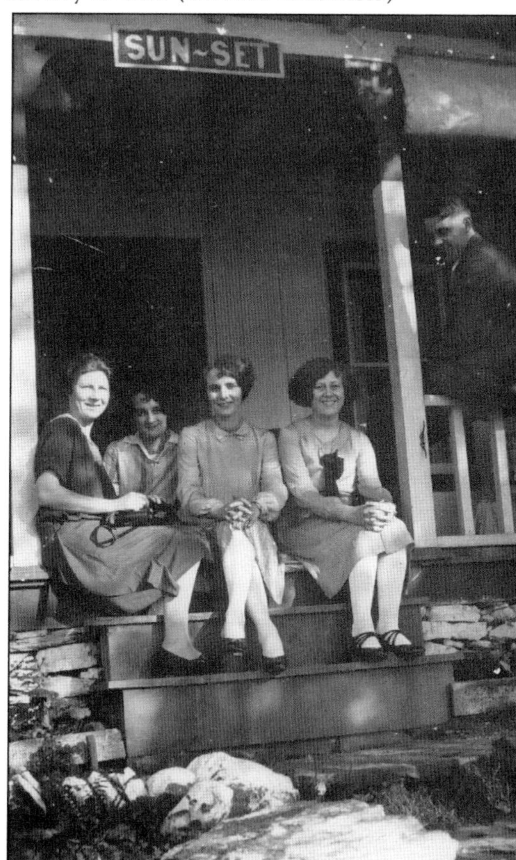

Courtship took place on porches before the automobile. These young people (from left to right), Irene Buckworth, Clara Stevenson, Margaret Newton, and Grace Stevenson, pose on the steps of Sun-Set cottage on the lake's east shore around 1925. Ted Enoch, Grace's suitor, sits on the railing beside them. (Yes, she married him.) Sun-Set was demolished in 1957. (Weaver collection.)

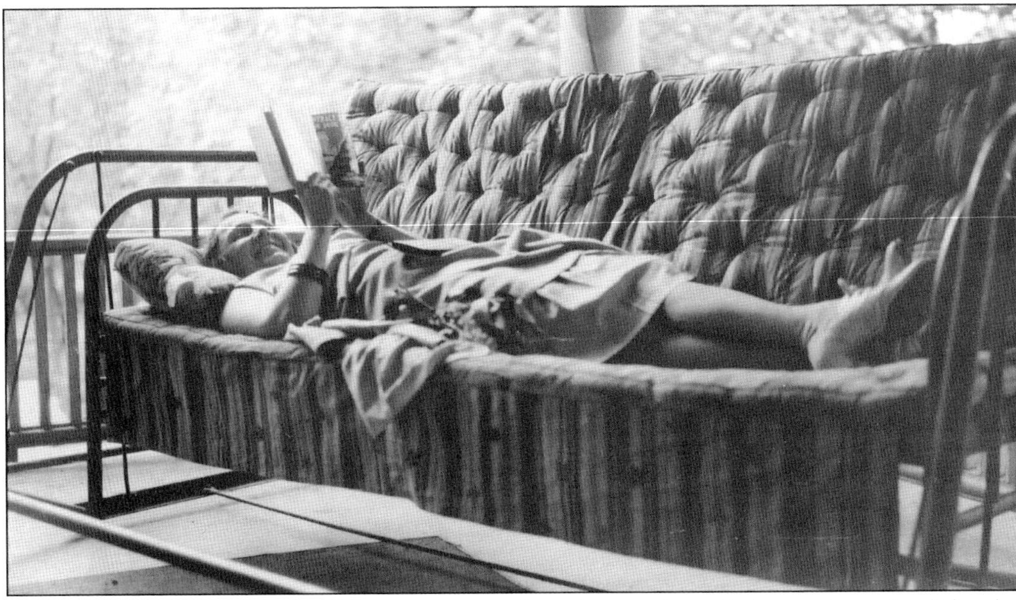

This guest of Bill and Ruth Quin appears to be relaxing in a Quinwood porch glider, but Mary Becker is actually boning up on her bridge game, reading a guide to contract bridge. (Tidball/Davis collection.)

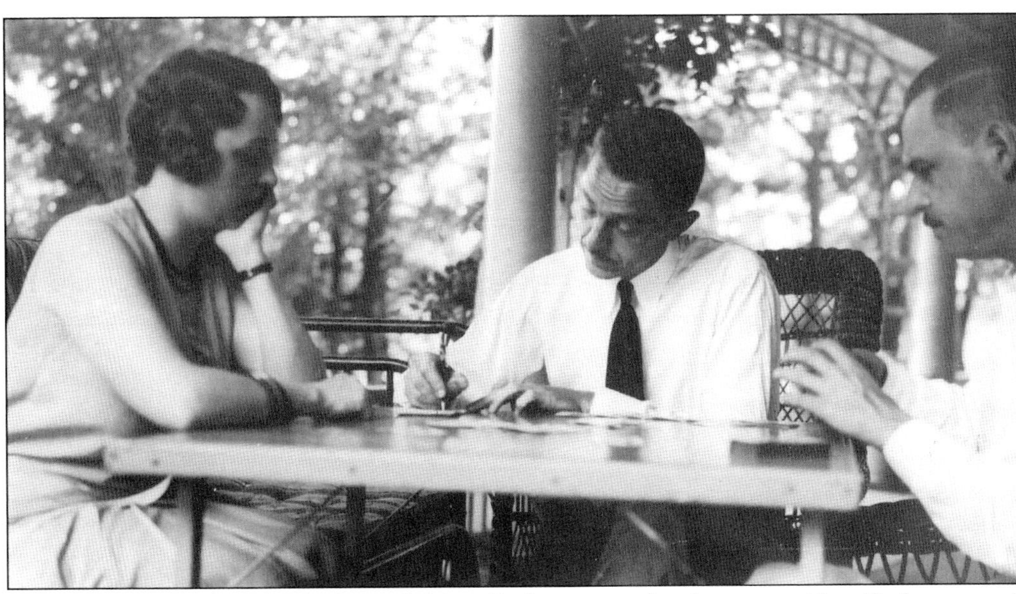

It appears to have done her little good. Mary Becker stares glumly as an unidentified man totals the score and her partner, Bob Quin, busies himself shuffling the deck. Bridge was a serious pastime at Quinwood where over 20 bridge tables were kept in readiness for bridge parties on the lawn. (Tidball/Davis collection.)

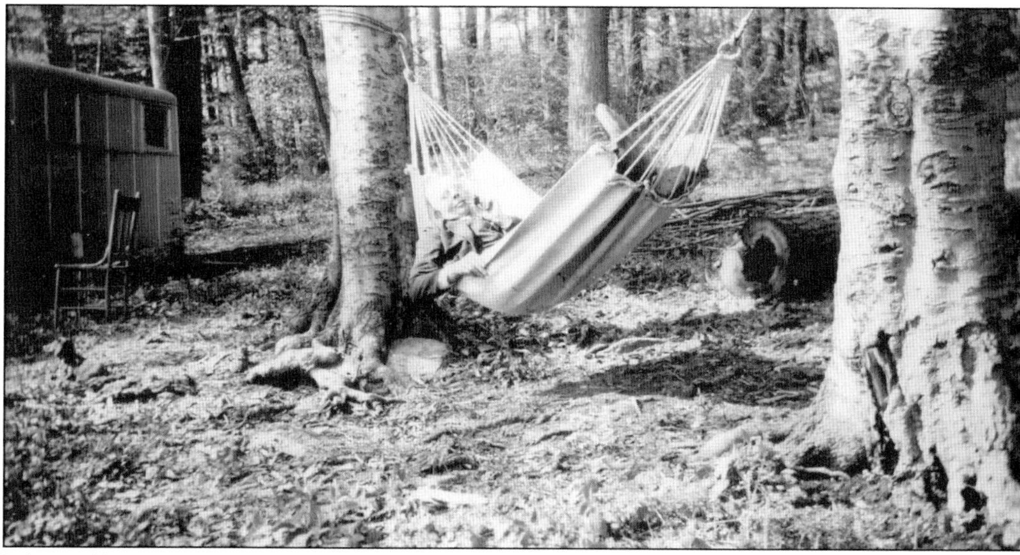

John Williamson, pipe in hand, relaxes in his navy surplus hammock in July 1945. The next year this Wilkes-Barre postal carrier roused himself and built Hemlock Haven for himself and his family with the aid of his young grandson Chuck Givler. (Givler collection.)

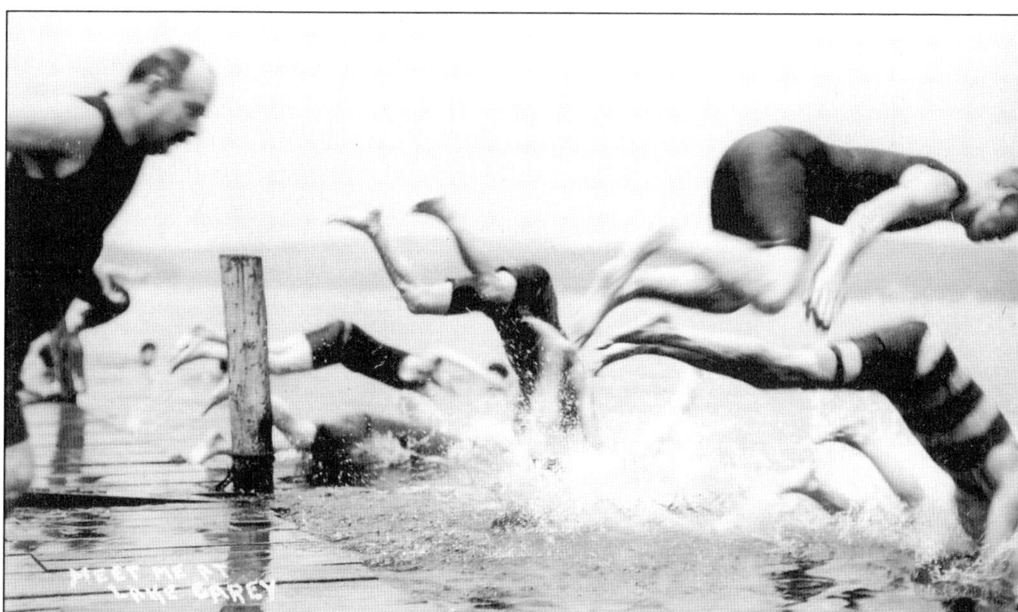

Swimming was always a major draw, as this real-photo postcard image by W. J. Harris acknowledges. Welsh-born Harris began his career in Wilkes-Barre but based his business at Lake Hopatcong, New Jersey, and St. Augustine, Florida. He made a trip to Lake Carey to make photographs for a postcard series in 1907. Despite its caption, this one does not appear to have been taken at Lake Carey. (Author's collection.)

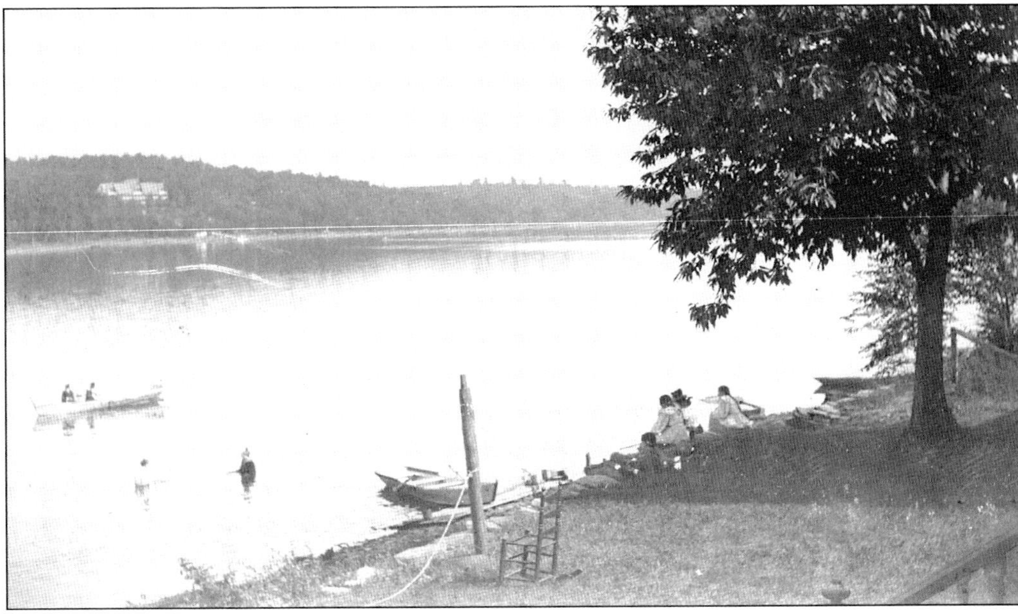

Members of the Dunn family swim and boat, while their elders sit in the shade in front of the west shore cottages built by family patriarch Henry Metcalf. The east shore's Fern Cliffe Hotel is visible on the left. (Wyoming County Historical Society collection.)

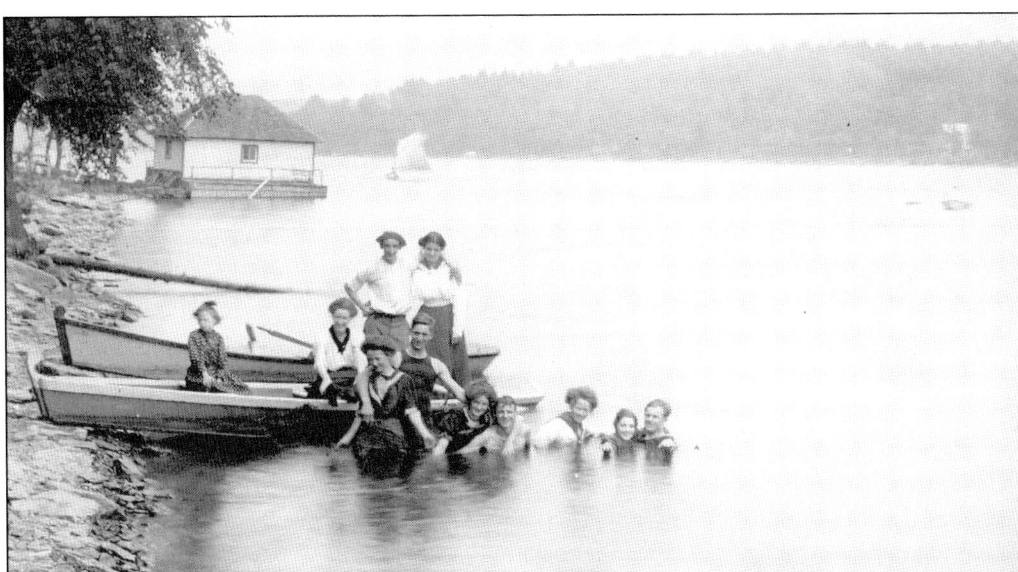

This racy crowd, half in the water and half in their Finch boat, are in need of a chaperone. Such physical intimacy was unusual when this photograph was taken around 1900. (The photograph's disapproving owner wrote on the back, "I have no idea who these people are.") Nimrod Lodge boathouse and a gaff-rigged boat are visible in the background. (Tidball/Davis collection.)

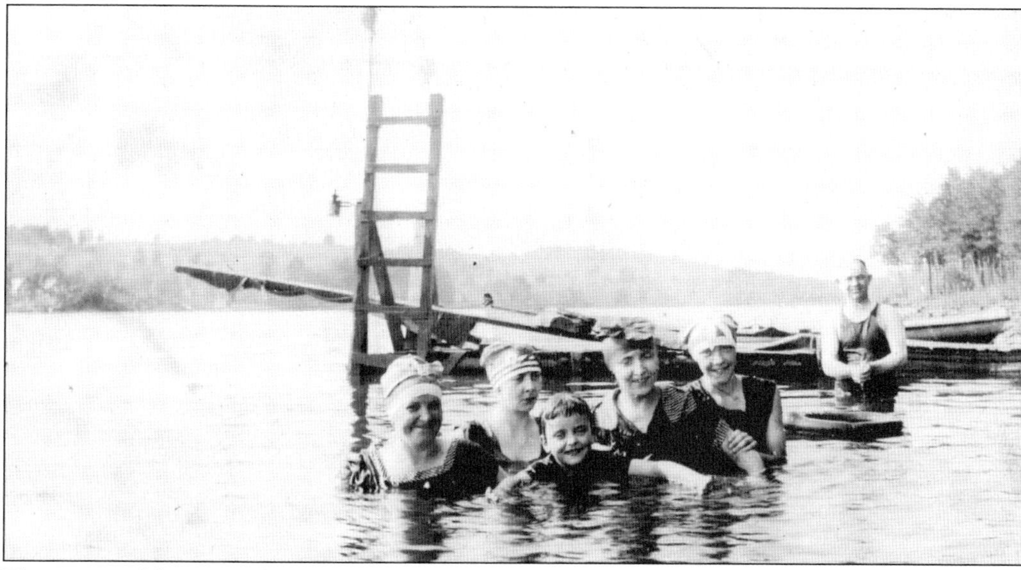

This party of five rented Harold cottage on the east shore in August 1921. Evidently the water is great for these members of the Carmody clan: from left to right, unidentified, Anne Carmody Huddy, unidentified, Ruth Connors McHenry, Margaret Carmody Conlon, and unidentified. Swimmers climbed the ladder to the diving board, covered with cloth to prevent slipping, and plunged in. Were the swimming caps a fashion statement? (Banis collection.)

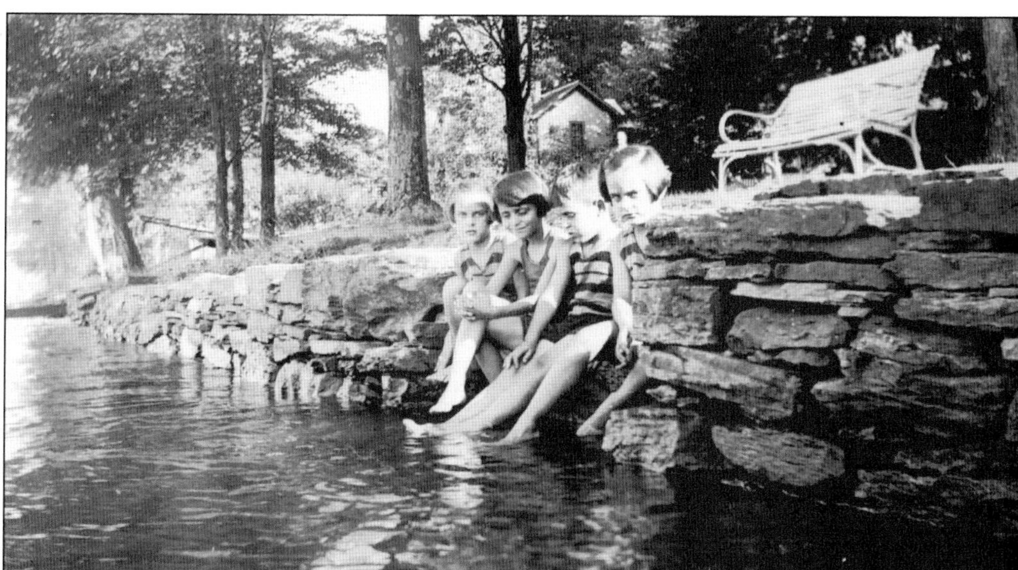

Sometimes it is best to just dip one's toes in the water. Electra, a "fresh air girl," and John Merritt sit between his twin sisters, Micky and Betty, in this photograph taken at the Matten cottage lakefront in 1928. (Pitkin collection.)

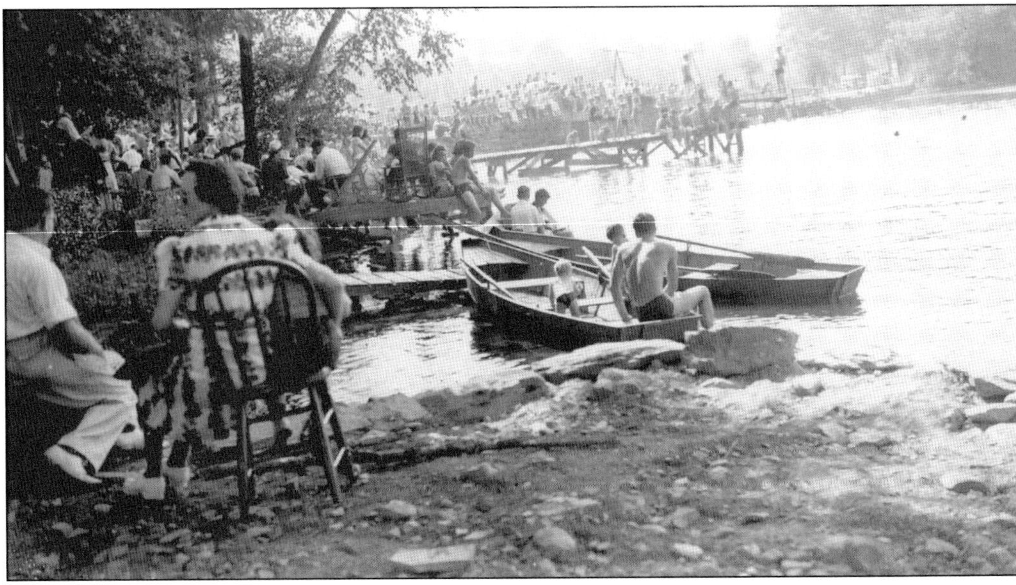

Crowds gather to watch this swimming exhibition held on Zaleppa's dock in the 1940s. (Weaver collection.)

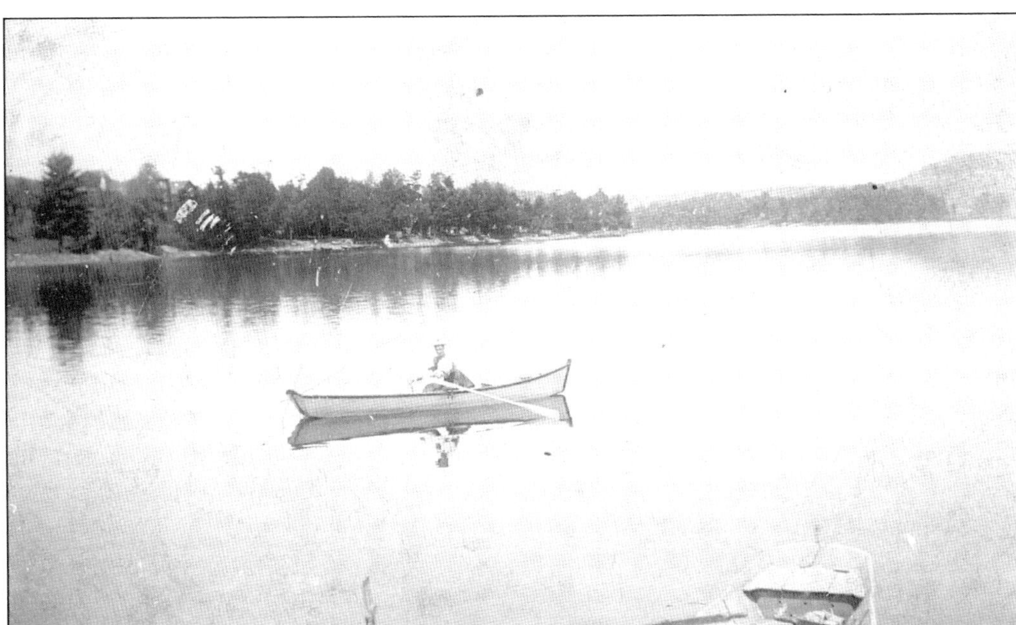

Boating was another attraction of lake life. Mary Rhone Marcy, Susan Stone Marcy's daughter-in-law, takes to her oars on a perfectly still lake in this 1896 photograph. (Pitkin collection.)

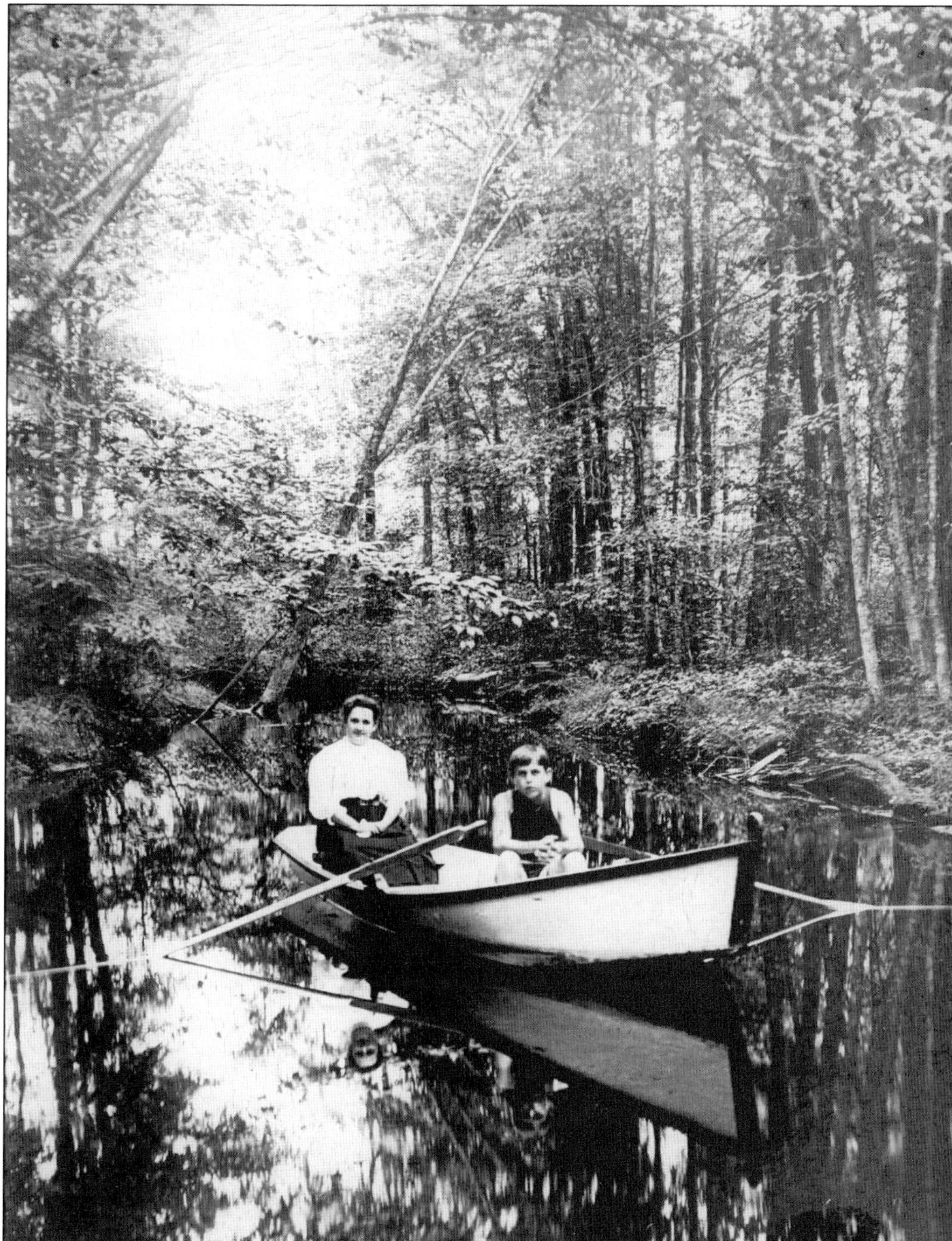

In time, Mary Marcy could rely on her son, Harry K., to man the oars. In this real-photo postcard, this appears to be the same Finch boat she rowed in 1896, eleven years before. Wooden boats were expensive, often locally made, carefully maintained, and kept in boathouses to protect them from weather. Finch made his boats near Harveys Lake, but one could buy a copy from a carpenter named Sykes on the Flow Pond. (Pitkin collection.)

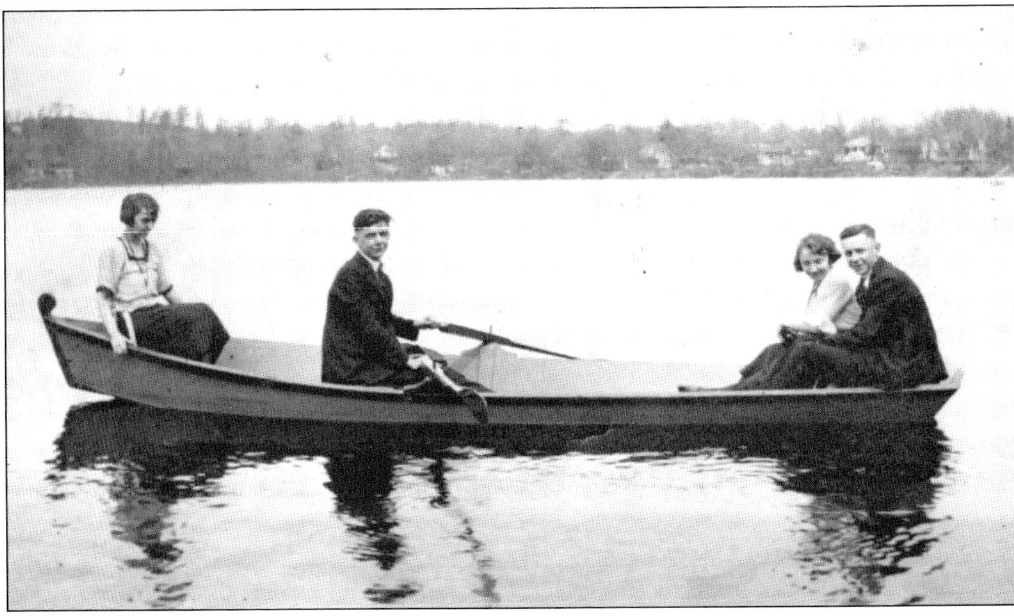

Dewey McHenry and his 17-year-old bride, Ruth Connors McHenry, spent their honeymoon in June 1920 at the Wrigley farmhouse then being rented out by its owners, the Coopers. (Ruth's sister, Elizabeth Connors Carmody, would later purchase the place.) Joe Carmody rows the Finch boat with the honeymooners in the stern; his sister, Betty, is along for the ride. (Banis collection.)

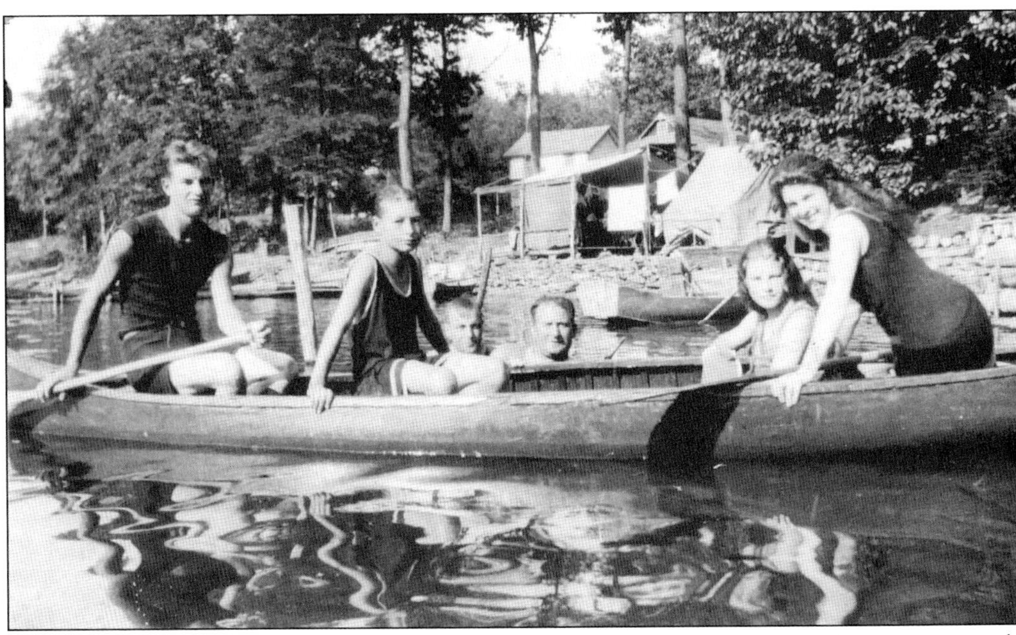

The Buckworth family pauses in and behind their canoe, their reflections shimmering in the water. Note the tent and lean-to on the east shore behind them in this photograph from about 1922. (Weaver collection.)

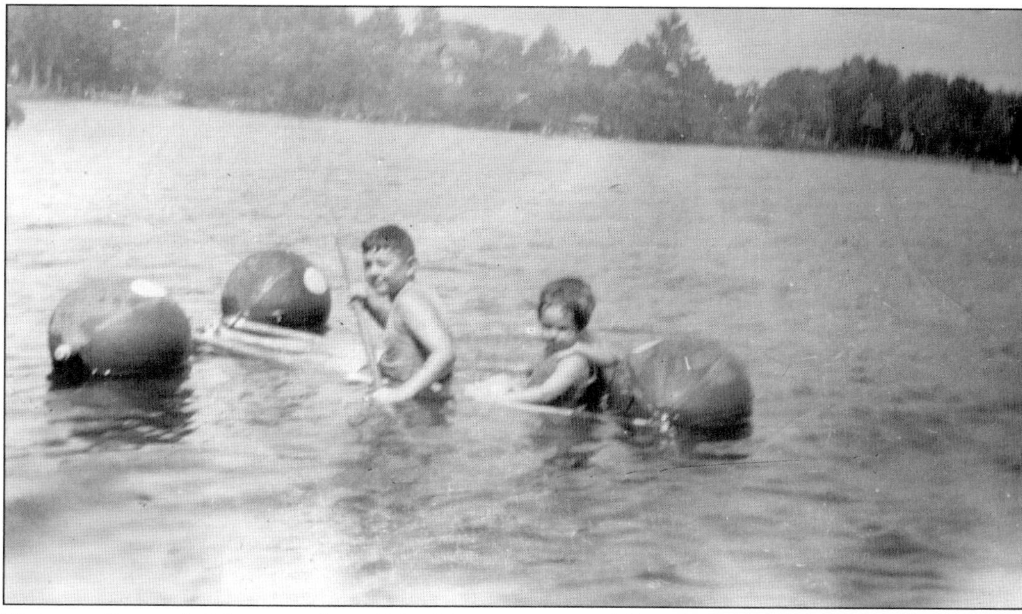

This peculiar craft did not catch on. John Merritt poses, paddle in hand, with his twin sisters, Micky and Betty (or is it Betty and Micky?), behind him. Family records do not reveal what John's father, a Wilkes-Barre pharmacist, was thinking when he made this 1926 purchase. (Pitkin collection.)

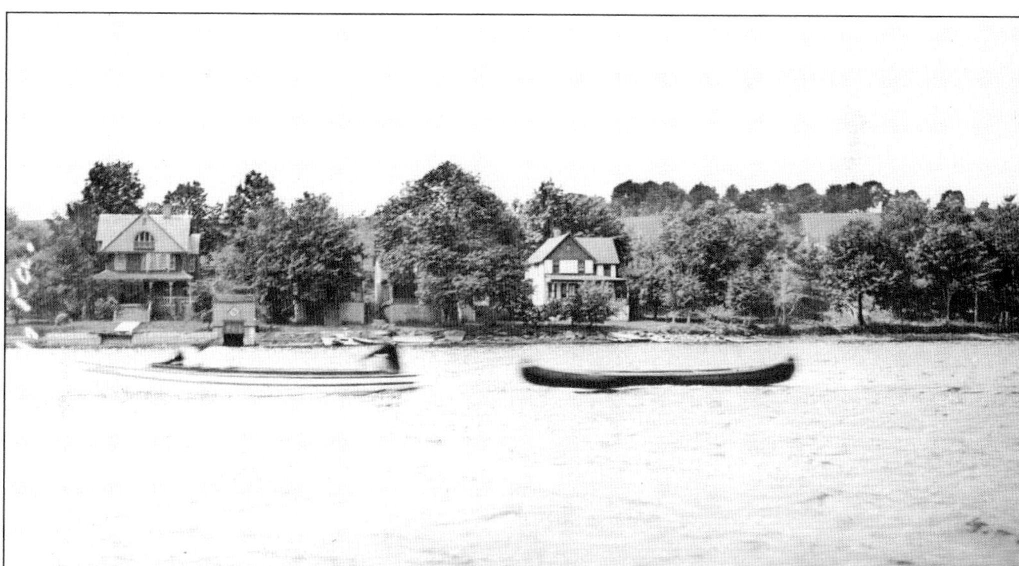

But motorboats did market well. This motorized launch appears to be towing a canoe at a speed too fast for slow film to capture. In time, "chug-chugs," as they were first known, would outnumber all the lake's canoes and rowboats put together. Elsemere and the Metcalf cottages are visible on the west shore across the lake in this real-photo postcard from around 1910. (Fellows collection.)

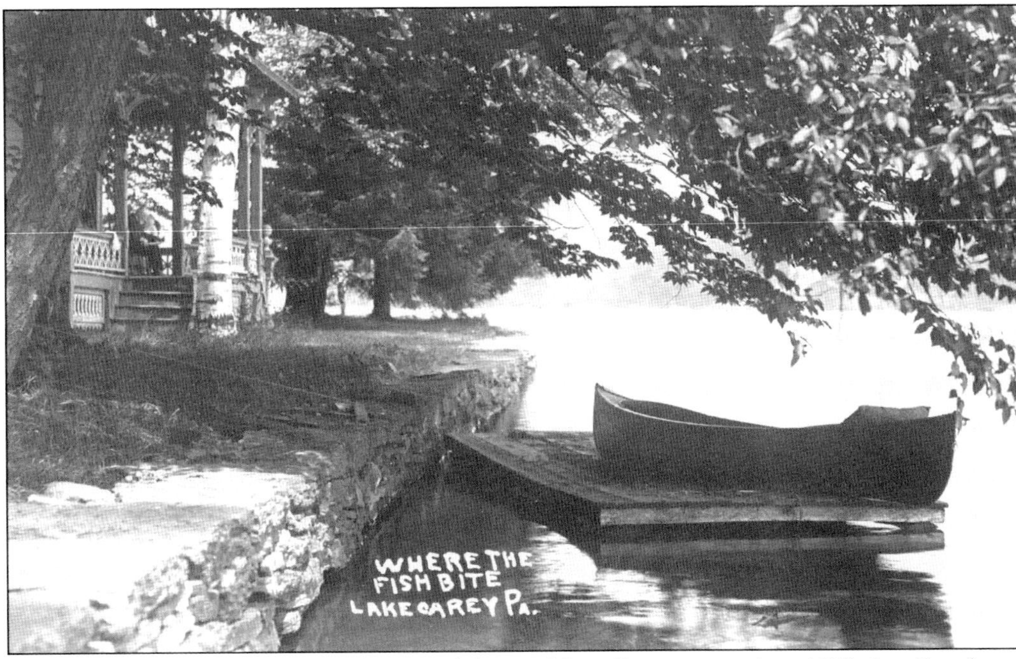

Lake Carey was often celebrated for its fishing. Alvin Day reported in 1875 that Frank and Rollin Stark of Philadelphia and Hendrick Wright of Wilkes-Barre caught "upwards of three hundred perch and catfish" one August day. This nicely framed real-photo postcard of a boat on a raft includes Beech Grove Camp's porch on the left. (Russell collection.)

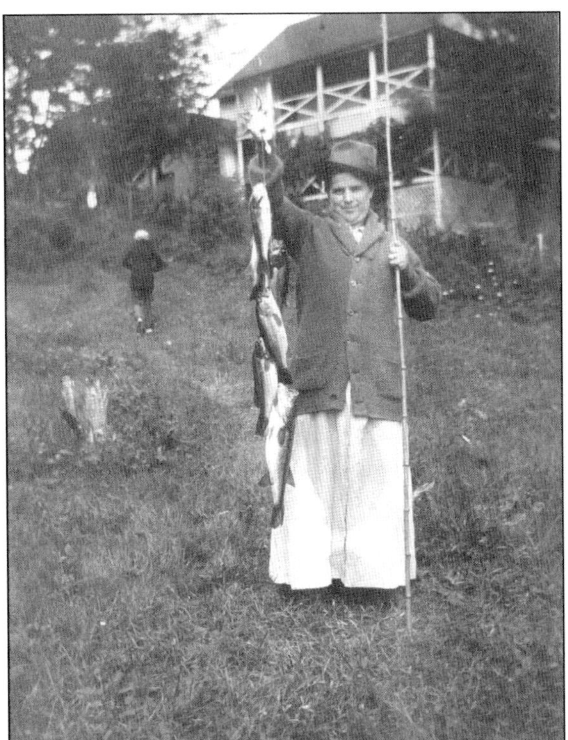

A member of the Geddes family, bamboo pole in hand, proudly displays her catch of largemouth bass and a walleye in a photograph from Anna Geddes's 1915–1918 scrapbook. Fishing was very popular among cottagers who often dined on fresh fish and potatoes. Nimrod Lodge is in the background. (Author's collection.)

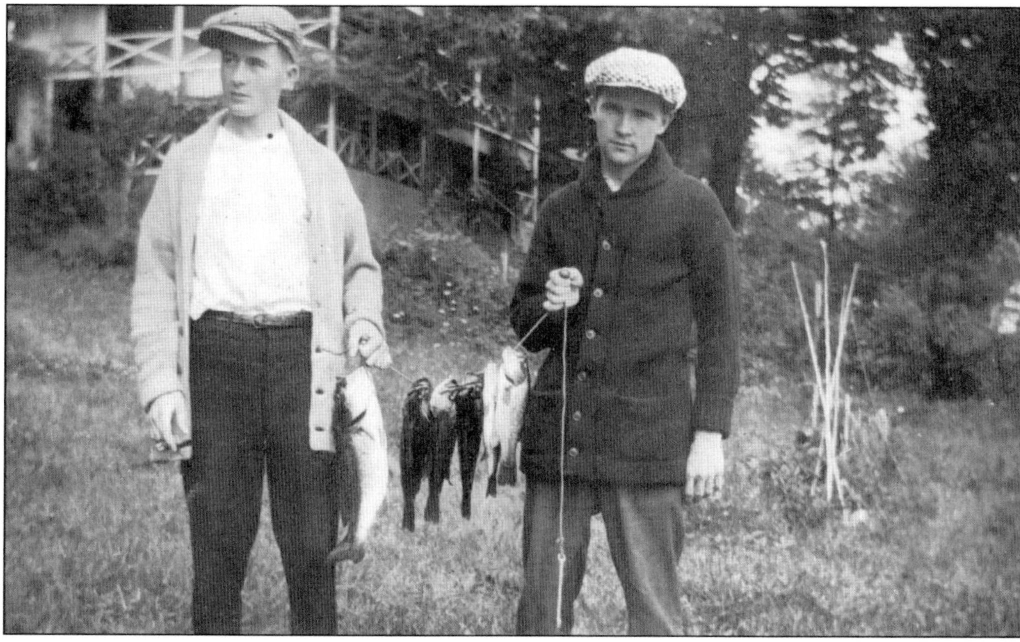

Two young men from Nimrod Lodge display their catch of pickerel and smallmouth bass in another photograph from Anna Geddes's scrapbook. The 1897 report of the state commissioners of fisheries reported that, in addition to pickerel and smallmouth bass, catfish, sunfish, and perch, as well as black and largemouth bass all were plentiful at the lake. (Author's collection.)

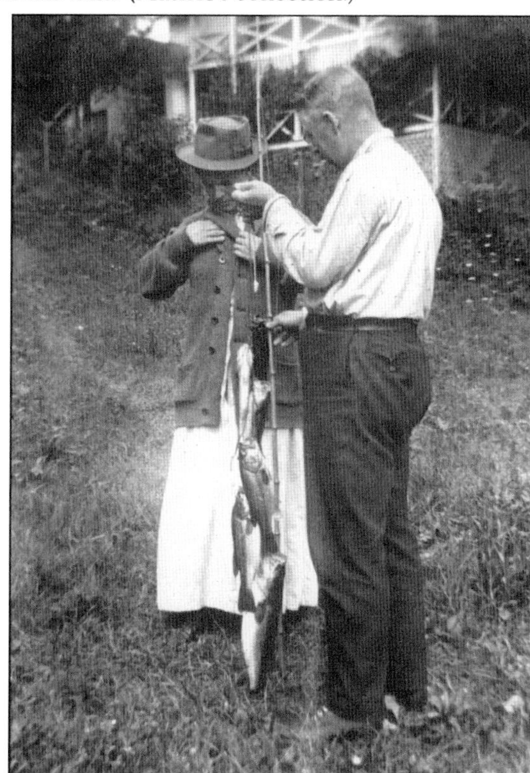

The caption from Anna Geddes's album for this photograph reads, "They didn't have to worry over fish stories." But the fisherwoman may have another worry; has she hooked herself? (Author's collection.)

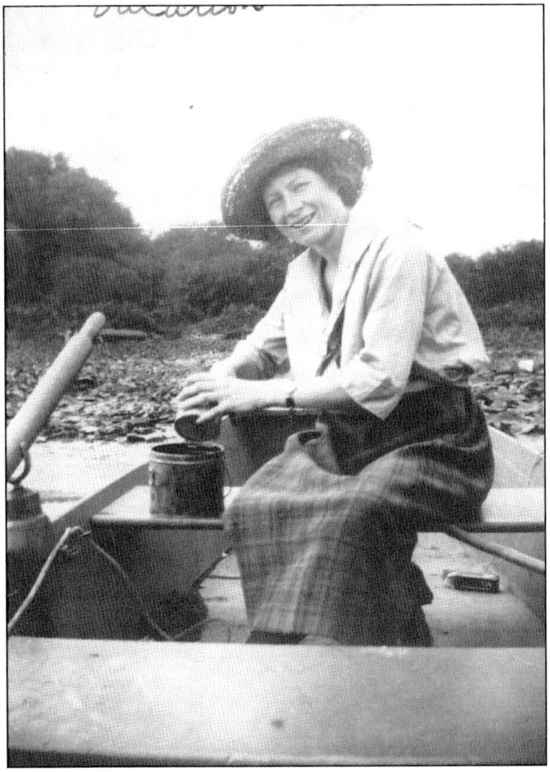

Irene Buckworth Lee prepares bait on the Flow Pond in the 1930s, smiling cheerfully because her boat is still dry. Her husband, a carpenter and boat maker, was known to his family as Bob the box maker—he seldom managed to produce a watertight boat, at least for them. He also worked for Adm. Harold R. Stark as a handyman. (Weaver collection.)

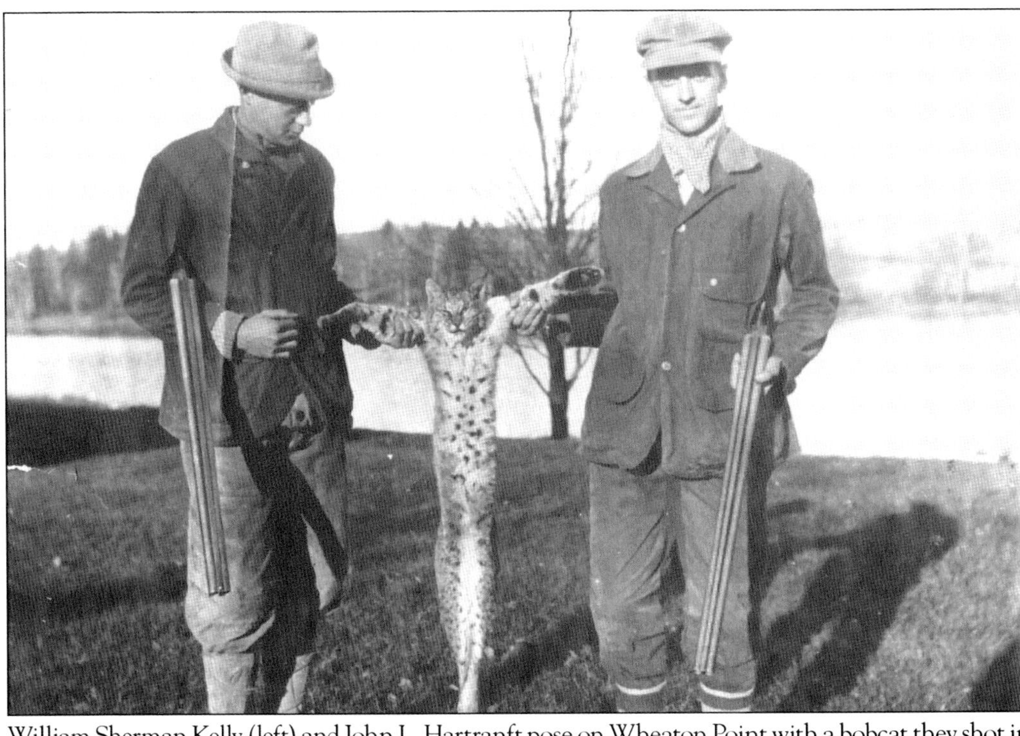

William Sherman Kelly (left) and John L. Hartranft pose on Wheaton Point with a bobcat they shot in the 1920s. If there was a lake recipe for bobcat burgers, it was not handed down. (Kelly collection.)

Thomas Buckworth holds a large snapper by its tail around 1927 as Tom Stevenson stares solemnly at the camera and a young Tommy Thomas recoils. Some folks ate snapper. Buck Kelly recalls his grandmother preparing snapper turtle soup with vegetables. After the head was cut off and the blood drained, the turtle was boiled until the meat could be separated from the shell. (Weaver collection.)

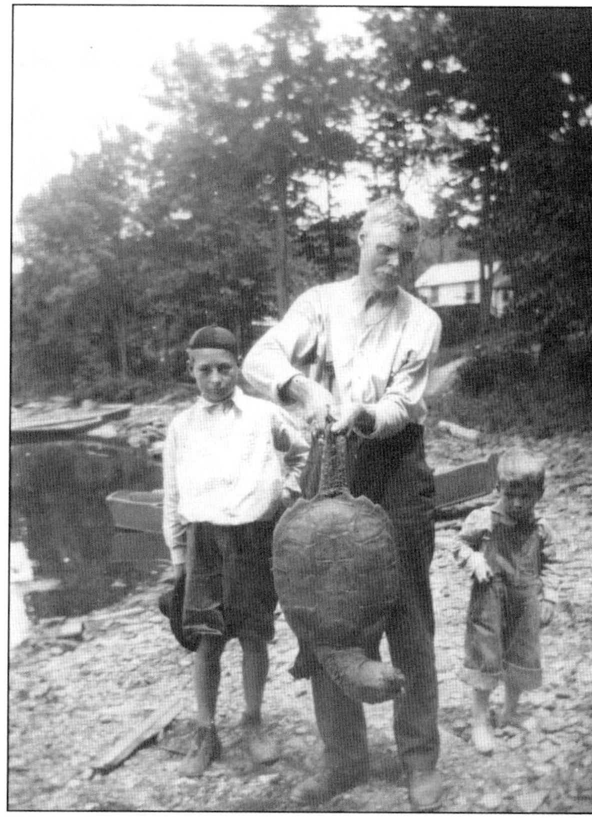

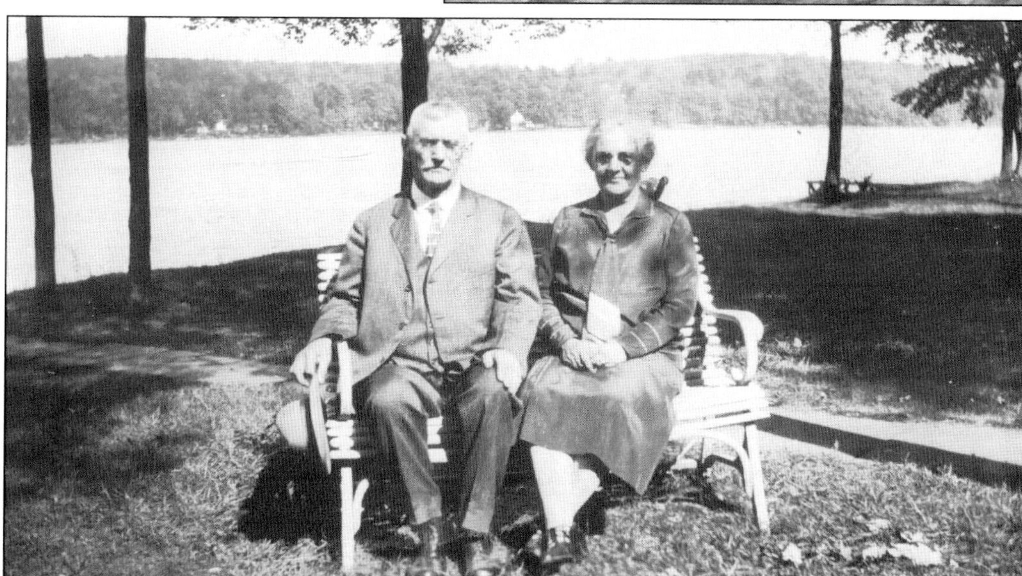

Posing for family photographs has long been a ritual of lake life. Here Mary Rhone Marcy sits beside her husband, Harry G. Marcy. Her son Harry K., with whom she is pictured on page 105 about 30 years before, graduated from Princeton where he crewed for the Tigers. Her daughter Ruth, pictured on page 48, forsook Curtis Logan to marry a young attorney, later judge, Robert W. Trembath. (Pitkin collection.)

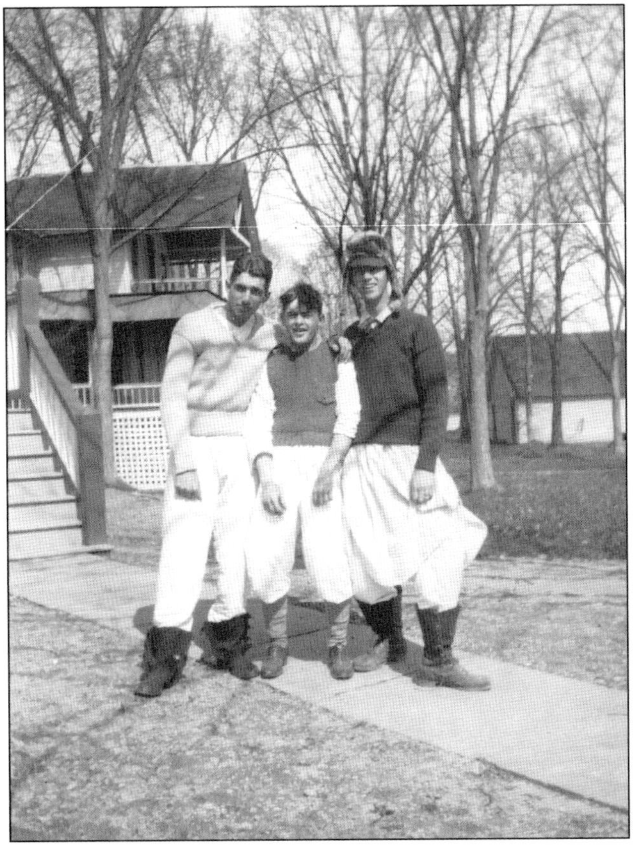

Some photographs were informal shots of friends. Here teenagers (from left to right) Carlton Gates, Bill Quin, and Jimmy Norris pose in front of the Schlingman cottage in the early 1920s. Norris appears in high-cut boots (some contained a pocket for a scout knife) and raccoon cap—it was the bee's knees! (Tidball/Davis collection.)

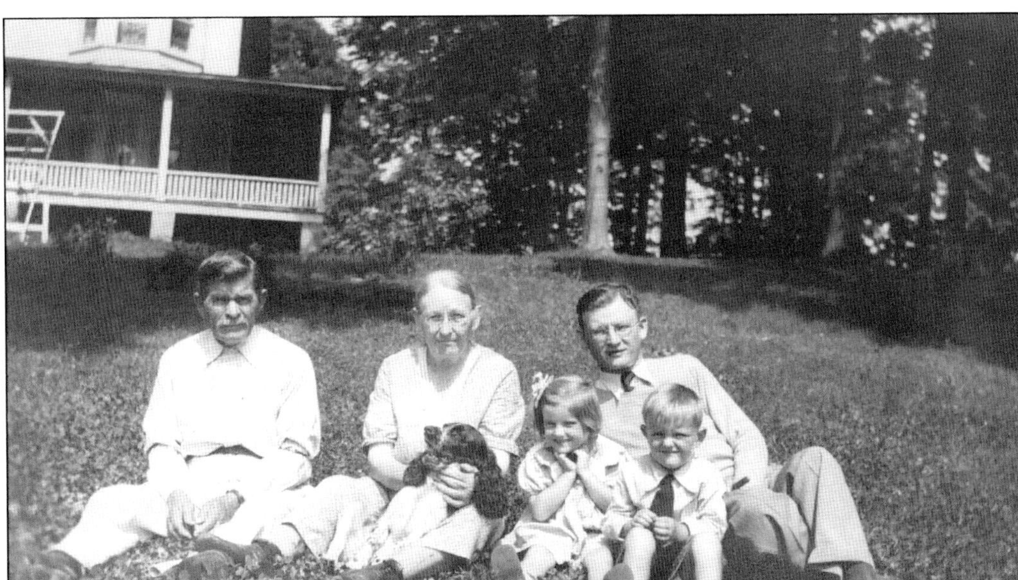

Across the lake, attorney Felix E. Bolowicz poses with his parents and his niece Betty Toole Robic and her twin, Col. C. J. Toole, in front of their east shore farmhouse about 1932. (Robic collection.)

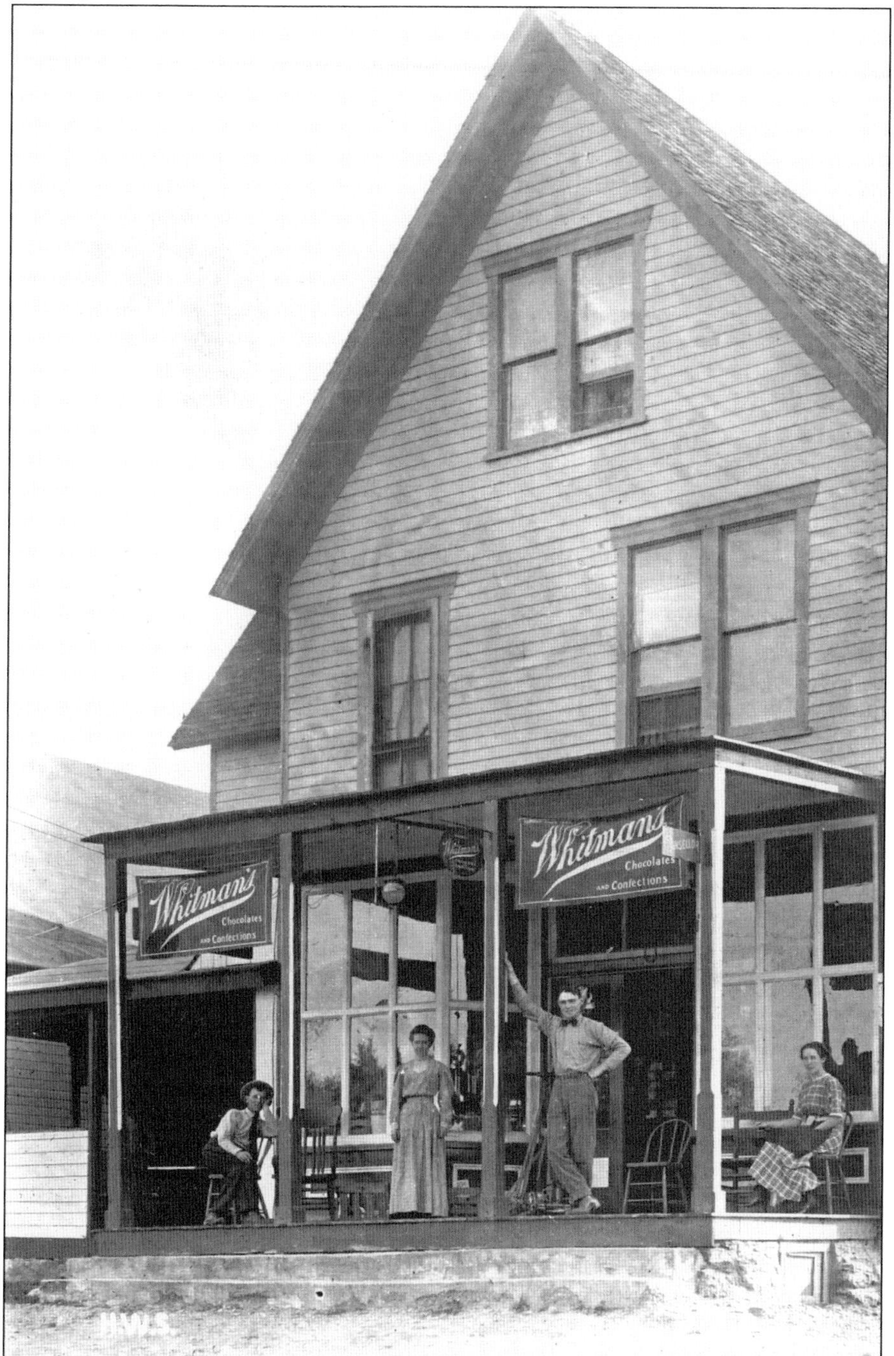

Cassedys west shore store and post office became an important institution. It featured Harrington's ice cream at the soda fountain and Whitman's chocolates at the counter. The post office, to the left in this real-photo postcard, was entered from inside the store. Walter Cassedy (likely the man leaning against the post) acquired the business in 1901 from B. W. Lewis and sold it 22 years later to Ross I. and Mary Weill. The store was later owned by the Clemens, the Mordents, and the Towners. It was destroyed by fire about 1960. (Russell collection.)

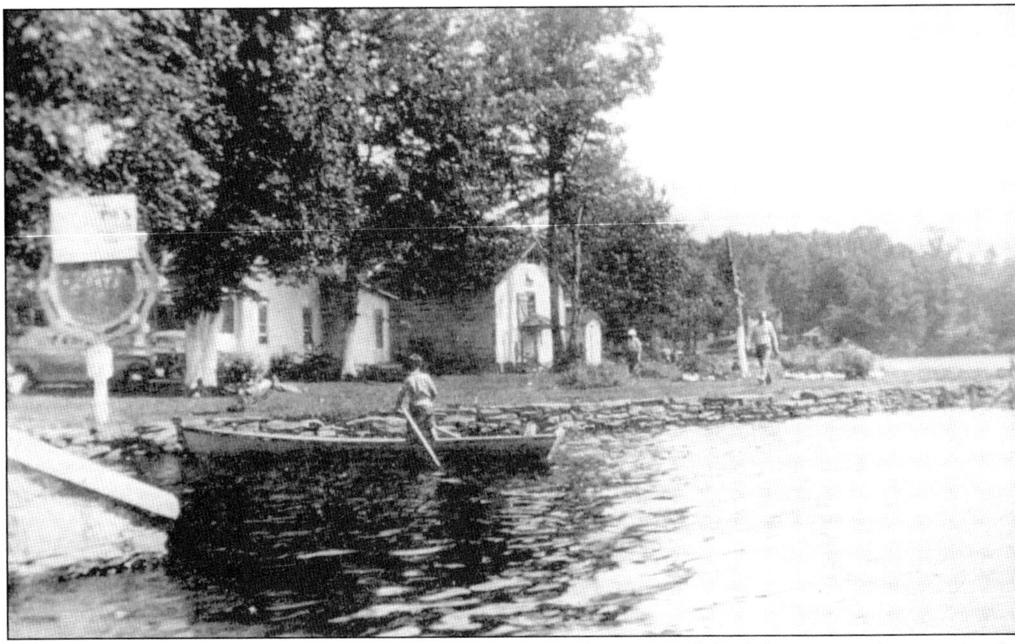

When not goofing around, boys could be sent on errands to one of the lake's general stores. In this postcard, a youngster docks at Zaleppas. He might have been sent for kerosene or for perishable foods. Eggs, milk, and meat had to be purchased several times a week before electricity and Frigidaires. Some staples also were delivered by hucksters to the cottage dock or door. (Pitkin collection.)

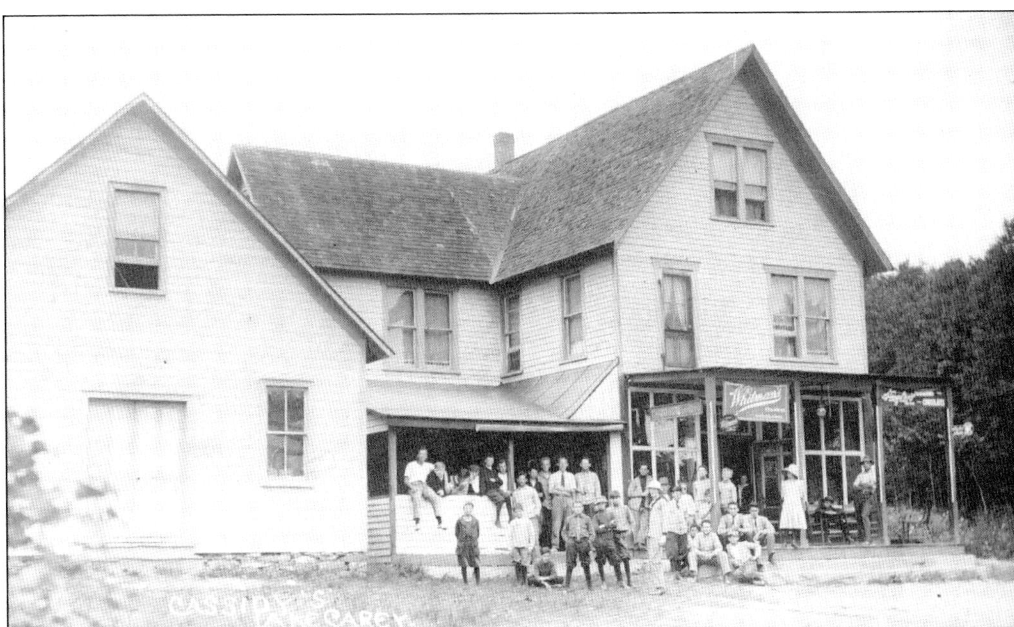

Cassedys was especially popular with teenagers. In this real-photo postcard, boys from Camp Pokanoket pose in front of the store. Teenage girls met here too. Typically the girls gathered on summer mornings—under the guise of picking up the family mail—"to plan their day." (Redding collection.)

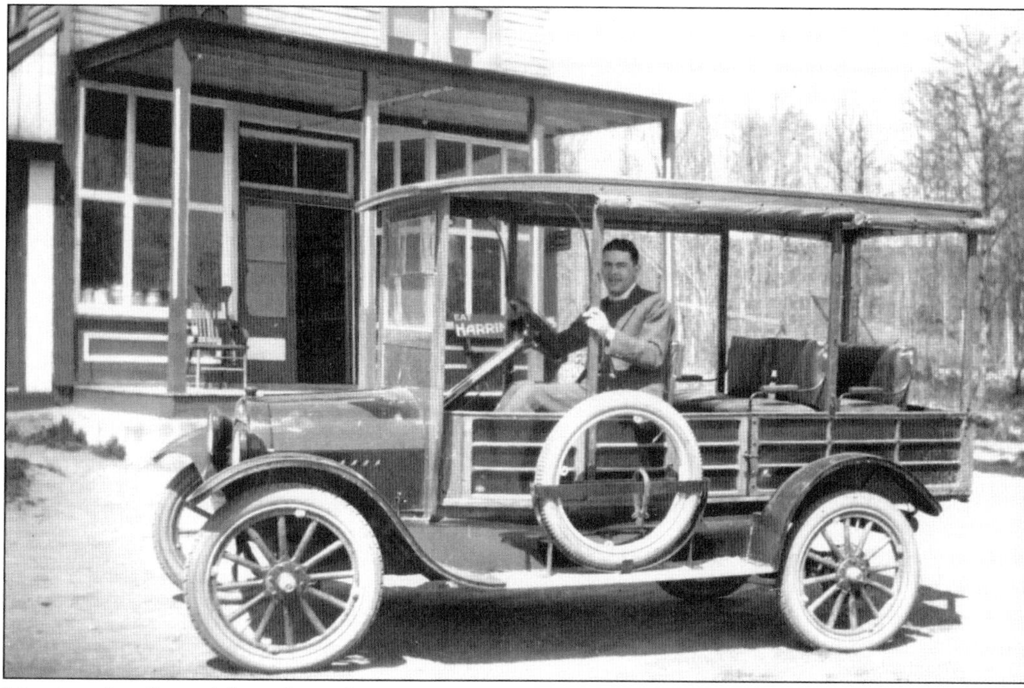

Meeting family and friends at the station was an important part of adult life. Bill Quin poses in his depot hack in front of what was then Weill's store in the mid-1920s. "Hack" bodies were manufactured in Pennsylvania and could be placed on the chassis of a Chevy, Ford, or Dodge. This ironic image captures the transition from fixed rail transportation to the freedom of the automobile. (Tidball/Davis collection.)

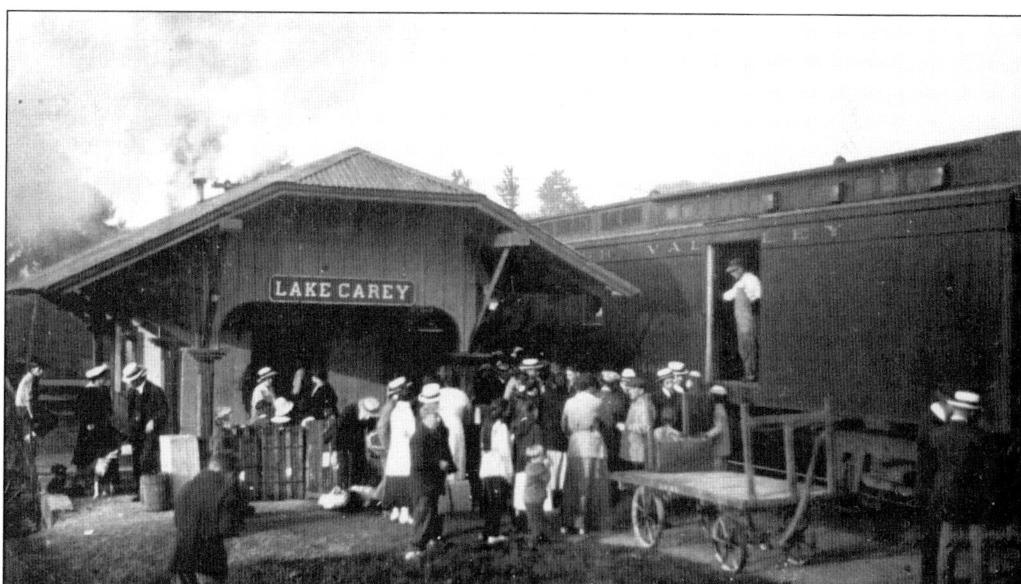

From Cassedys, the girls might progress to the nearby station to see who was arriving on the morning train. Here the 6:00 a.m. train from Montrose pulls into Lake Carey on its way to Tunkhannock in 1918. (The girls would probably have checked out a later train.) (Russell collection.)

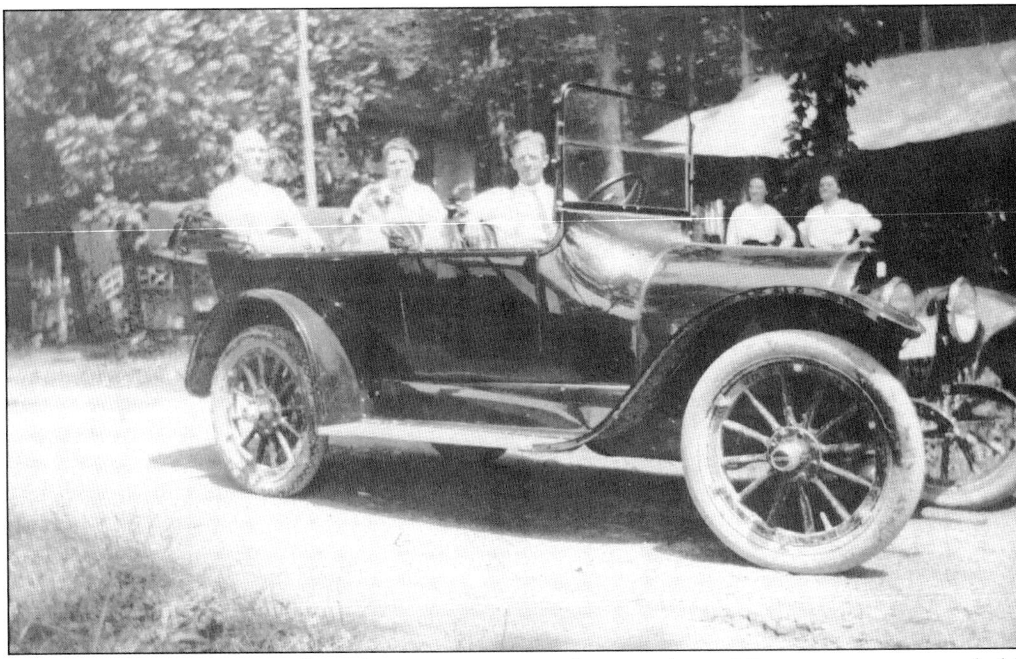

Jack Townsend poses proudly in his touring car on the east shore. His passengers are probably his parents. Automobiles would change lake life greatly. Now one could travel when and where one wished. Northeast Pennsylvanians who once filled Lake Carey's hotels and picnic spots instead toured the region in their automobiles, stopping in cabins along concrete highways. (Bell collection.)

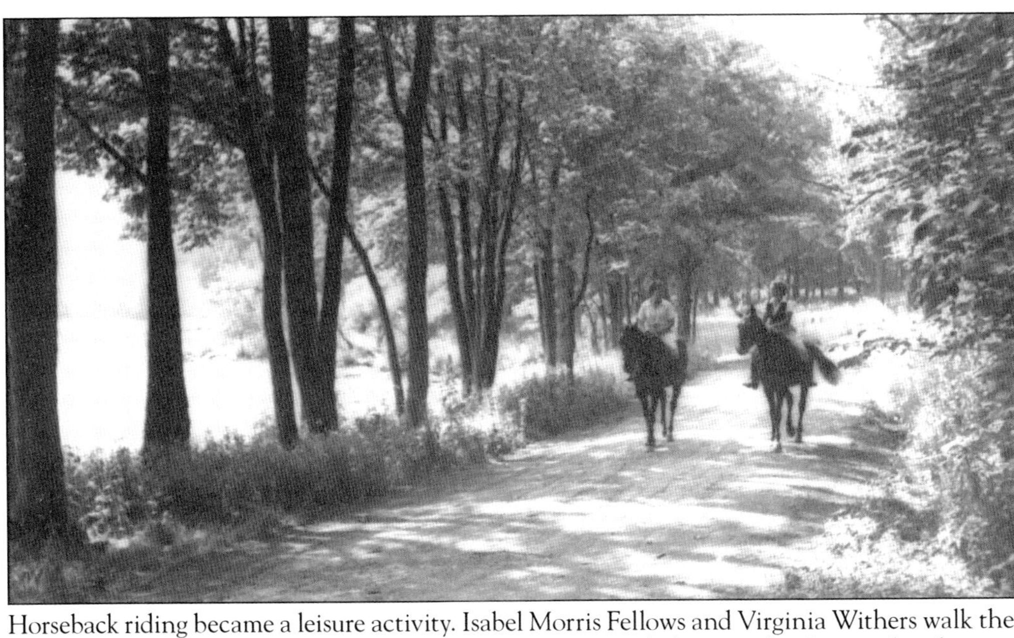

Horseback riding became a leisure activity. Isabel Morris Fellows and Virginia Withers walk their horses down an east shore road dappled with afternoon sunlight near the Cooper farmhouse in the 1930s. A riding academy was maintained for several years about this time in the Spring Grove Inn stables by Stan and Elizabeth "Bumpy" Dewitt. (Fellows collection.)

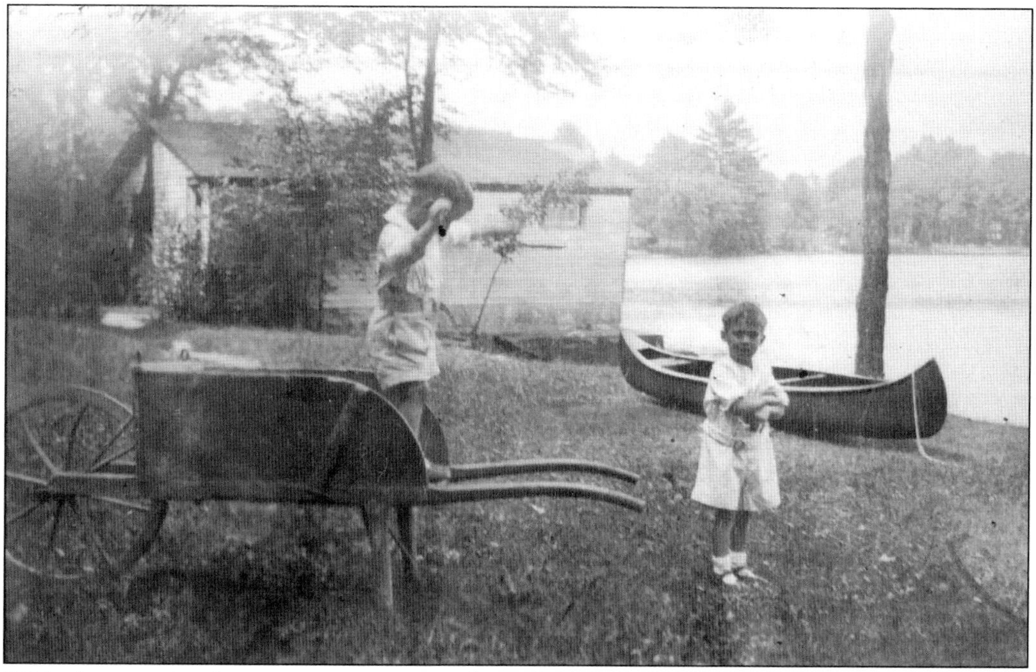

With the crowds of summer visitors gone from the lake, cottagers turned to quieter pastimes. Here John Merritt practices wheelbarrow jumping while Dick Kehoe, still having trouble with his technique, nurses a bruised elbow. (Pitkin collection.)

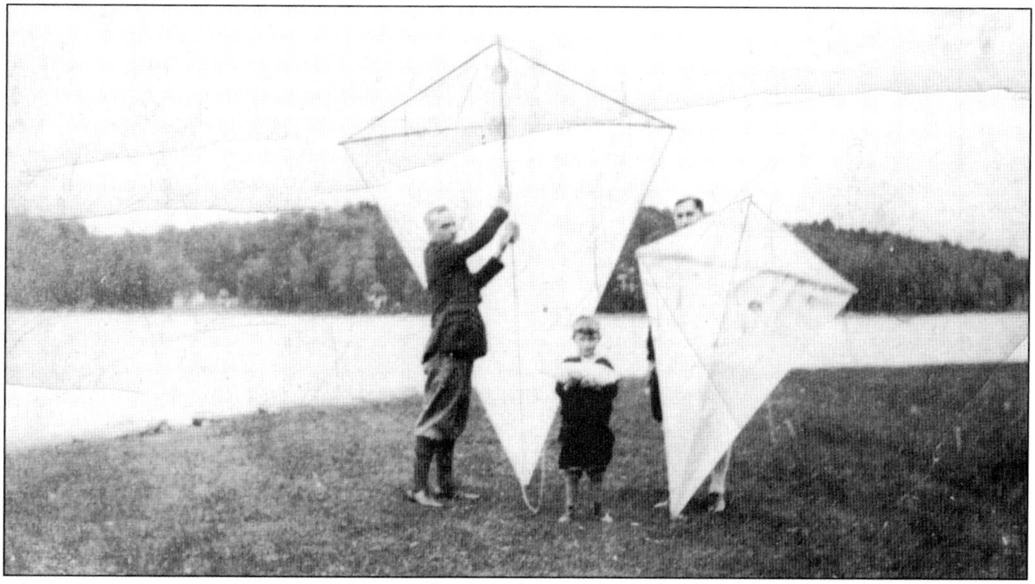

These kites on Wheaton Point are tailless Malays. Roscoe Moore, a mechanical engineer at Wilkes-Barre's Vulcan Steel, prepares a large Malay for flight while Beanie Rhodes (holding a lot of cord) and Harley Wheaton stare at the camera. On one occasion, Buck Kelly reports his Uncle Roscoe attached a camera with which he took aerial photographs of unsuspecting cottagers below. (Kelly collection.)

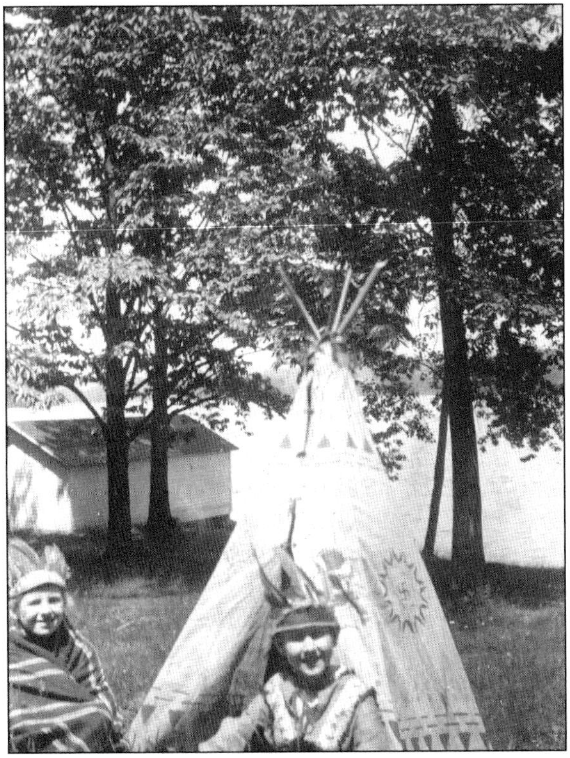

In this photograph from Anna Geddes's album, two unidentified boys pose in feather headdresses before a painted wigwam on the shores of Lake Carey. Tom Mix may be waiting on the other side of Nimrod Lodge from these unsuspecting braves. (Author's collection.)

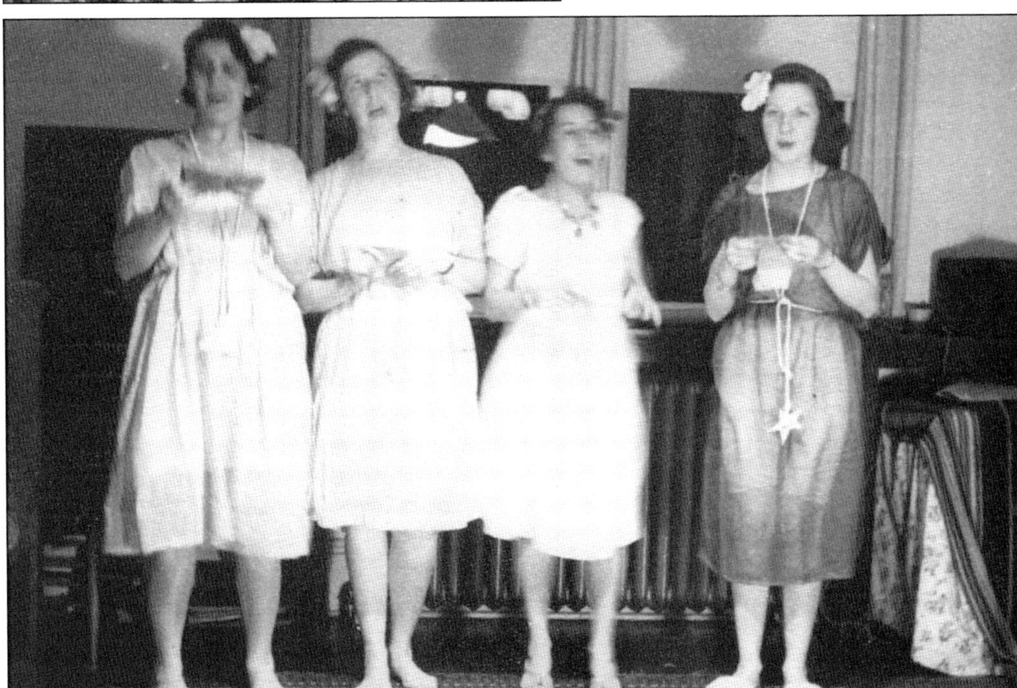

Neither age nor gender could protect unwary cottagers from silliness. The four women performing barefoot or in slippers in the Quinwood living room are thought to be (from left to right) Ruth Marcy Trembath, Ruth Quin, Jo Boston, and Sally Davis Farr. (Tidball/Davis collection.)

Arthur Schrage (left) and Bill Kelly (right) support Roscoe Moore, whose approach to yard work at Wheaton Point is strictly hands off. (Kelly collection.)

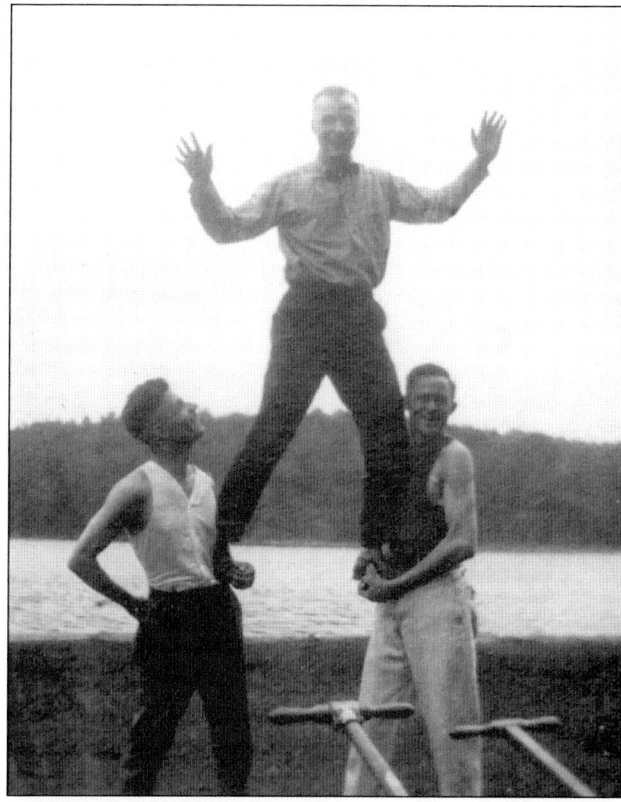

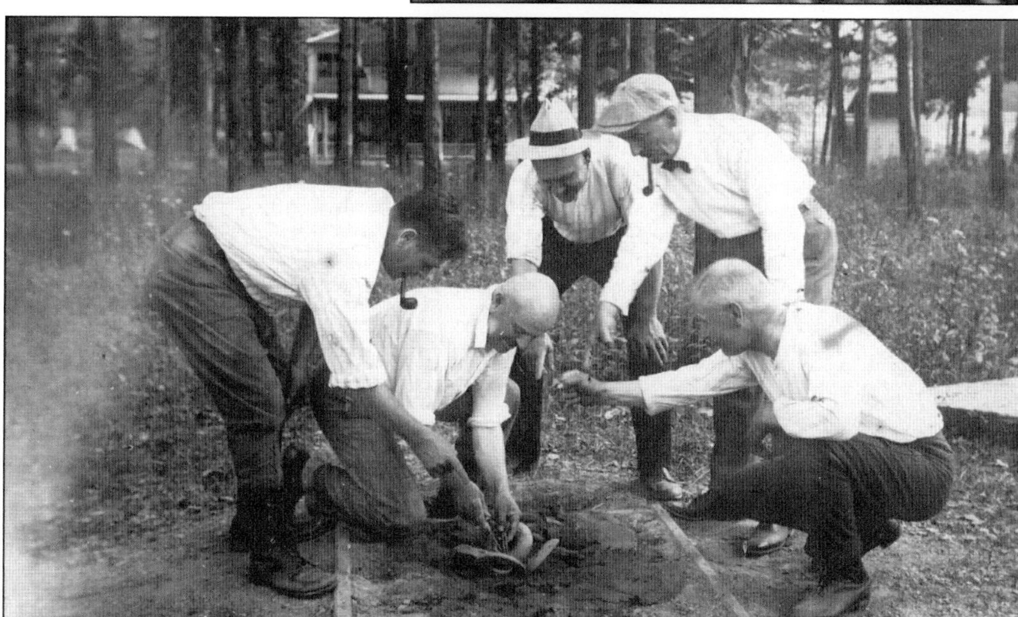

Quoits were popular for many years. This photograph captures (from left to right) John Kilcoyne, Dr. Harry Matten, John Habicht, Robert Quin, and J. Wallace Davis as they debate the deciding point. These west shore "reprobates" gathered every Sunday at 10:00 a.m. while their wives attended services at the Union Chapel. (Tidball/Davis collection.)

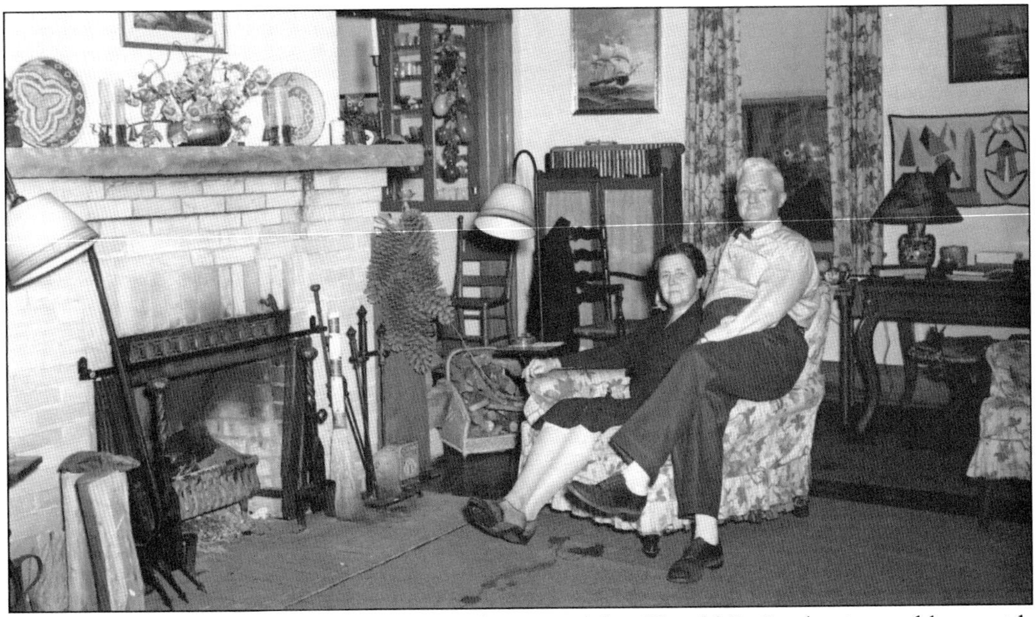

The lake's most famous and influential resident was Adm. Harold R. Stark, pictured here with his wife Kit in their comfortable cottage living room. Stark grew up on the lake where he met his future wife, Katherine Rhodes, at age four. (Kelly collection.)

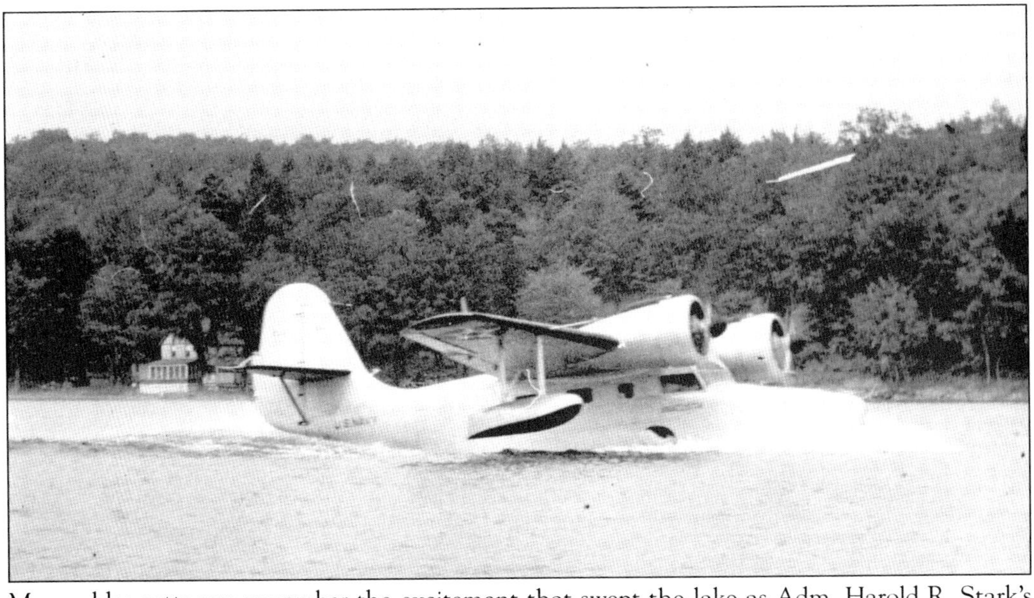

Many older cottagers remember the excitement that swept the lake as Adm. Harold R. Stark's sea plane, *Anacostia*, circled before landing. Once on the lake, many would row out to greet him. (Chambers store is visible in the background.) (Tidball/Davis collection.)

Here the *Anacostia* has come to rest before the Fellows cottage. The admiral is about to step into a waiting rowboat. (Kelly collection.)

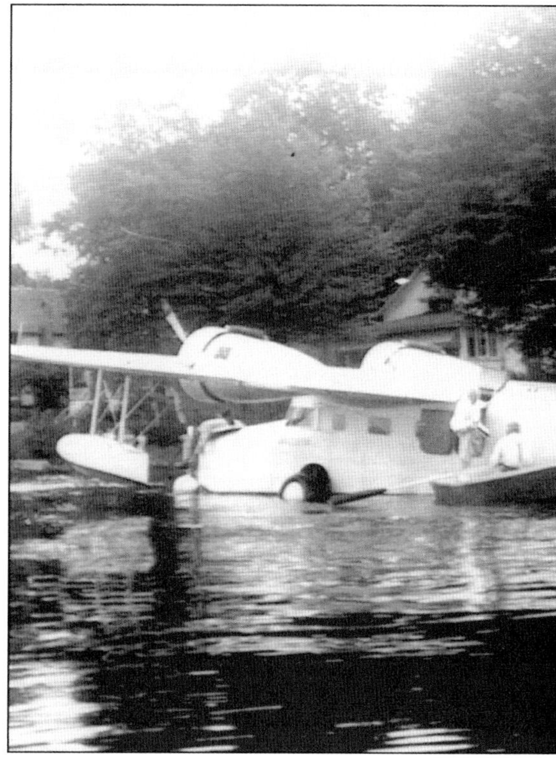

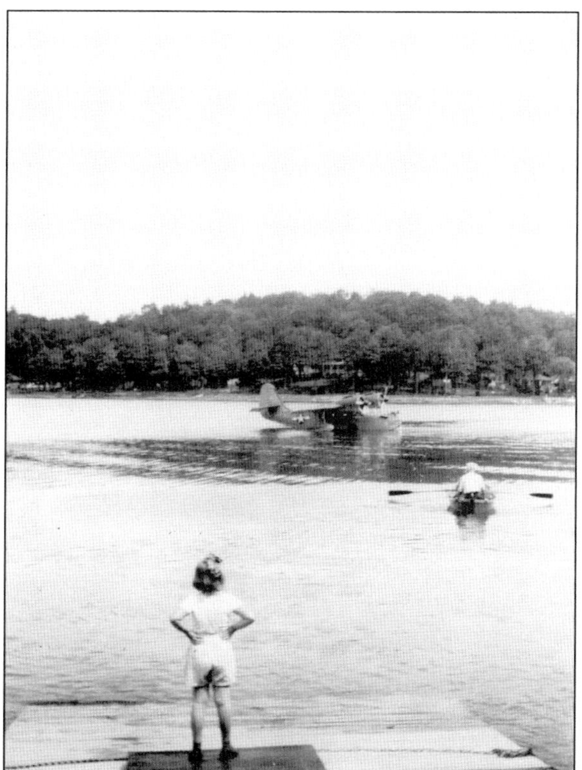

Sally Bruce Gillespie waits to greet her grandfather as he is rowed ashore in August 1944. (Kelly collection.)

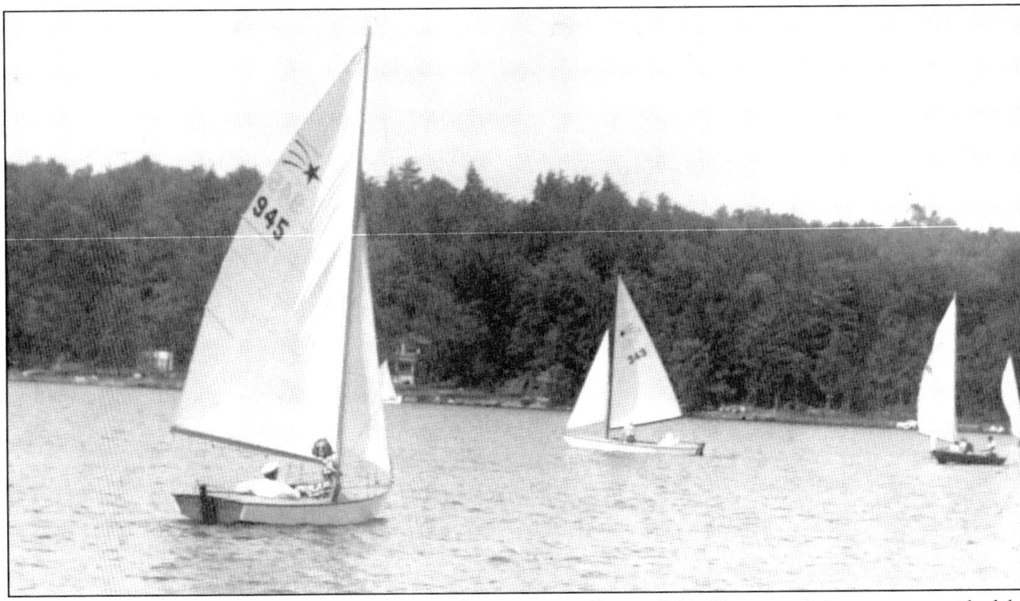

Sailboat racing began in 1934. By 1939, there was a fleet of 11 Comets. Many were sailed by husband and wife teams, as in the case of Hank and Eleanor Dunn's 945 pictured here. Competition was keen, and tempers sometimes flared. Some boats were named to forestall martial conflict; *Harmony* and *Argue-Not* were two. (Dewitt collection.)

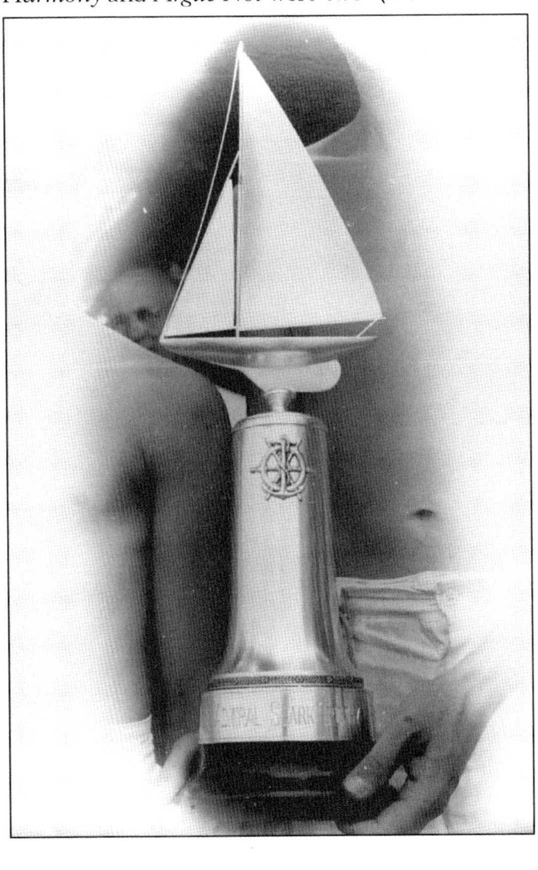

In 1939, Adm. Harold R. Stark donated a trophy to be awarded the winner of the Labor Day regatta. Before then, the winner was awarded a blue and white Lake Carey pennant. Participants had to be members of Lake Carey Comet Fleet No. 30 and agree to abide by NAYRU (North American Yacht Racing Union) racing rules. The trophy is now in the Stark Learning Center of Wilkes University. (Stevens collection.)

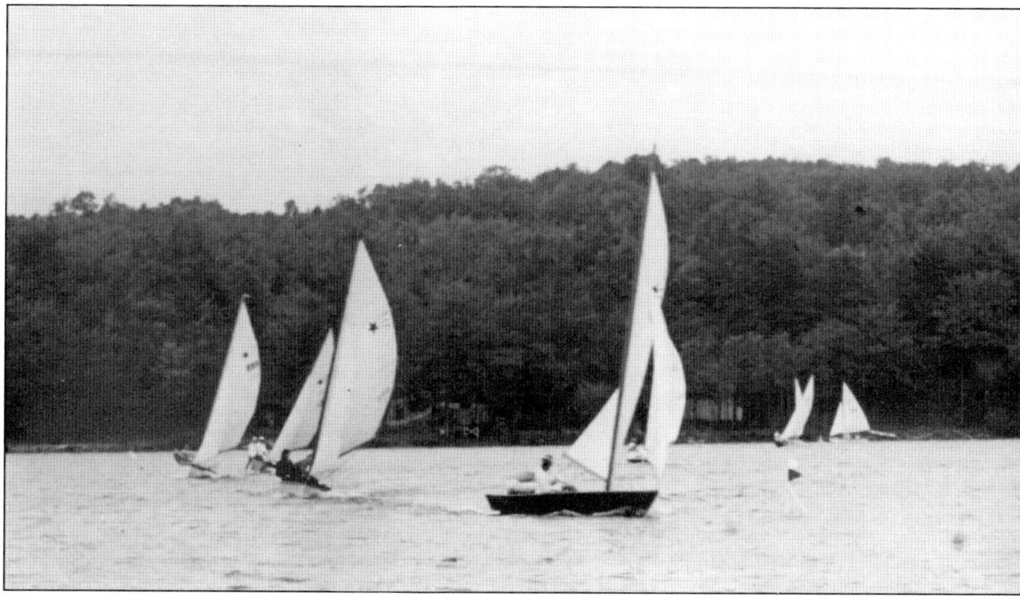

A race is in progress here as four Comets, heeling nicely on a starboard tack, prepare to round the buoy on the right. The summer's sport culminated on Labor Day weekend with two races on Sunday and a third on Monday. The weekend ended with a dinner dance at the Lakewood Club. (Tidball/Davis collection.)

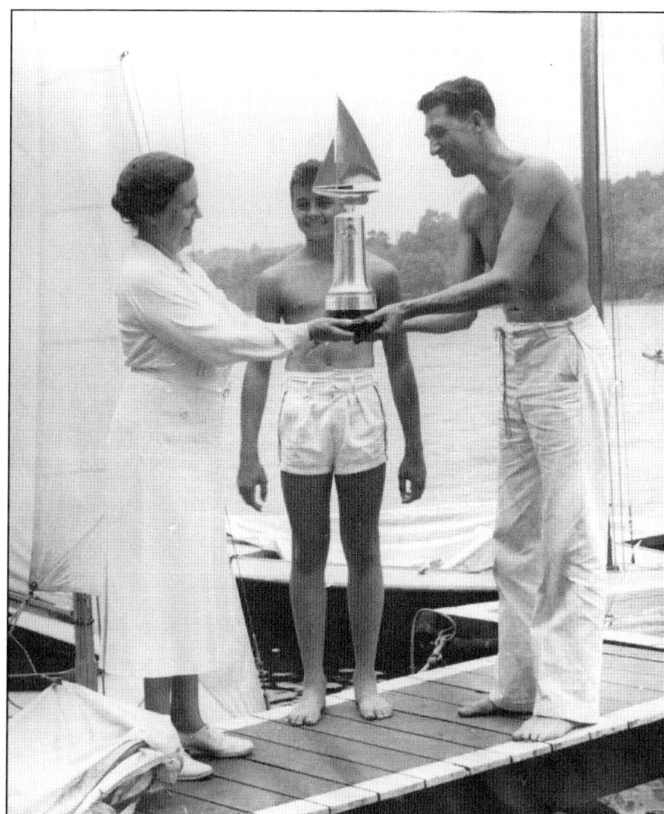

Kit Stark, standing in for her absent husband, presents his trophy in 1939 to Ab Folsom, skipper of the winning Comet, the *Sequence*. Bob Stevens, his crew, looks on. There was also a trophy for the most number of points in the summer's series of races, won that first year by Harden and Lindsey Coon. (Stevens collection.)

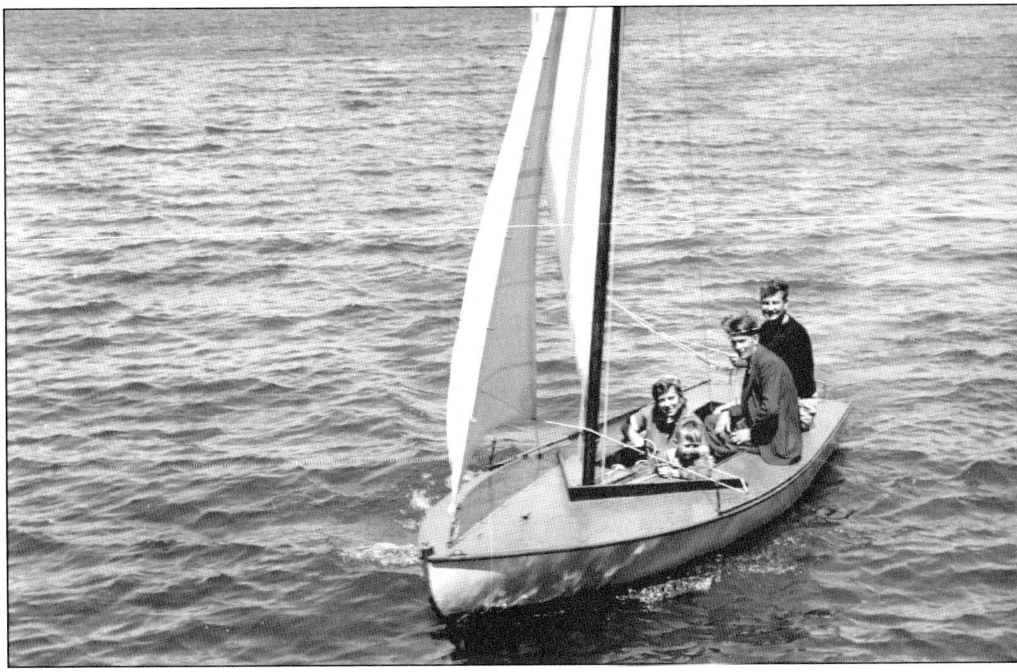

While Comets were popular, other designs, such as this Snipe, were sailed on the lake. Charles Buckworth, an Annapolis sailing instructor, is at the helm while his wife, Marge, crews for him around 1940. A young Bob Lee is along for the sail, and John Taylor sits on the deck. (Weaver collection.)

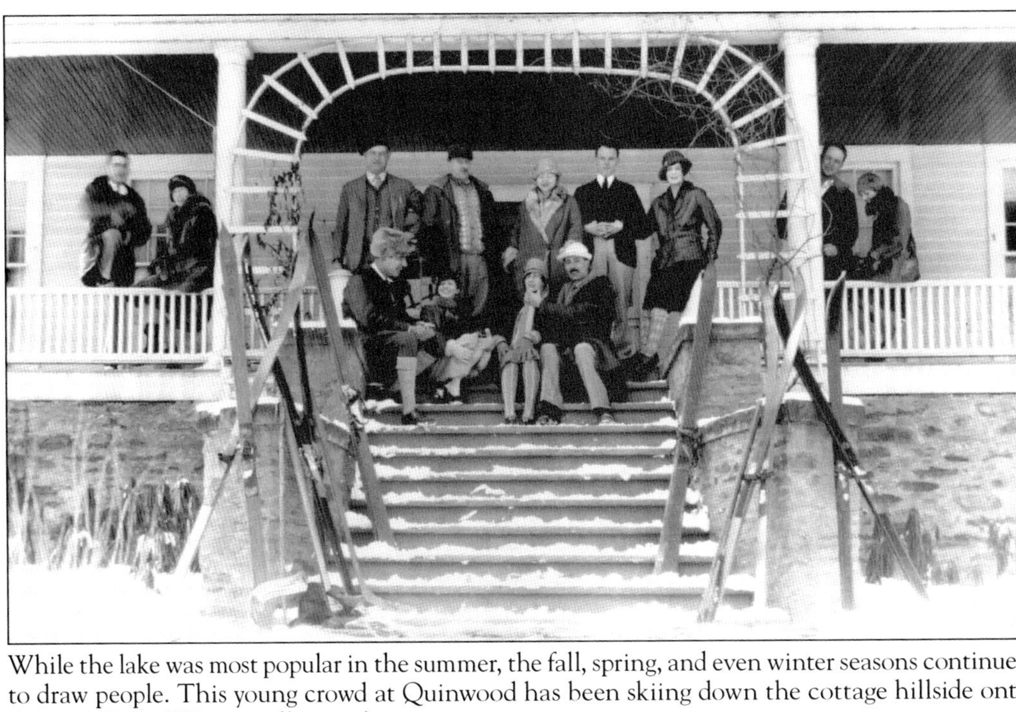

While the lake was most popular in the summer, the fall, spring, and even winter seasons continued to draw people. This young crowd at Quinwood has been skiing down the cottage hillside onto the ice. (Tidball/Davis collection.)

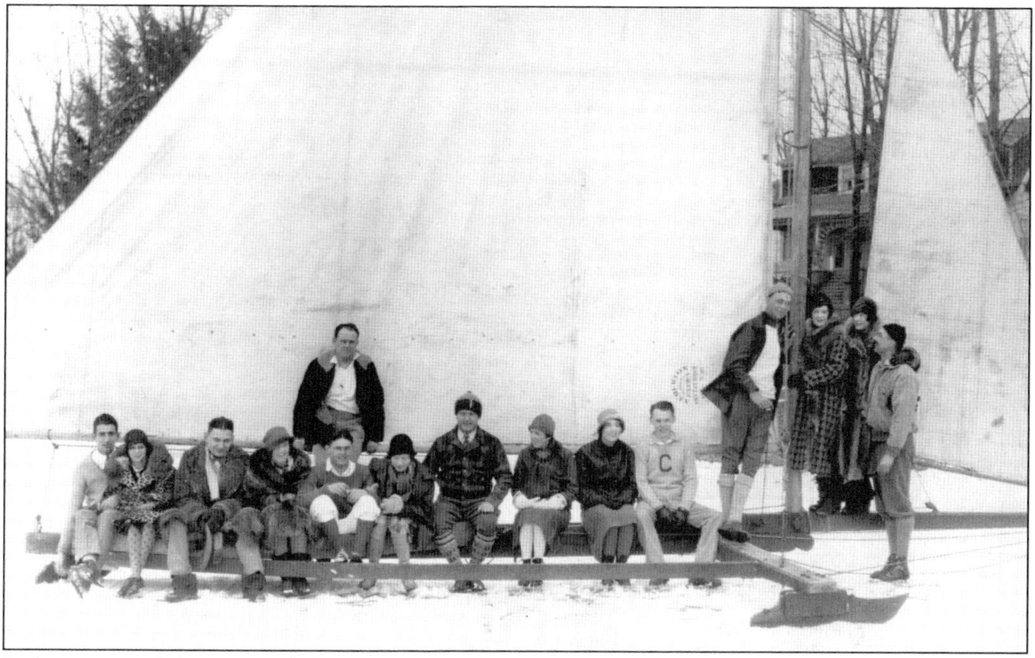

Iceboating and skating made better use of Lake Carey's natural features. This group of Bill Quin's friends poses on his iceboat around 1925. Quin, in white linen pants, sits beside the girl in the raccoon coat and in front of his good friend Seth Beatty. (Tidball/Davis collection.)

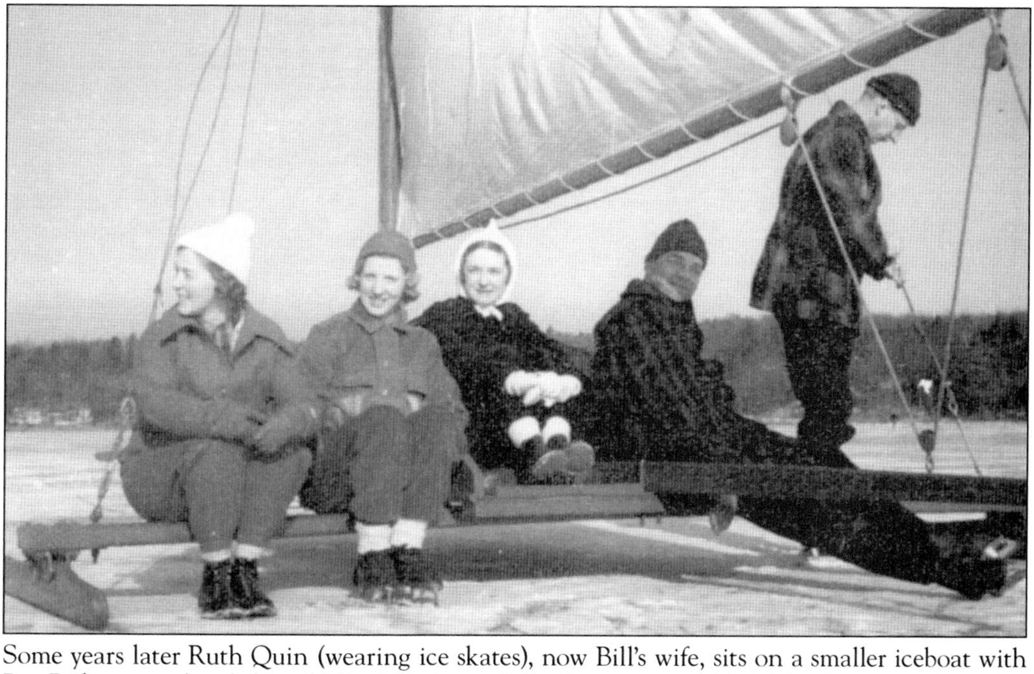

Some years later Ruth Quin (wearing ice skates), now Bill's wife, sits on a smaller iceboat with Peg Ridgway to her left and Elin Northrup, Bob Trembath, and Dick Ridgway to the right. (Tidball/Davis collection.)

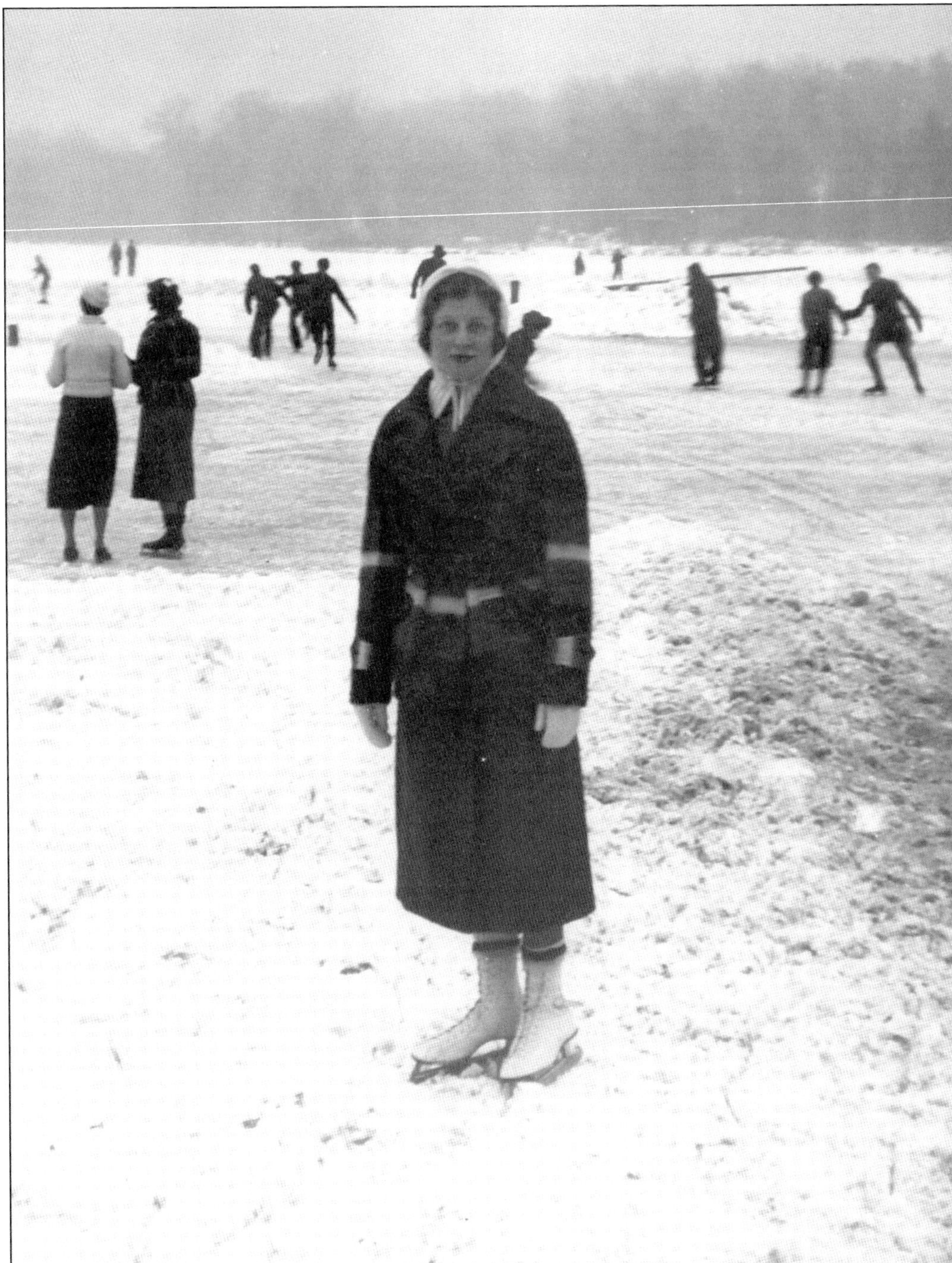

Dorothy Dickinson Mitchell pauses on her way to the lake on an overcast winter's day around 1935. In a moment, she will be lost among the skating figures behind her—returned to the Lake Carey of the past. (She was first seen when she posed as a child with her parents beside Jonesy's shack on page 85.) (Weaver collection.)

BIBLIOGRAPHY

Bogdan, Robert, and Todd Weseloh. *Real Photo Postcard Guide: The People's Photography*. Syracuse, NY: Syracuse University Press, 2006.

Gilborn, Craig. *Adirondack Camps: Homes Away from Home, 1850–1950*. Syracuse, NY: Syracuse University Press, 2000.

Krewson, Cece, and Mary Krewson. *Wyoming County Salutes the Millennium: An Historic Overview of Wyoming County, Pennsylvania, 1700–2000*. Vol. 2. Tunkhannock, PA: MK Publications, 2000.

Larson, Paul Clifford. *A Place at the Lake*. Afton, MN: Afton Historical Society Press, 1998.

Levine, Barbara, and Stephanie Snyder. *Snapshot Chronicles: Inventing the American Photo Album*. New York: Princeton Architectural Press, 2006.

Petrillo, F. Charles. *Harvey's Lake*. Rev. ed. Wilkes-Barre, PA: Wyoming Historical and Geological Society, 1991.

Van Slyck, Abigail A. *A Manufactured Wilderness: Summer Camps and the Shaping of American Youth, 1890–1960*. Minneapolis: University of Minnesota Press, 2006.

Wyoming County Historical Society. *Wyoming County 1842–1992*. Tunkhannock, PA: Mulligan Printing, 1992.

Consistent with our mission to preserve history on a local level, this book was printed in South Carolina on American-made paper and manufactured entirely in the United States. Products carrying the accredited Forest Stewardship Council (FSC) label are printed on 100 percent FSC-certified paper.

MADE IN THE USA